FAIR OR *FOUL*

THE COMPLETE GUIDE TO SOCCER OFFICIATING IN AMERICA

WORLD CUP EDITION

by

Paul E. Harris Jr.

&

Larry R. Harris

SOCCER FOR AMERICANS,
BOX 836 MANHATTAN BEACH,
CALIFORNIA, 90266

Cover photo by Christopher Shaw
Design by Ron Norris

Library of Congress Catalog Number 77-73484

ISBN 0-916802-07-8

Book design, type and production by Volt Technical Corp., Anaheim, CA
Cover by Ron Norris

Printed in the U.S.A.

DEDICATION

This book, as before, is still dedicated to all of those people who are working for the good of soccer in America.

FAIR OR FOUL has been adopted as the official Referee's manual at many different levels of soccer. It currently remains as the official manual for the American Youth Soccer Organization (AYSO), 111 South Oak Street, Inglewood, California 90301. All inquiries outside of AYSO should be directed to SOCCER FOR AMERICANS, Box 836, Manhattan Beach, California 90266 (213) 372-9000.

ACKNOWLEDGEMENTS

TO: The Soccer Referee . . . . . both in and out of America

With special thanks to:

The American Youth Soccer Organization . . . . And Everyone in it

Ken Aston . . . . .FIFA Referee, Instructor, Member of the Referee's Committee

Don Phillipson . . . . Chairman of the USSF Referee's Committee

Gordon Hill . . . . Always with an idea

Anthony Smulders. . . . . The Brother who was "collared" to do the index

Joe Bonchonsky . . . . Who has the conviction to try new things

Ron Norris. . . . . Patient and talented designer

Bill Mason . . . . Thorough and sensible criticism

Ken Mullen . . . . Who comes through every clinic with a smile

George Cross . . . . Mini-book analysis from Scotland

Rene Court and H. Kaser . . . . Our "go-betweens" in FIFA

FIFA . . . . Governing the world game and in support of Referees everywhere
and for permission to reprint the laws

AN INTRODUCTION . . . . SOME PERSONAL WORDS

If someone had said we would be pressed to revise only 30 months after the second edition, we might have given up long ago. The single factor which led to an early revision was not declining interest in the book or in refereeing, but a need to say certain things in a changing world.

The world of soccer since 1975 has changed, and more than ever the importance of the Referee seems no less than that of the coach. We should never forget that once the teams are assembled and ready for the kick-off, the game is in our hands. Many of you have told us that you need help, not so much in learning laws, but in gaining a broader understanding of what it really takes to apply them in a game.

Referees should no longer be in the background, hesitant to advance an idea or admit a mistake. There is no longer room for Referees who spend time in "covering up" or in making excuses for inconsistent behaviors. We are vital to the game as it moves into the place it richly deserves in the American sporting world. With this in mind, we have introduced some Referee personalities who should inspire you. Yes, there are giants among us, and you should be proud to be a Referee. If you think that what you are doing is "thankless," then go on to another responsibility in soccer.

Rather than detail the changes awaiting you in the 1978 World Cup Edition, we'd like to tell you why we're here again.

1. We've tried a lot of ideas, whistled over 500 games, conducted camps, clinics, and classes for over 1000 Referees since the last edition. Referees of many persuasions have crossed our path, and we've learned from you.

2. Helpful conversations with many experienced, discerning Referees have shown us the complex nature of our job.

3. Added contact with first-rate coaches has brought new insights into "how others see us."

4. Referees as coaches, coaches as Referees, youngsters as Referees, and Referees as people brought us around to the idea of bringing the human touch back to the chosen art.

The World Cup Edition symbolizes an event, one which is refereed by few but enjoyed by many. It is the showcase of our game, and we pay tribute to it and to its participants. To the many who will never read a soccer book, it is the most visible event in soccer. The best that is refereeing is, of course, the best that is within you. We know that your satisfactions will be great and hope that in some small way we've contributed to your personal enjoyment.

O. Maxmilian

"Shake my hand and I'll let you keep the ball."

TABLE OF CONTENTS

I.   **I, YOU, THE REFEREE.** 1
     The Decision to Referee 2
     Your Fitness for Refereeing. 4
     Equipment. 9

II.   **BEFORE THE GAME** 11
     Field Inspection 12
     Pre-Game Instruction. 12

III.   **THE DIAGONAL SYSTEM OF CONTROL** 17
     The Diagonal System 19
     Linesmen. 25
     The One Referee System. 34

IV.   **DURING PLAY** 39
     The Use of the Watch. 40
     The Use of the Whistle 42
     Signals and Signaling 45
     Referee/Linesman Data Card. 48
     Thoughts on Game Control. 50
     Warnings, Cautions, and Ejections. 53
     The Goalkeeper . . . Rights, Privileges and Responsibilities. 57
     9.15 Meters, Please!. 60
     Injuries 65
     What to Do at Halftime 66

V.   **DON'T JUST DO SOMETHING . . . STAND THERE!** 69
     The Advantage Clause 70
     The Other Advantage. 72

VI.   **REALLY KNOWING FAIR FROM FOUL.** 77
     Referee Composition 78
     Concentration. 83
     The 10 Most Difficult Decisions. 87
     12k . . . Have You Forgotten It?. 90
     You've Got to Feel the Foul 91
     Fouls that Mean Trouble for You. 92
     Big Games and Television 94

VII.   **AFTER IT'S OVER . . . BEFORE IT BEGINS AGAIN.** 97
     Referee Meetings. 98
     Coaches' Referee Evaluation 100
     Writing Game Reports 105

TABLE OF CONTENTS (Continued)

VIII. THE WORLD CUP 111
        World Cup Facilitators 112
        Refereeing at the World Cup 119

IX. YOU MEET THE GREATEST PEOPLE 123
        Ben Glass. 124
        Shelly Whitlock. 126
        Gordon Hill 128
        Jose Teixeira de Carvalho 130
        Jimmy Walder. 132

X. THE RULES ALMANAC 135
        The Field of Play 138
        Conversions 141
        The Ball. 143
        Players 144
        Substitutions 145
        Illness/Injury 146
        The Goalkeeper. 148
        Equipment/Apparel 150
        Referee 152
        Advantage Clause 153
        Termination of Game. 153
        Timing 154
        Kick-Off 155
        Drop-Ball. 156
        Outside Agent. 159
        In/Out of Play 160
        Scoring 161
        Off-Side. 162
        Fouls and Misconduct 171
        Warnings 172
        Cautions 173
        Ejections 174
        Entering/Leaving the Field 175
        Free-Kicks — General 176
        Indirect Free-Kick 177
        Ungentlemanly Conduct 178
        Dangerous Play 181
        Direct Free-Kick 183
        Charging 185
        Penalty-Kick. 187

TABLE OF CONTENTS (Continued)

Throw-In 193
Goal-Kick 195
Corner-Kick and Corner-Flag Post. 196

XI. TESTING YOUR KNOWLEDGE 199
Basic Referee's Test 200
Key and Critique. 210
The Advanced Referee's Test. 214
Key and Critique. 222

XII. YOU AND THE YOUTH 229
When You Referee Youth Games 231
The Referees of Tomorrow Should Be the Referees of Today 234
Every Player Is Different. 237
A Test for Young Referees 239

XIII. FOR THE GOOD OF THE GAME 241
Making Something Out of Violence. 242
A Note on Protests 244
Notes to Coaches, with Test 246
Advice to Players. 251
A Coach Looks at Refereeing. 252
Women Referees and Women's Soccer. 254
The Indoor Game 256

XIV. THE LAWS OF THE GAME 259
The FIFA Laws. 260
The International Board . . . How Soccer's Laws Are Changed 279

XV. THE AMERICAN SCENE. 281
The Two Referee System (Dual System) 283
The Modified Diagonal (MOD). 297
Youth Soccer Rules. 311
High School Differences from FIFA 314
College Differences from FIFA 318
The Timekeeper 322
United States Soccer Federation. 323
The Highest League in America 331

APPENDICES 333
Glossary, Definitions and Terms 334
Index of Films 339
Bibliography 340
Index 342

"It's you and I together."

I

I, You,
The Referee

THE DECISION TO REFEREE

One of the changes in our lives since the last edition is an increasing contact with the larger world of soccer, and that includes the domain of the player and coach. The most tolerant, understanding coach will say, "I don't envy any Referee. It's a thankless task." While the view is sympathetic and no doubt springs from the daily pressures on the Referee, the positive Referee does not view the task as "thankless." The game is now emerging from 100 years of semi-darkness into the light, and with this emergence soccer refereeing is coming of age. More and more, the Referee is being supported, helped, understood, and sometimes admired.

The road from the bottom, your first game, may seem very long, depending on your ambitions. If you are realistic about it, you may even know after your first game if refereeing is for you. You are positively "hooked" on your task when you find yourself looking at each game as if it were the championship. Books, movies, television, clinics, and other forms of communication can bring exemplary Referees and professional guidance to you and your group. You can progress very rapidly.

We are well aware that your ambitions may be limited, and that age, occupation, or outside interests may prevent you from refereeing professionally. Most of the players are amateur, and most of the coaches and Referees should be as well. You can, however, do a professional job in your amateur game. Each time you accept an assignment, walk out on the field, and blow a whistle, the standard of officiating must exceed that of play.

"He has that certain knack of being a player's Referee."

2

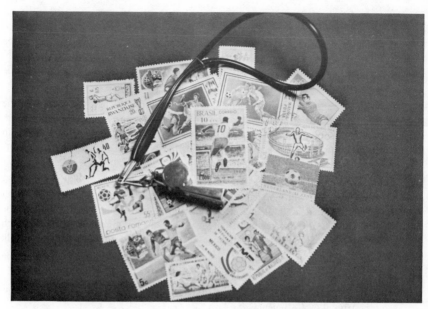

The Referee puts his stamp of approval on the game.

☆★☆★☆★☆★☆★☆★☆★☆★☆★☆★☆★☆★☆★

When you become a Referee in soccer, you will never again see the game as a mere spectator.

☆★☆★☆★☆★☆★☆★☆★☆★☆★☆★☆★☆★☆★

YOUR FITNESS FOR REFEREEING

It has been repeatedly observed that vast individual differences appear in Referee dress, attitude, experience, and ability. Conditioning and training present no exception. Some Referees train, almost religiously, for their task, yet others let the games provide the setting for their training.

If you are a fanatic for conditioning, don't try to outrun the ball, the players, or the play. Also, don't try to set a record by whistling nine games in a day, as one Referee did. Conversely, if you take conditioning lightly, you will probably not progress very far in refereeing. So . . . what is a realistic approach to the physical task that is before you?

In an earlier edition of this book we stated that condition was 50% of refereeing. We no longer believe that. At best, it is 25%, and maybe only 15%. The Referee who is confidently "in shape" will feel able to perform in the last minute as in the first. Other Referees will find that as the game clock runs down, so will the physical clock. The demands made upon the Referee are often greatest in the last minutes of the game, with frustrated players and desperate, fatigued, less-than-fully-coordinated moves by all.

Officials in various sports will find varying demands made upon them, depending on the game itself. The realities of your job will tell you that:

- You will spend a great deal of your time moving at medium speed, at a slow, easy, trot, at 60% efficiency.

- At least ten times in a game you must run full-speed, for 30 yeards or more, to view a quick attack on goal.

- Much of your effective running must be backwards, or sideways.

- You must have mobility to avoid players and the ball.

- Even the shortest game is stopped at least 50 times for throw-ins, goal-kicks, corner-kicks, free-kicks, goals, injuries, substitutions, etc. Don't let anyone tell you that soccer is continuous. When you do have these breaks in play, don't rush into your next position. Save your strength.

Lest you feel complacent, thinking that the job is not physically demanding, the following chart is offered:

	Referee	Linesmen
Two Referee System	7 – 8 miles	
Diagonal System	6 – 7 miles	2 – 3 miles
Modified Diagonal	5 – 6 miles	3 – 4 miles
One Referee System	8 – 10 miles	

These distances refer to the amount of "moving about" that an average Referee would do in a normal 90 minute game, and would, of course, be dependent on the size of the field.

Your training is individual, largely dependent upon your physical makeup, your games, and your lifestyle. Many Referees advocate Interval Training, the interspersing of repetitions of a prescribed exercise with periods of rest. For those readers who have insisted on some kind of an exercise program for Referees, the following is presented as a guideline.

Warming-Up Period

Jog lightly for 200 meters (including 50 meters sideways and 50 meters backwards)

Walk briskly for the same distance

Repeat, four times

Stamina Program

Wind Sprint Intervals

> Walk 25 meters, jog 25 meters, then sprint the same distance
>
> Repeat ten times
>
> Increase to 50 meters
>
> Repeat five times

This simple daily program, coupled with normal activity of games and an average physical life, will prepare you adequately for games and for the Physical Fitness requirements of the United States Soccer Federation. (See Chapter XV on USSF requirements.)

FIFA RECOMMENDATION

200 Meters — less than 3 minutes 15 seconds

100 Meters — less than 15 seconds

High Jump — 3 feet 7 inches

Long Jump — 11 feet 6 inches

Have you ever refereed four games in a day?

Comment: There has always been a shortage of Referees in the game. Not enough Referees are interested in going out to recruit others. They would rather whistle more games, even at the expense of the players, and their own health. More than two games in a day deprives others of reffing and diminishes your effectiveness. If you *must* be active, evaluate other officials in the extra time you would be on the field.

HINTS

1. Before the game, run from one goal to the other as you inspect the nets. This effort will "warm you up" in cool weather and will impress both players and spectators with your enthusiasm and alertness.

2. A ball travels faster than any player or Referee can run. Keep up with the play, not with the ball.

3. Prior to the opening of a regular season, ask league officials for practice game assignments. This will aid in both mental and physical conditioning.

4. Through experience you will learn to avoid unnecessary running on the field, thus saving your energies for sudden breakaways on goal, when you must not be caught in the middle of the field.

5. Never smoke in view of spectators or players.

6. Never lean on a goal upright during a game stoppage.

7. Use the half time period for rest and for game discussion with your fellow officials.

Oto Maxmilian

Dante Maglio (right), a FIFA Referee, leaves the field, apparently more fatigued than the players. He is in top condition, and has given his all in this game.

6

The Referee gets a brief physical respite during the taking of a penalty-kick.

☆★☆★☆★☆★☆★☆★☆★☆★☆★☆★☆★☆★☆★☆★

A famous player once approached a Referee after a controversial decision. "I've wanted to tell you for some time that
you are the second-best official in this league. The Referee's
curiosity got the best of him, and he asked the identity of
#1. The answer: "All of the others are tied for first."

☆★☆★☆★☆★☆★☆★☆★☆★☆★☆★☆★☆★☆★

Oto Maxmilian

"Toros, these new Referee   "Why thank you, Emmett."   "No es para tanto"
boots of yours are simply   (BIG DEAL).
smashing."

EQUIPMENT

"When the occasion is worth dressing for, it's worth the best in dress."

The most obvious part of a Referee's equipment is his uniform, which shall consist of the following:

1. A long or short sleeved black shirt, with white collar and cuffs, with the crest of the Referee's association on the left side of the chest.
2. Black shorts, with length 4 to 5 inches above the knee.
3. Black stockings, with or without white at the top.
4. Black studded shoes, with black or white stockings.

It is recommended that a transparent or black waterproof jacket be worn in rainy weather. A black visor/cap helps protect the Referee who wears glasses from the rain. It is also handy as a sun shade. When it is determined that one team's colors are in conflict with the standard black of the Referee, the Referee shall change to a shirt of contrasting color or pattern. A striped basketball shirt (as used by soccer officials in the East) and the basic Referee shirt with the black and white reversed are two popular alternatives.

The Referee's equipment must also include a Referee data card (see Chapter IV) or a small pocket notebook and the following:

Whistles (2)	Coin
Watches (2) (one must have stop action)	Red and Yellow Cards (1 set)
Pencils (2)	

Many Referees have the following items in their equipment bag:

Glasses with yellow lenses	Increases contrast and visibility for games played at night, in rain, fog, or when very overcast.
Spare set of red and yellow cards	
Law Book	
Set of linesman's flags	
Shoe polish	
Spare pair of shoes	Screw-in cleats are best for a wet field.
Inflating pump and valve needle	
36" of a cloth tape measure	
Shoe laces — black and white	A spare pair. If you function as a linesman, you can change to match the Referee.
String/cord and a knife	For the emergency repair of nets.
Masking/Adhesive tape	To repair nets and to hold up ones stockings.
Captains' arm bands	
Screw-in cleat tool	
Band-aids and chapstick	
File for burrs on cleats, etc.	

Oto Maxmilian

"Come, come, Gentlemen . . . can't you at least wait until the game has started?"

10

II

Before
The Game

FIELD INSPECTION

The Referee is evaluated the moment he enters the field of play. His trademark is *not* his whistle, but the respect he commands for the unobtrusive and silent way he moves about the field, always with full authority.

When the Referee enters the field of play, his first job is to make a thorough inspection of the grounds. If field markings are poor or inadequate, this time before the game begins is to be used to correct these deficiencies. In particular, the penalty-spot should be stepped off to determine the condition of the spot and its exact location. If the spot is in a hole, it must be corrected by filling in the hole. Nets should be checked for holes or loose tie-downs, and corner and midfield flags inspected. This is to be followed by a general inspection of the field for dangerous water drains, holes, rocks, or other irregularities. If some conditions exist that cannot be corrected, a reminder of such conditions to captains and team managers is a courtesy, followed by a written report to the proper authorities.

If the Referee is working a game with another Referee or with two Linesmen, all of the above should be accomplished cooperatively and with a minimum of talk to players and managers. The Referee must be satisfied that the field is in playable condition before calling the captains to the center of the field.

A FIELD IS PLAYABLE WHEN:

1. The field is properly marked according to Law I, with nets and corner-flags secure.

2. The Referee can see one goal while standing at the other, or he uses the lesser requirement of seeing both goals while standing within the center-circle.

3. The ball, when dropped from the shoulder, will bounce. If wet areas exist, they should be few in number.

4. The ball, swhen placed on the ground, will remain so without being disturbed by the wind.

PRE-GAME INSTRUCTIONS

After the field has been inspected and the Referee has conferred with his fellow officials, he shall call the team representatives (captains and alternate captains) to the middle of the field for pre-game instructions and for the coin toss. (This is done on "open fields" or stadiums which do not have dressing rooms available for the players.)

The discipline of team managers and captains is highly important in ensuring game control, and these instructions should be the first indication to the players that the Referee is fair, brief, firm, and precise. It is a well-known fact that Referees vary in their pre-game formalities, ranging from "no instructions" to a recitation on the seventeen laws of the game. The intention here is to inform Referees of the many possibilities available, with the advice that game control is often established *before* the opening whistle! It is recommended that the only instructions given are those (if any) the Referee feels may be applicable to *that specific* game.

Listed below are some suggested reminders that Referees may use in instructing players. These are all matters of personal preference, and questions of age, experience, and reputation of players and teams must be taken into consideration.

SUGGESTED POSSIBLE PRE-GAME INSTRUCTIONS

1. No disagreements with a Referee's or a Linesman's decision will be tolerated, on or off the field.

2. A team captaincy implies responsibilities, not privileges. The captain does not have the legal right to address the Referee on any aspect of the game or on its progress. Duties of the captain are to maintain discipline and fair play among his players.

3. All substitutes must enter and leave from the middle of the field, and only when the Referee signals for the substitution.

4. Play the Referee's whistle, for only this whistle may stop the game.

5. The team coach is responsible for the conduct of the team's supporters.

6. All indirect-free-kicks are indicated by an upraised arm. There is no signal for the direct-kick.

7. Any attempt to delay the taking of a free-kick will result in a caution.

8. Deliberately reaching out and stopping the ball with the hands or arms, or catching the ball in the hands in order to prevent an opponent from gaining an advantage will result in a caution.

HINTS FOR REFEREES

1. Some Referees prefer to identify captains through the use of armbands, or identifying adhesives, to be worn on the upper arm, just below the shoulder. This is a purely optional procedure, as are all procedures in this chapter, with the exception of the tossing of the coin. Some captains consider this gesture as giving the captain a special mark of distinction, which is right. If, however, the captain refuses to wear the armband, the Referee shall not force him to do so.

2. The Referee should request that his neutral Linesmen be present during pre-game instructions, and they should be introduced to team captains.

3. Do not talk with one captain before the game until the opposing captain is present, for everything that is said must be heard by both parties.

4. A captain or coach may not eject a player from the field, but he is required to send the player off after the Referee has ejected him from the game.

5. The use of the yellow card for cautions and the red card for ejections is highly recommended. Never use a two-faced card. (See section 13 warnings, cautions, and ejections.)

6. Very few players or club officials are well-schooled in the laws of the game. Do not attempt to flaunt your own knowledge in order to correct this deficiency.

7. *All* players' equipment shall be examined before the game. Equipment such as headbands may be worn if the Referee feels they do not present a hazard to players. Necklaces, casts, rings, and wrist watches are usually not permitted. Armcasts are sometimes allowed by Referees (never for high school and youth), if they are wrapped in heavy sponge rubber or similar material.

8. It is sometimes helpful to illustrate a point with an example, in point 4, under *Suggested List of Pre-Game Instructions*, a Referee may say, "This week I had to award a penalty-kick because a defensive player thought he heard a whistle, and he picked up the ball in the penalty-area."

9. It is considered courteous to ask the players if there are any questions, but this is not required. Do not allow players to grill you on the laws of the game in order to test your knowledge.

10. In the event of disagreement between the teams, the Referee selects the game ball. It must pass his criteria for weight, size, composition, condition, and air pressure.

11. The coin toss shall be conducted at the conclusion of the pre-game instructions. The visiting team captain shall call the coin "heads" or "tails" while in the air, and if he wins he shall have the choice of direction or kick-off.

    If the coin is to be caught, the captain should be told that it will be re-tossed if it falls to the ground. This precludes any problems of the coin landing on edge in the grass.

    An acceptable gesture is to have the home team captain toss the coin. If this is done, use a 50-cent piece or silver dollar, due to its heavier weight. Let it land on the ground.

12. The Referee shall note the captains' numbers and record the team kicking off, so that the other team may kick-off in the next period. It is advisable to ask the captain for the number of a substitute or alternate captain.

13. Just prior to whistling for a period/overtime opening kick-off, it is suggested that the Referee receive a signal from each G.K. indicating they are ready.

*A Referee should not enter a game with preconceived notions about players and teams. It is his duty, however, to inform himself of the habits and manners of players, from personal observation and from the observations of fellow officials. The good Referee places himself at an advantage by observing teams in games and in forming his own opinion on how to best control a game.

"Alright, now that I know your name, what's your phone number?"

☆ ★ ☆ ★ ☆ ★ ☆ ★ ☆ ★ ☆ ★ ☆ ★ ☆ ★ ☆ ★ ☆ ★ ☆ ★ ☆ ★ ☆ ★ ☆ ★ ☆ ★ ☆ ★ ☆ ★ ☆ ★ ☆ ★

You have accepted an assignment, and someone calls with a more attractive one. What do you do?

Comment: If you take refereeing at all seriously, you will probably someday be given the position of making assignments. Do unto others. Your share of the good games will come to you, in time.

☆ ★ ☆ ★ ☆ ★ ☆ ★ ☆ ★ ☆ ★ ☆ ★ ☆ ★ ☆ ★ ☆ ★ ☆ ★ ☆ ★ ☆ ★ ☆ ★ ☆ ★ ☆ ★ ☆ ★ ☆ ★

☆ ★ ☆ ★ ☆ ★ ☆ ★ ☆ ★ ☆ ★ ☆ ★ ☆ ★ ☆ ★ ☆ ★ ☆ ★ ☆ ★ ☆ ★

"I used to think violence against Referees was deserved, until they went after me."

—Eric Sellin
Author of *The Inner Game of Soccer*

☆ ★ ☆ ★ ☆ ★ ☆ ★ ☆ ★ ☆ ★ ☆ ★ ☆ ★ ☆ ★ ☆ ★ ☆ ★ ☆ ★ ☆ ★

One, two, three . . . Kick!!

III

The Diagonal
System Of Control

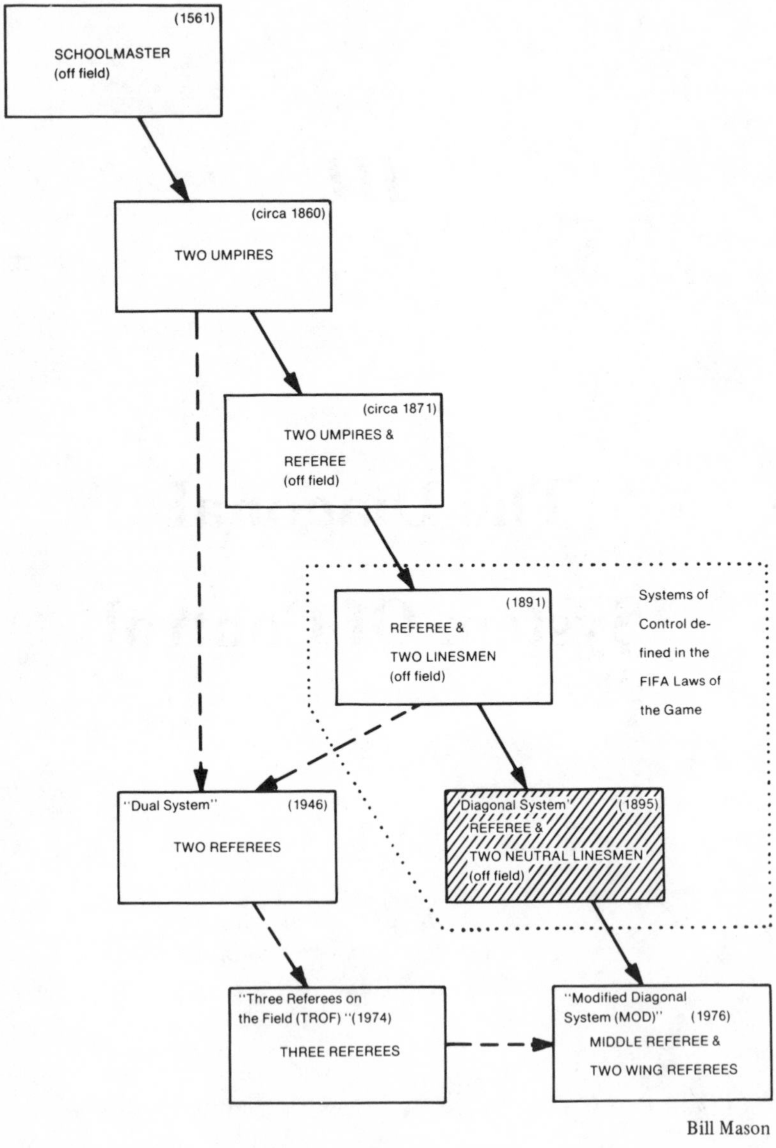
(1561)
SCHOOLMASTER
(off field)
(circa 1860)
TWO UMPIRES
(circa 1871)
TWO UMPIRES &
REFEREE
(off field)
(1891)
REFEREE &
TWO LINESMEN
(off field)
Systems of Control defined in the FIFA Laws of the Game
"Dual System" (1946)
TWO REFEREES
"Diagonal System" (1895)
REFEREE &
TWO NEUTRAL LINESMEN
(off field)
"Three Referees on the Field (TROF)"(1974)
THREE REFEREES
"Modified Diagonal System (MOD)" (1976)
MIDDLE REFEREE &
TWO WING REFEREES
Bill Mason

The Evolution of Soccer Officiating

THE DIAGONAL SYSTEM

Although the laws of the game neither prescribe a system of field control nor contain specific instructions on field positioning during a game, there is a system which has received worldwide approval. This method, called the *diagonal system,* makes the most effective use of the Referee and two neutral Linesmen, and is commonly used in club, professional, and international games. The key to efficient game control under the diagonal system is Linesman cooperation (Law VI). The Referee must know and respect his Linesmen, and Linesmen should respect and support the decisions of the Referee.

Referees should not necessarily keep to one diagonal on the field of play, and must adjust their positioning according to weather and grounds conditions.

The following diagrams will indicate the basic system of control, followed by referee positioning at various stages of play development. (Reprinted with permission of the Federation Internationale de Football Association.)

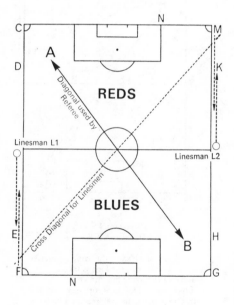

Diagram 1

The imaginary diagonal used by the Referee is the line A–B.

The opposite diagonal used by the Linesmen is adjusted to the position of the Referee: if the Referee is near A, Linesman L2 will be at a point between M and K. When the Referee is at B, Linesman L1 will be between E and F; this gives two officials control of the respective "danger zones", one at each side of the field.

Linesman L1 adopts the *Reds* as his side; Linesman L2 adopts the *Blues;* as *Red* forwards move toward Blue goal, Linesman L1 keeps in line with second last *Blue* defender so in actual practice he will rarely get into Red's half of the field. Similarly Linesman L2 keeps in line with second last *Red* defender, and will rarely get into Blue's half.

At corner-kicks or penalty-kicks the Linesman in that half where the corner-kick or penalty-kick occurs positions himself at N and the Referee takes position (see Diagram 4 – corner-kick; Diagram 9 – penalty-kick).

The diagonal system fails if Linesman L2 gets between G and H when Referee is at B, or when Linesman L1 is near C or D when the Referee is at A, because there are *two* officials at the same place. This should be avoided.

(N.B. – Some Referees prefer to use the opposite diagonal, viz., from F to M, in which case the Linesmen should adjust their work accordingly.)

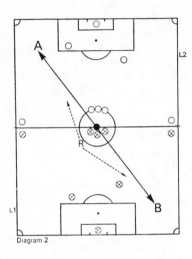

Diagram 2

Diagram 2
START OF GAME

Position of Referee at Kick-off – R.
Position of Linesmen – L1 and L2:
in position with second last defender
Players – ○ and ⊗.
Diagonal followed by Referee A–B.
Referee moves to diagonal along line
←——→ according to direction of attack.
Ball –●.

Diagram 3
DEVELOPMENT OF ATTACK
(From Diagram 2)

Ball moves out to left wing, Referee (R)
slightly off diagonal to be near play.
Linesman (L2) level with second last defender.
Two officials, therefore, up with play.
Linesman (L1) in position for clearance
and possible counter-attack.

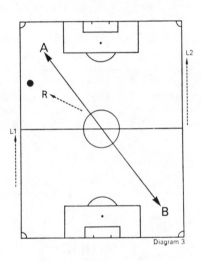

Diagram 3

Diagram 4

Diagram 4
CORNER-KICK

Positions of officials the same no matter
at which corner-area the kick is taken.
Referee (R) along line shown.
Linesman (L2) – in accordance with the
instructions from the Referee the Linesman
(L2) shall be near the corner flag or on the
goal-line near the corner flag, to observe
whether the ball is properly played, whether
the opposing players are at proper distance
(10 yards), whether the ball is behind the
goal-line, or whether incidents have happened possibly hidden from the Referee.
Linesman (L1) in position for clearance
and possible counter-attack.

20

Diagram 5
THE COUNTER-ATTACK
(Following Diagram 4)

Referee (R) sprints to regain correct position on diagonal along path --------> .
(Note: The Referee who is physically fit is able to do this easily.)
Linesman (L2) hurries back to his correct position on the touch-line.
Linesman (L1) level with attack and in position to see infringements and indicate decisions until Referee regains his position.

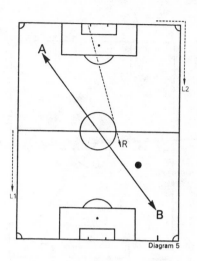

Diagram 5

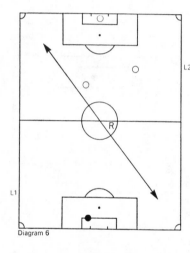

Diagram 6

Diagram 6
GOAL-KICK

Referee (R) in midfield adjacent to central point of diagonal.
Linesman (L1) exercising watch over goal-kick, positioned in line with the penalty-area.
Linesman (L2) in position in line with second last defender pending a possible attack by side taking goal-kick.

Diagram 7
FREE-KICK IN MIDFIELD

Players line up for kick ○ and ⊗. Referee (R) and Linesman (L2) in respective diagonal positions, level with players and able to judge accurately any questions of off-side or foul play. Linesman (L1) sees that kick is taken from correct position and also is in position for possible counter-attack.

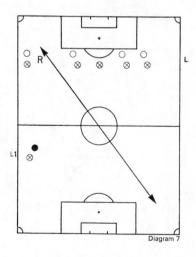

Diagram 7

21

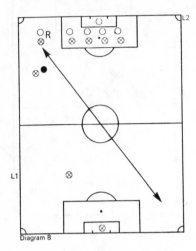

Diagram 8

Diagram 8
FREE-KICK NEAR GOAL
(Just outside penalty-area)

Players ⊗ and ◯ line up for free-kick.

Referee (R) takes up his position just off his diagonal so that he is placed accurately to judge off-side. Linesman (L2) is more advanced but can watch for off-side and fouls and also is in a good position to act as goal judge in the event of a direct shot being taken.

Diagram 9
PENALTY-KICK

Players ⊗ and ◯ with the exception of the goalkeeper and kicker are shown outside the penalty-area and at least 10 yards from the ball – goalkeeper on goal-line.

Referee (R) is in position to see that kick is properly taken and that no encroachment takes place.

Linesman (L2) watches goalkeeper to see that he does not advance illegally and also acts as goal judge

Linesman (L1) is in position should the goalkeeper save a goal and start a counter-attack.

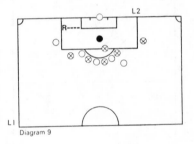

Diagram 9

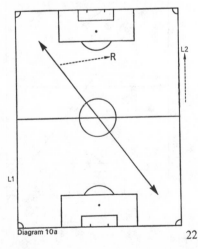

Diagram 10a

Diagram 10a
THROW-IN

Ball out of play and Linesman (L2) is in position with second last defender indicating position of throw and to which side.

Referee (R) crosses from diagonal to centre of field, in the same manner as a defence covering a throw-in.

Linesman (L1) in position in line with his second last defender for the possible counter-attack.

22

Diagram 10b
THROW-IN

Linesman (L1) is away from the throw-in but should be able to judge feet and probably to indicate which side is entitled to throw. He also maintains his position in line with second last defender in the event of a clearance.

Referee (R) can judge other throw-in infringements and veers slightly from his diagonal towards touch-line.

Linesman (L2) is in position with second last defender in his half of the field of play, and can see any infringement occurring before Referee can turn to follow play.

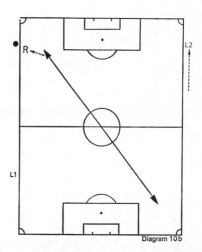

Diagram 10b

☆★☆★☆★☆★☆★☆★☆★☆★☆★☆★☆★☆★☆

The Diagonal System is so named because of the relationship of the Referee to Linesmen, not so much because of the "diagonal" method of running. There are countless situations where running a "diagonal" will remove the Referee from the reality of play.

☆★☆★☆★☆★☆★☆★☆★☆★☆★☆★☆★☆★☆

☆★☆★☆★☆★☆★☆★☆★☆★☆★☆★☆★☆★☆

"Lining is an art in itself and in my view a more difficult one than that of Refereeing."

—Denis Howell, English Referee

☆★☆★☆★☆★☆★☆★☆★☆★☆★☆★☆★☆★☆

23

Find the Referee. In times like this, the Referee needs all the help he can get.

LINESMEN

"I am not a Linesman.
He is not a Referee.
We are a team."

Signals

The basic signal is to raise a motionless flag high and directly overhead. The Linesman should stand rigid and straight, facing the field of play near where the violation or out-of-bounds occurred. You must always look at the Referee before flagging a foul. After having gained the Referee's attention, indicate which way the free-kick or throw-in should be taken. The arm and flag should be at 45 degrees and held rigid.

When Not Signaling

Proceed at all times with the flag unfurled at your side, pointed toward the ground (NASL holds the tip of the flag against the stick). Never run with an upraised flag.

Out of Bounds/Throw-In

If the ball is out-of-bounds and the Referee has not seen your flag, never put it down. This is a decision based on fact.

If the ball has obviously gone out of bounds, there is no reason to flag, similarly, if one team has clearly last played the ball, the flag does not need to be pointed.

The Linesman usually watches for 'foot in the field' or for throws not originating from behind the head.

An infraction is indicated by holding the flag in the basic signal position (straight up). After acknowledged, give a signal indicating the type of throw-in violation (e.g., raising a foot or stepping into the field).

After a throw-in, immediately move to the off-side position of your choice.

The Off-Side

To indicate — Give the basic signal for approximately three seconds. If whistled, stay exactly in line with the position from which the free-kick is to be taken and point with the flag to the point of infraction (near, middle, or far side of the field).

The NASL variation is to keep the flag raised and to point to the offending *player* with your free hand.

If the ball went out-of-bounds on the Referee's diagonal, do not indicate the direction of the throw unless asked for by the Referee. (A common signal is placing the hand on his stomach.)

25

Methods of monitoring offside:

- Standard – Stay even with the second to last *defender*. (FIFA) This is the best method for new Linesmen. The main weaknesses are:
  1. Poor trail coverage, particularly when the defender lags.
  2. Defenders are harder to follow than attackers due to sudden shifting of positions.
- Option A – Stay even with the leading *attacker*.
- Option B – Stay even with the second to last *player*. (NASL)

The main drawback to the exclusive use of either Option A or B have to do with the Linesman getting into a position which results in his viewing play from a poor visual perspective.

Fair or Foul – Recommendations for experienced Linesmen are to stay even with the leading attacker in every case *except* when he has passed (gotten behind) the second to last defender. Whenever this occurs, you are to stay even with the second to last defender.

Wait a fraction of a second to determine the flight of the ball before calling the off-sides.

You may wish to move into the field a bit, if your visual perspective is poor.

Do not merely signal an off-side position each time it occurs. Signal only when the player is taking advantage of that position.

During Play

Follow every long ball to the goal-line or to the goalkeeper, no matter how futile this may appear.

Linesmen may occasionally go 10 to 15 yards into the other half of the field for superior positioning on infractions.

When the ball has not completely gone over the touch-line, the Linesman may indicate that the ball is still in play by pointing toward the field with his free hand.

Play On/Advantage

The safe sign (baseball) with the free hand is an indication of there being no foul. The advantage is indicated to the Referee with the free hand pointing in a straight ahead direction, parallel with the touch-line.

Providing Assistance on Fouls

Questions asked before flagging.

- If I don't raise my flag, do I fail the Referee?
- If I do raise it, will I embarass him?

When indicating infractions, raise the flag vertically and move it slightly to the right and the left – *once only* to attract the Referee's attention and to ensure a full flare of the flag. When acknowledged, point the direction at a 45 degree angle and indicate with the free arm, or by body movements, what type of infraction is being called. Then, having completed the signal, if the foul results in an IFK, give that signal.

If the Linesman flags an offense that was committed in the penalty-area he *does not* point to the penalty-mark but rather walks briskly to a position near the corner flag and awaits developments.

If the Referee calls an infraction quite close to the penalty-area that the linesman feels does not warrant a penalty-kick, he stands at ease with the flag out of sight behind his back.

Free-Kick Close to the Goal

Linesman runs to the goal-line but only *after* the Referee has either moved into position for judging the off-side or has indicated goal coverage by a brief wave of his arm.

Scoring a Goal

If the Linesman feels the goal should not be awarded he looks at the Referee, keeps his flag down, and remains motionless. If he feels it is good, he walks back toward the halfway line. After the Referee signals the goal, the Linesman runs toward the halfway line. If a goal is scored on a close situation (e.g., ball hits cross bar or GK steps completely within the goal), the linesman should indicate that the ball has totally crossed the goal-line by standing on the goal-line and giving the basic signal. When the Referee acknowledges, then the Linesman points and runs toward the halfway line. This close situation, like the ball going out of bounds, is a decision of fact and should be treated accordingly.

- Verbal abuse is indicated by pointing to the player concerned with your free hand, then tapping the index finger on your lips.

Undetected Events

- Signal for fouls that are not observed by the Referee, but only when the flag can be observed by him.

- Report all incidents that are not observed by the Referee.

- Signal to the Referee in order to draw attention to the other Linesman's flag. This will usually happen during a temporary stoppage of play for "off-the-ball" situations, crowd control problems, or other disciplinary measures that must be handled by the Referee.

- To indicate the need to discuss a transgression which has escaped the Referee's attention on the field, hold the bottom of an unfurled flag parallel to the ground either waist high or overhead.

27

Indicate Your Support of the Referee

When the Referee whistles a foul relatively near to your position, immediately flag the foul to indicate your assent with the call.

Providing Added Assistance

If a violation is *about* to occur, try to take care of yourself, rather than placing the burden on the Referee. (e.g., prohibiting encroachment on all nearby corner-kicks/free-kicks and maintaining control through friendly warnings during play.) Let the players know that you are there. Don't be silent.

Never . . .

- Shout at the Referee.
- Leave your position behind the touch-line to retrieve a ball.
- Point to your watch to indicate the passage of time. Have a prearranged signal. One method is to point the flag toward the center of the field; another is to cover your Referee patch with your hand.
- Fail to immediately join the Referee at the conclusion of a period.
- Fail to support the Referee on all of his decisions, even if he overrules you.

Always . . .

- Attempt eye contact before making goal-line decisions.

The USFA Cup Final was taken seriously in 1915, too. The officials were from Massachusetts, New York, and Pennsylvania. The stadium was Taylor Stadium in Bethlehem, PA. Notice that the Linesmen are carrying American flags!

LINESMEN'S GUIDE (DIAGONAL SYSTEM)

Occurrence	Lead Linesman	Trail Linesman
KICK-OFF	In line with the second-to-last defender. (FIFA) In between the halfway line and the second-to-last defender. (NASL) On the halfway line until the ball is played (ASL) *(Fair or Foul)*	In line with the second-to-last defender. (FIFA) On or 3 yards behind the halfway line. (NASL) On the halfway line (NASL) (ASL) *(Fair or Foul)*
GOAL-KICK To indicate: Move on the touch-line so as to be in line with the edge of the goal-area.	In line with the second-to-last defender. (FIFA) In line with the halfway line or the most advanced forward. *(Fair or Foul)*	1. In line with the edge of the goal-area for ball placement, then . . . 2. In line with edge of Penalty-area to see that the ball leaves the area, then . . . 3. Quickly getting in line with the second-to-last defender prior to the adoption of a position for correctly monitoring off-side. An infraction of (1) or (2) is indicated by the basic signal.
CORNER-KICK To indicate: Move rapidly around the corner flag on the goal-line.	1. If a near-side corner, he checks out the placement of the ball within the quarter circle, then . . . 2. He goes ten yards in from the quarter-circle along the goal-line. If defenders attempt to encroach, call out "10 yards back" to the players. For any violation, he indicates it by using the basic signal.	At the halfway line in position for clearance and a counter-attack.
PENALTY-KICK If you flag for the foul, don't point direction. Move toward the corner-area.	On the goal-line at the intersection of the penalty-area line. (FIFA) On the goal-line — 10 yards from the goal post. (Ref is at the intersection of the goal-line and the goal-area.) (NASL) He acts as goal judge and watches for GK foot movement. If the GK has moved, this is indicated by giving the basic signal. *(Fair or Foul)*	At the halfway line in position for clearance and a counter-attack. (FIFA) In line with the edge of the penalty-area to check for encroachment. *(Fair or Foul)* When there is encroachment, use the basic signal, the upraised flag.
	The Linesman gives his signal for encroachment only when it would result in that kick having to be retaken.	

29

LINESMAN SIGNALS

The Linesman's signals are for the Referee. They must be consistent. After they are viewed by the Referee, the flag is no longer appropriate, and must be lowered.

For any type of infraction, the Linesman must point to the area of the field where the incident took place. This aids in quick and accurate ball placement.

An off-side signal.

Some Linesmen prefer to switch hands for indicating a throw-in to the side where the flag is not being carried.

There is no doubt about this signal for a throw-in. Remember that all signals are for the Referee, but can be an aid to the players.

A corner kick is awarded. The Linesman moves directly to the corner area.

The basic signal for the awarding of a goal-kick.

After the Referee has stopped play for an off-side, the Linesman indicates that the player who was off-side was on the far side of the field.

REFEREES

1. The Referee and Linesmen should discuss all matters involving mutual cooperation. The following Referee Instructions should be fully covered (takes about 20 minutes).
   a. Their duties prior to the game (Field Inspection, etc.)
   b. Who shall be senior Linesman in case of need. (Red Flag – NASL and ASL)
   c. The side and end of the field each Linesman will take during each half of the match.
   d. The positions taken for various types of play resumptions.
   e. Signals to be used.
   f. Watch synchronization.

2. Have your Linesmen present, and introduce them, during pre-game instructions to captains.

3. Instruct your Linesmen to enter and to abandon the field with you as a unit, and not as individuals.

4. Before signaling for a goal, always check with your Linesmen.

5. Whenever possible, face your Linesmen as play progresses, keeping the play between the two of you.

6. Never allow your conversations with Linesmen to be overheard.

7. It is recommended that the Referee change his diagonal and that Linesmen change sides but not ends of the field at halftime. If the Referee retains his same diagonal, the Linesmen should remain on their original side of the field.

8. Where a special disciplinary problem may exist or be anticipated, the Referee may change diagonals and switch his Linesmen in the middle of the game.

ADVANTAGES AND DISADVANTAGES OF THE DIAGONAL SYSTEM

Advantages

1. This system is universally accepted by players and coaches, as well as by most countries.

2. The single authority on the field brings consistent interpretation of laws.

Disadvantages

1. Requires three equally qualified Referees who are thoroughly schooled in the laws of the game.

2. To operate most effectively, requires Referee "teams" of three, which are very difficult to assign.

3. Requires Referee to alternate his attention between monitoring play and glancing at his Linesmen to see if they are signaling.

4. Referee is forced to turn his back to a Linesman in order to view play thus missing some "off the ball" fouls.

5. Referee often not close enough to play.

6. Linesmen often feel unimportant, and if overruled, will become inattentive.

7. Linesman easily overruled by Referee. Can lead to lack of confidence in both Referee and Linesman by players.

COMMENTATOR

* Explains all his calls.

* Talks to fans on the sidelines.

* Tells everyone that politics keeps him from getting good assignments.

* Yells "Play On" everytime there is any type of contact.

* Takes a player under his wing and coaches him during the game.

* Interprets **Fair or Foul** for anyone who will listen.

* Never gets a sore throat.

* Gives advice to God.

* Wife wears ear plugs.

THE ONE REFEREE SYSTEM

A commonly experienced game control situation, unfortunately, involves the "One Referee System," where no neutral Linesmen are present. Under these difficult circumstances, the Referee must be prepared to make all decisions himself. The fact that Club Linesmen are not neutral greatly increases the responsibility of the Referee, and does in fact reduce his effectiveness.

When a Referee finds himself as the only qualified official in a match, he must appoint two Club Linesmen. Their duties are to signal when a ball is out of bounds, either over the touch-line or the goal-line. They shall *not* signal for off-side or for any other violation, nor shall they signal directions for throw-ins, goal-kicks, or corner-kicks. The Referee shall instruct both Linesmen in the above duty before the game, encourage them to keep up with play, not to be distracted in any way from their responsibility and that regardless of their personal opinion, the decision of the Referee is final and must not be questioned.

In whistling under this system, the Referee must make several adjustments in his method of officiating. The following pattern of control is advised:

THE FLEXIBLE DIAGONAL

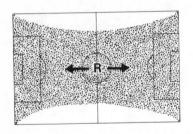

The Referee **(R)** runs either the left-wing or right-wing diagonal, whichever is most appropriate at that moment. It is a 'watered down' diagonal because **(R)** is continually gravitating toward the center of the field, where he will be in a favorable position to recognize infractions. The obvious disadvantage is that he will have to look quickly from side to side to judge offside, but this is unavoidable. He will not be in perfect position to judge every offside but should be able to properly judge the more flagrant violations.

SUGGESTED PREGAME INSTRUCTIONS

"Play the whistle at all times, particularly when a player may be off-side. If your team plays the 'off-side' trap, you do it at your own risk, for a single Referee will sometimes miss an off-side."

The above is an attempt to have the players keep playing, thus cutting down on the amount of suspiciously off-side or claimed off-side goals.

KICK-OFF   and   GOAL-KICK

— As per FIFA Guide —

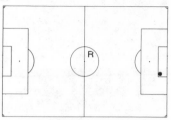

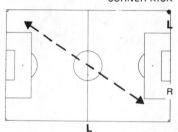

CORNER-KICK

CORNER-KICK

(R) should be *past* the far post. This allows him to see the whole of the corner-kick and the general playing area. He should be on the goal-line so that he is in the best position for judging the ball that temporarily goes out of play on an outswinger, acting as goal judge, and observing any obstruction of the goalkeeper. In any event he must be prepared for an all out sprint when the expected counter-attack materializes.

PENALTY-KICK

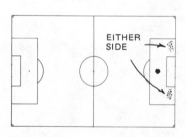

EITHER SIDE

The position for the kick is somewhere between the goal-line and the edge of the goal-area. He is 10-15 yards out from the goal post.

He alone is responsible for the monitoring of encroachment, GK movement, and acting as a goal judge.

THROW-IN

- *Near midfield and defensive throws* – Since many attacks and counter-attacks are made following this type of a throw-in, **(R)** should move within 10-15 yards of the thrower and slightly downfield in order to obtain a favorable viewing angle.

- *Attacking, near opponent's penalty-area* – Similar to the above. Do not go to the opposite side of the field, as it places you in a difficult position for match control.

35

"One Referee, one player . . . . . everyone else went home."

POINTS TO REMEMBER

1. Always play the angle. Try to avoid coming up from directly behind play. Visual perspective is even more important in this system.

2. For all free-kicks, the Referee should position himself downfield, and may use a second whistle to recommence play so that he may position himself correctly.

3. The Referee will often be in doubt on an off-side, and there is no solution to this problem, except that superior field positioning and a careful study of team tactics and abilities is imperative. Do *not* decide to give the advantage to the defense if you are undecided.

4. The off-side more often results from long, rather than short passes. Try to anticipate when a long pass is to be made, and position yourself accordingly.

5. Do not travel to the extreme corners of the field unless it is absolutely necessary. This leaves the opposite corners untended, and violations will be difficult to detect.

6. The Referee may dismiss Club Linesmen at any time, but others must take their place.

7. This system has no advantages over other systems of control, except that with one Referee there is no possibility of disagreement between officials. In the interests of the game, the One Referee System is to be avoided when possible.

"I threw out my club Linesman and I'll throw you out too if you question another one of my calls."

George Tiedemann

"Me first!"

IV

During Play

THE USE OF THE WATCH

(For High School and College Differences See Chapter XV — The American Scene)

As with the whistle, the properly equipped Referee carries two watches during the game, at least one of which is a stopwatch. After he has synchronized watches with his two Linesmen and noted actual time of the kickoff on a regular watch, he may sound his whistle for the commencement of the game. The game begins and he starts his stopwatch at the moment the ball has legally traveled its circumference. The Referee is the sole time-keeper on the field, and he may check time with his Linesmen for accuracy or for any other reason. Although an average of more than 100 stoppages occur on the field during the game, his watch must not be stopped, except for unusual circumstances.

WHEN TO STOP THE WATCH

Yes	No
Treatment of injuries, when a player cannot be safely removed from the field.	Ball out of bounds.
Lost ball, or ball that must be replaced.	On administering a caution or ejection. (Yes for High School.)
Deliberate wasting of time by either team, whether or not they are at an advantage.	After a goal. (Yes for High School and College.)
	After a foul.
	For the taking of a penalty-kick. (Yes for High School and College.)

HINTS FOR REFEREES

1. Since it is quite difficult to observe the game and your watch at the same time, you must observe your watch only during stoppages. If the period is about to end, count down the remaining seconds as you observe play, and check quickly before sounding the whistle to end the period.

2. Arrange a signal system with your fellow Referees so there will be no discrepancies on time of game.

   Your fellow officials can be signaled regarding time remaining by using a hand held unobtrusively at the side. Use one finger for each minute remaining up to five minutes and a closed fist for half-minute increments. A hand covering the Referee patch indicates that time has expired.

3. Do not indicate when you are making up time. Players who see a Referee checking his watch will deduce that he is aware of an unnatural stoppage.

4. A period can end when a ball is out of play.

5. When time runs out, the period is over, even if the ball is in the air.

6. If a regular watch is used instead of a stopwatch, at the start of each half set the minute hand so that half will end with the minute hand at 12:00 o'clock. For a 45 minute half, set it 15 minutes after the hour.

7. The carrying of two watches is extremely important. The second watch, set to regular time, is used to back up the primary watch. It sometimes happens that a Referee will stop his watch for some reason and then not properly restart it. The back-up watch then allows him to end the game properly and on time, making any allowance for time lost.

8. A skin diver's watch is an excellent second watch, since it has rotating outer bezel that allows exact starting time to be noted. A chronograph is also very good.

9. The Referee should periodically check his watch for accuracy, at least once every three months.

STOPWATCHES

- Be sure that the 'reset' function doesn't operate when the watch is running.
- Avoid a watch with a 30 second sweep.
- Avoid one that can be stopped accidentally.
- Conventional stopwatch recommendations . . . Heuer and Minerva.
- The Ingersol is a setable stopwatch that is made in England. The first 45 minutes have a green background and it is very difficult to stop accidentally.

DUAL PURPOSE WATCHES (WRIST/CHRONOGRAPHS)

Seiko Quartz Chronograph
- Time of day
- Stopwatch with split action

Seiko Tri-Alarm
- Countdown timer with alarm
- Two time of day alarms (24-hour time)

Citizen Multi-Alarm
- Countdown timer with alarm
- Two time of day alarms
- Stopwatch

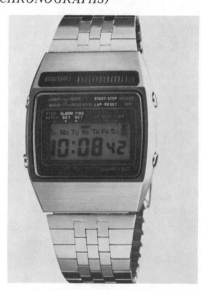

THE USE OF THE WHISTLE

It has been previously observed that the properly equipped Referee must have two whistles. It is recommended that the spare whistle be very accessible, as it is intended for emergencies when the game whistle is defective.

Most experienced Referees carry the whistle in the hand, rather than in the mouth, for the following reasons.

1. A Referee should allow himself time to think and to change his original quick decision. A whistle carried in the mouth is often sounded too hastily.

2. A whistle carried in the mouth is inviting danger.

3. A whistle carried in the mouth makes breathing difficult and unnatural.

4. Heavy breathing with a whistle in the mouth can cause an accidental whistle. If you choose to run with a whistle in your mouth, keep your tongue in the opening of the whistle.

5. A whistle carried on a string around the neck discourages running, for it will bounce, and is distracting. If placed around the neck and held while running, it inhibits free movement on the field. It also detracts from the appearance of the Referee.

It should be obvious that the whistle is the Referee's tool, not his weapon. He should whistle only when necessary, for each time he does, the attention of the participants and spectators switches from game to Referee. One strong short and decisive whistle is usually all that is required. Any Referee who sounds the whistle unnecessarily is seeking attention. It is advisable to whistle longer and louder for a severe foul, and the whistle should say, "I won't allow this to happen again."

HINTS

1. Referees should sound a whistle for the taking of a penalty-kick. This audible signal is for the goalkeeper and for the kicker as well, for they are studying each other and should not have to be distracted from their concentration by having to look at the Referee for a hand signal. If the penalty-kick is taken before the whistle is blown, the kick must be retaken, regardless of the outcome.

2. For emphasis, some Referees prefer to whistle for a goal. This is not recommended, for unfortunately this is sometimes done prematurely, and if the whistle is sounded before the ball is entirely over the goal-line, a drop-ball must be given at the position of the ball when the whistle occurred. Furthermore, an unwhistled goal makes the disputed goal a somewhat easier solution, in that consultation with the Linesman can be carried out with the players' knowing that the Referee has not yet made up his mind on the legality of the goal.

3. The authors recommend the following whistles: the Balillas: Al, Micro, Arbiter, and Balilla/2 (plastic); Acme Thunderer (plastic) and Acme Thunderer Valsport (wide mouth metal).

WHEN WHISTLE SHOULD BE BLOWN

*= Required

Before all kick-offs
- start of game*
- start of half*
- put in play after a goal

For any violation of the Laws of the Game
- improper throw-in*
- to award free-kicks*
- to award penalty-kicks*

Out of Bounds, resulting in . . .
- throw-in ⎫ Unless it is clearly out of
- goal-kick ⎭ bounds
- corner-kick

To put into play . . .
- a penalty-kick
- after a substitution
- after an injury
- a free-kick if the attacking team has asked for the 10 yards. (They shouldn't have to.)
- just prior to dropping the ball

Period Endings*
- half — It's often conventional for the Referee to blow his whistle two times.
- game — Blow whistle three times and point to the center of the field.

If the Referee mistakenly whistles — resume play with a DROP-BALL.

If play is interrupted by a Non-Referee's whistle — PLAY ON.

At first stoppage, have captain of the home team take the necessary action to identify and remove the person blowing the whistle. The Referee has the authority to order the removal of a problem spectator.

*High School/College — The Referee shall blow his whistle whenever the ball is out of play.

DICTATOR

* Is inflexible and a sadist.

* Doesn't allow the coach to walk across the field 20 minutes before kick-off.

* Thinks it's his field.

* Wears multiple Referee badges.

* Tells players and coaches how lucky they are to have him.

* Overrides all of the other officials' calls.

* Makes player move the ball two feet to the left for a free-kick taken at midfield.

* Never heard of *Fair or Foul.*

* Is God.

* Beats his wife.

SIGNALS & SIGNALING

The laws of the game list only one required hand signal for Referees, this being the upraised arm for the indirect free-kick. The benefits of this signal are obvious, particularly when a kick is to be taken near the goal. The signal is solely for the players, so they will know the options open to them as they attack and defend the goal when the kick is taken.

A whistle is sounded on the field . . . is it for pushing? holding? off-sides? obstruction? The Referee will sometimes point in the direction where the ball is to be kicked, but this is the only signal that is normally given. When this happens, players, coaches, spectators, and sometimes other officials are all kept uninformed of the situation and of the infraction. When asked, sometimes the Referee will explain to the player the nature of the violation. This, however, is not recommended, even to the team captain, for it leads to further conversation and to more questions.

The purpose of this section is to recommend a series of signals that a Referee may use in the course of a game, signals which will neither slow the game nor call undue attention to the Referee. Rather, they will convey information in a concise and direct manner to both player and spectator. Furthermore, they will improve Referee-player communications, nonverbally.

With the exception of the accepted signal for "play on," signals are best used immediately after the whistle and prior to the Referee's pointing the direction of the kick. While the Referee is using his handsignal, he will be doublechecking in his mind, making sure that he does not erroneously point in the wrong direction. The proper use of these signals will in part lift the veil of secrecy that sometimes exists between violator and Referee (and violated!), and will further extend the Referee's authority on the field. All Referees must again be reminded that these signals are offered here only as suggested improvements for the game.

NON-FREE-KICKS

SCORING

Goal
or Point to the
Center Circle.

No Goal

Goal-Kick
Point toward the
halfway-line with
one hand and to the
location of the kick
with the other.

Corner-Kick
Point to corner-flag
on side kick is to be
taken.

Penalty-Kick
Point to penalty-mark.

INDIRECT

Dangerous Play

Charging
At inappropriate time

Off-Side

Misconduct

Obstruction
Hit the chest with palms

**Goalkeeper
Steps**

DIRECT

Handling Ball

Tripping

Kicking
Show red card

Pushing

Holding

**Charging Violently
Charging from Behind**

Striking

Jumping at

MISCELLANEOUS

Advantage

"Play-On"

Time-Out

46

HINTS

- Obvious fouls need only the whistle. Everyone knows what has happened. Don't point or gesticulate.

- Subtle fouls, such as an obstruction preceding a charge, need a definite, clear, and immediate signal. Walk or move quickly away from the player (unless you sense possible retaliation), for you will no doubt have the possibility for dissent in such decisions. Players never consider the possibility that you are right.

- Get the habit of walking or moving toward the direction of the team that fouled. This shows everyone that the kick will be taken toward their goal.

- A hand signal indicating direction of kick is all right in most cases. However, do not keep it up after players have fully accepted the direction. Otherwise, the advisable 60° angle of the arm could possibly be interpreted as an IFK signal.

- Do not get in the habit of pointing where the ball should be placed for a kick. "Over there, near the bare spot" is enough. Like the whistle, the hand and arm must be used only when needed.

- Pointing to the goal area and the corner area for kicks is fine, but when everyone knows what's happening, don't do it just "for kicks."

- A penalty-kick, always unwelcome by the defense, demands your pointing to the penalty-spot.

- Keep the "play on" signal to a minimum. Usually no one is looking and no one cares. In most cases you are trying to justify not calling a foul.

☆ ★ ☆ ★ ☆ ★ ☆ ★ ☆ ★ ☆ ★ ☆ ★ ☆ ★ ☆ ★ ☆ ★ ☆ ★ ☆ ★ ☆

In 1954, a World Cup game was played by the national teams of Yugoslavia and Brazil. It was probably the first time in the history of the World Cup when the spectators could walk away and say, "Today the Referee was Faultless." Yes, it's true, the name of the Referee was Mr. Faultless, and he was from Scotland.

☆ ★ ☆ ★ ☆ ★ ☆ ★ ☆ ★ ☆ ★ ☆ ★ ☆ ★ ☆ ★ ☆ ★ ☆ ★ ☆ ★ ☆

☆ ★ ☆ ★ ☆ ★ ☆ ★ ☆ ★ ☆ ★ ☆ ★ ☆ ★ ☆ ★ ☆ ★ ☆ ★ ☆ ★ ☆

Don't talk about your good games. Let them speak for themselves.

☆ ★ ☆ ★ ☆ ★ ☆ ★ ☆ ★ ☆ ★ ☆ ★ ☆ ★ ☆ ★ ☆ ★ ☆ ★ ☆ ★ ☆

REFEREE/LINESMAN DATA CARD

The Data Card is a structured format designed to replace the traditional notebook of blank paper. It is scaled to fit on a 4" x 6" card which is folded in half for convenient pocket insertion. After the match, it can be placed into any standard 4" x 6" card file for future reference.

Colors of the teams are of primary concern. Misconduct and goal information on the left side of the card pertains to the Red team and that on the right to the White team. Numbers of the team captains and their alternates are directly beneath their respective team colors.

An "X" is placed into the appropriate box the the team taking the kick-off. To start the second period, the opposite team kicks-off. The direction the ball is to be kicked-off in is noted in the box marked "Direction." A permanent landmark could be used instead of compass direction if desired. Kick-offs starting a period during regulation play are taken in the same direction.

Time of Day (the backup to your watch with stop action) is recorded on the upper left hand portion of the card. The difference between End Time of the 1st half and Start Time of the 2nd half tells you what the actual halftime interval was.

Match Self Evaluation is accomplished in the upper right hand portion of the card. An overall rating is made (0–10) as well as pertinent comments which may act as the impetus to modify your behavior.

48

The Misconduct portion is centralized. It tells you the name and number (#) of the player who was cautioned (C) or ejected (E), the reason, and the time in minutes when the offense occurred (Min.). An added feature is recording the opponent's number (Opp. #) of the player who was the target of the violator's action. Sometimes (as in the case of #6 on the White team), an instigating player can be identified and actively monitored, thus heading off the ejection which unfortunately occurred in the 84th minute.

Your status (R = Referee, L = Linesman, W = Wing Referee (MOD)) is indicated in the box at the bottom labeled 'Status-Self'. Directly to the right of this is located the status and name of your fellow official(s).

The back of the card is a Tie Breaker Kick Record for use when the match is decided by either kicks taken from the penalty-mark or a shootout (as used in the NASL).

Team colors are entered for the winner of the toss (they must kick first) and their opponent. Each kicker has recorded his name, number (#), if he made the shot or not (X = Score, – = Miss), and what the cumulative (running) totals are.

The results are entered on the front of the card (PK Results) directly beneath the Final Score box.

TIE BREAKER KICK RECORD

WINNER OF TOSS				OPPONENT			
PLAYER NAME	#	X —	RUNNING TOTAL	PLAYER NAME	#	X —	RUNNING TOTAL

Team colors are entered for the winner of the toss (they must kick first) and their opponent. Each kicker has recorded his name, number (#), if he made the shot or not (X = Score, – = Miss), and what the cumulative (running) totals are.

The results are entered on the front of the card (PK Results) directly beneath the Final Score box.

THOUGHTS ON GAME CONTROL

The problem of game control cannot be over-discussed in Referee clinics, and deserves the closest attention of every soccer official.

The success of every soccer Referee will largely depend on the attitude he carries with him toward the game and its players. The Referee is evaluated from the moment he enters the field of play. He is judged by everyone on his dress, his voice and confidence, and his general demeanor. He should be thorough without reciting the laws, enthusiastic without appearing high strung and nervous, polite without appearing too friendly, and firm while being fair.

The Referee's best friend on the field is not his whistle, for his whistle must be used when all else fails. Anyone can blow a whistle, and many fouls occurring in soccer are obvious. Unlike his whistle, his voice will serve him best, and bring him closer to the players. The good Referee will never let a hard foul go without a word to the player. These warnings help prevent cautions, as cautions help prevent ejections and ejections help prevent player riots. These words of advice to a player should always be direct, and positive: "Let's keep the hands down when going for the ball," or "This isn't the kind of tackle I allow," instead of "Don't use your hands going after the ball," or "If you tackle like that again, you'll be cautioned."

Positioning is vitally important when the Referee talks to a player. He should not always approach the player directly, for this will call attention to the Referee's action. Rather, he should move alongside the player, or he may be moving away from the player while talking. There is no "punishment" involved, and the Referee is saying, "I want to get on with the game, but you first must know how I will react to your acts." Words are administered, if possible, so that both offended and offender can hear. This prevents retaliation, and the offended knows that the Referee is on the field to protect the rights of the players. Even when advantage is allowed, the Referee may say, "Play on, watch the tripping #10." On such an occasion the Referee leaves no doubt that he has seen it, allowed the advantage, and noticed the number of the player who fouled. He has thus gained the respect of both players, and others within earshot, and he probably will not have to warn this player again.

The testing period for the Referee is in the first few minutes of play of each period. If the Referee is firm, the testing period will then be over, and the players will settle down to a fair game. If the Referee fails the testing period, for whatever reason, the game will proceed, but with players waiting for the opening when they can gain the unfair advantage. For the Referee, the game is won in these precious minutes. For the players, they must wait the full duration of the contest.

HINTS:

1. Superior field positioning is essential to good game control. Most players will accept a questionable call when a Referee is in a favorable position to call an infraction. They will always suspect even an inconsequential whistle if the Referee is far from play.

2. There are times when the Referee is best-advised to keep distance from players, and at the same time require them to stay away from him. When a penalty-kick is awarded, dissent usually is prevalent except with the most disciplined of teams. After calling the infraction, and while waiting for players to position themselves, the Referee should move to some isolated portion of the penalty-area, where players seldom congregate. He has created distance between himself and the players. If players try to approach him, he may say, "The foul has been called and it is a penalty. I will not change it. If you approach me, you will be cautioned for dissent." (Ungentlemanly conduct)

3. A smile from the Referee should be seen at least once after he has entered the field. This will prove he is human. Too many Referees assume their responsibility with never a smile nor a bit of humor. This method can break the tension in a game, but should never be attempted when it could be misconstrued as being at the expense of a player.

4. The Referee's main responsibility lies in protecting law abiding players from those who don't.

Your problems in a game may snowball on you. Meet Alan Snowball, Referee, from Spartanburg, South Carolina.

51

Oto Maxmilian

"It was him . . . . Number 15."

WARNINGS, CAUTIONS, AND EJECTIONS

(See Chapter X — Rules Almanac)

The consistent and disciplined attitude of the Referee is best exemplified in his handling of warnings, cautions, and ejections. Since the Referee whistles the game not for the players or spectators but in order to apply the Laws of the Game, he must take extreme measures when a single disruptive act or constant infringement of the laws takes place.

Law XII states rather clearly the conditions under which a player is to be cautioned, and those conditions under which he is to be removed from the game. The Referee should memorize the four basic conditions where a player shall be cautioned and the three where he shall be ejected from a game. He should not hesitate to employ these laws.

The World Cup of 1970 brought a partial answer to communication difficulties on the field, where in international competition an Argentine referee may be trying to caution a Moroccan or a Czech player. Obviously, the language difficulties are great, greater perhaps than the tensions of the game. A system of yellow cards for cautions and red cards for ejections was employed, for the benefit of players, coaches, and spectators alike. If a player was being cautioned, a small 3" x 5" yellow card was held high by the Referee, followed by the booking of the player. No words were to be spoken, in any language. Similarly, a red card was used for a more serious situation, when a player was being sent off the field. Whether it was the threat of the cards, the quality of the refereeing, or the players themselves no one will know for sure, but the red cards were not needed, and a World Cup without serious incident was soon history.

Other soccer organizations have accepted the cards, citing among other reasons the example that is made of the offender as the card is held high. Whatever the reasons, this idea is a very constructive step toward game control, and is highly recommended for all levels of soccer.

The word "warning" appears nowhere in the laws of the game, yet comes up frequently in referee discussions, and sometimes on the field. Warnings as such are rather nebulous, and are usually the easy way out for a Referee who for some reason is hesitating to issue a caution. For our purposes here, a warning is a "soft caution." In his efforts to minimize conversation on the field, the Referee must keep his warnings at a minimum, and with little explanation. It is the Referee's desire to avoid and to anticipate troubles on the field, and he may occasionally warn a player that his actions could lead to something more serious. Play should not be stopped to issue a warning, but these few well chosen words should come during a natural stoppage, and, as with cautions, in a place where players may not gather around the Referee. The warning is enough for most players, but if not, the caution will come as less of a surprise.

HINTS FOR REFEREES:

1. A free-kick, particularly one near the goal, is often the subject of much delay and consternation on the part of both Referee and players. Defenders who stand over or in front of the ball, without yielding ten yards must be cautioned. Other defenders, farther from the ball, often rush forward before the ball is kicked. When they do, the whistle must be sounded immediately, and the offenders cautioned. The Referee must *not* apply the advantage clause and await the outcome of the kick. He shall not prevent the kick from being taken unless asked by the players to step off the ten yards.

2. A player who has been sent off must leave the field. It is not recommended that he be seated with substitutes on the bench.

3. If an expelled player comes back on the field, he is no longer considered a player, and is a foreign object (regardless of his nationality). If he handles the ball, a drop ball is called.

4. If a captain is ejected, a substitute captain must be named among the remaining players.

5. If an extreme situation develops on the field, where cautions and ejections seem only to lead to more problems, the Referee may call both teams or both captains to the center of the field. He may then warn them that further violence will result in termination of the game.

6. The Referee should go to the player to administer a caution or an ejection. To require him to come to you is to abuse him.

7. When a player is cautioned or ejected, the name of the offender, and not just the number, must be recorded, as well as the offense and time elapsed.

8. Carry your two cards in separate pockets. This eliminates the problem of confusion and embarassing mistakes.

9. While it is sometimes advisable to be slow (ceremonial) in issuing a card, needless delay is unwise. Remember, that time is not out for such sanctions.

☆★☆★☆★☆★☆★☆★☆★☆★☆★☆★☆★☆★☆

We think it's a positive move . . .

In Argentina, an addition was introduced to the Laws of the Game. When a player holds the arm or any other part of the body of an opponent, the Referee automatically cautions the offender, and also makes the appropriate gesture to caution the whole team. From this moment, any other player from the cautioned team who commits a similar infringement will immediately be sent off the field by the Referee.

☆★☆★☆★☆★☆★☆★☆★☆★☆★☆★☆★☆★☆

AGITATOR

* Makes mountains out of mole hills.

* Does his best to aggrevate players, coaches, and fans.

* Tells the coach that this is the poorest field he has ever reffed on.

* Insults GK about his gloves during the coin toss.

* Tells fellow official that he has a cheap looking uniform.

* When he is in the stands, yells at the Referee.

* Tells his fellow official(s) at half time that they stink.

* Shows everyone a 'typro' he found in *Fair or Foul*.

* Argues with God.

* Is divorced.

Do you know what a goalkeeper may and may not do?

THE GOALKEEPER . . . RIGHTS, PRIVILEGES, AND RESPONSIBILITIES (See Chapter X, Rules Almanac)

Law III states that the teams consist of "not more than eleven players, one of whom shall be the goalkeeper." He is the usual last line of defense and as a participant with special privileges governing his movement and boundaries, he deserves special comment here.

The goalkeeper must wear a different color from all of the other players on the field and the Referee, including the color of the opposite goalkeeper. He may exchange places with any other player from his own team on the field, as long as the ball is dead (out of play), and the jersey is exchanged with said player, if the Referee has been previously notified of the change.

Q. Where may the goalkeeper handle the ball?

A. The goalkeeper may handle the ball at any location in the penalty-area, and the legality of his handling depends solely upon the position of the ball. He may be standing outside of the penalty-area, either in the goal, behind the goal-line, or on the field, and still handle the ball legally so long as some part of the ball is within the PA.

Q. When does the goalkeeper have possession of the ball?

A. He has possession when one or both hands or arms is holding the ball. Holding the ball and pinning it to the ground with any part of the hand is considered possession.

Q. How many steps may the goalkeeper take with the ball?

A. He may take four steps while in possession of the ball, and until played by another player. His first step is not counted until he regains his full balance after having pursued the ball. Steps are counted even if he bounces the ball. If he puts the ball on the ground and rolls it with his hand so it can be safely played by an opponent or dribbles it with his feet, the ball is in play, and steps are not counted.

Q. May the goalkeeper throw the ball into the opponent's goal and score?

A. Yes, as long as the ball was legally thrown from within his own penalty-area.

Q. When may the goalkeeper be charged?

A. He may be charged in the goal-area if he is obstructing, has possession of the ball, and if he has one or both feet on the ground. Outside of the goal-area, he may be charged the same as any other player. However, when he has the ball, opponents may not prevent him from putting the ball into play, nor may they obstruct him in any way.

Q. How long may the goalkeeper retain the ball in his possession?

A. The Referee will allow him a reasonable period of time to rid himself of the ball. If he does not, after being warned, he will be cautioned, and an indirect-free-kick will be awarded against him.

Q. **May the ball be played when a goalkeeper rolls the ball on the ground, throws it to himself in the air, or dribbles it with his foot or bounces it with his hand?**

A. Yes. When the ball is thrown by the goalkeeper to himself, steps are counted, even though it may be played.

Q. **May the goalkeeper travel to any part of the field?**

A. Yes, he has full rights to any part of the field, and may participate in throw-ins and in the kicking of penalty-kicks as well.

Q. **May the goalkeeper be obstructed while waiting for a corner-kick to be taken?**

A. Yes, but as the kick is taken, the obstructing player must make a movement toward the ball, or obstruction is immediately whistled.

HINTS FOR REFEREES

1. On the taking of a corner-kick, do not watch the flight of the ball, for this is the duty of the Linesman. Watch the goal-mouth, as there is often unfair charging or obstruction of the goalkeeper or jostling of other players at this time. When this occurs, and the ball is in play, the whistle should be sounded immediately, and an indirect or direct-kick, depending on the infraction, is to be awarded.

2. No teammate (player or substitute) may exchange shirts with the goalkeeper without notifying the Referee. If the new goalkeeper does this . . .

   If he was currently a *player* . . . The Referee cautions both as soon as the ball goes out of play.

   If he was a *substitute* . . . Caution the new GK and if the game is stopped to administer the caution, restart with an IFK from where the ball was.

3. The goalkeeper occasionally places himself in a dangerous position as he lunges through the air after the ball. He does this at his own risk, and is not to be called for dangerous play, even though the opponent may hesitate due to the action of the goalkeeper.

The goalkeeper provides a series of worrisome problems for the Referee. Two areas which constantly arise concern the rolling of the ball and obstruction. Both are judgment calls, and we can only provide guidelines.

A. **The Rolling of the Ball.** The goalkeeper who rolls the ball with the hand so that another player may safely play the ball shall not have steps counted. A step is counted each time he retains possession after rolling the ball. If the ball is tapped or rolled along so that he is only gaining space with no one having a chance to safely play the ball, steps are counted. Only you can judge that one.

B. **Goalkeeper Obstruction.** Occasionally you will see players standing in front of the goalkeeper. Law XII IBD 8 is directed toward these players. Many differing opinions exist on this subject. Our recommendation is to verbally discourage players from standing in front of the goalkeeper, and if they persist, caution.

These two pictures, taken in the same game, indicate the only legal alternatives open to the offensive player when the goalkeeper has possession. The player (top) has pursued the ball, but chooses to run past the goalie once she is in possession. She is seen at a discreet distance (below), allowing the goalkeeper to safely clear the ball. Which situation could pose problems for the Referee?

9.15 METERS, PLEASE!

Make no mistake about it, the administering of free-kicks (including penalties) is probably the single act which separates the superior from the average Referee. Since free-kicks are "set" situations, which, if properly executed, result in goals, the defense may use a variety of "gamesmanship" moves to prevent the goal.

Defensive players are required to be 10 yards (9.15 meters) away from the ball for the taking of all free-kicks and corner-kicks. The alert Referee must know that some players have been coached to distract the offense, delay the game, and generally to cause confusion so the defense may be made ready. This is particularly true with all "ceremonial" kicks near goal, where the wall is being set up and where offensive players are equally as confused. In fact, there usually seems to be guesswork on the part of the attacking team . . . who will take the kick, and how will it be taken?

WHEN THE FOUL IS AWARDED

1. Immediately point the direction of the kick. If it is indirect, raise the arm and say, "Indirect kick."

2. Indicate the place where the kick is to be taken.

3. Move away from the play, so you will not interfere with a quick free-kick. While you are doing so, if necessary, remind the defense to quickly retreat, or they will be cautioned.

IF YOU ARE ASKED TO MARK TEN YARDS
(Only the kicking team has the right to ask)

1. Indicate, "All right, but wait for my signal (FIFA recommends a whistle) before kicking." (They have now reduced the chances for surprise.)

2. Mark it off by quickly running 5-6 steps (or, you should be able to estimate the distance of ten yards within less than 2 feet). Never stride it off. Never push players back with hands or arms.

3. Say, "They're back. They won't encroach." (Players who hear this won't *dare* encroach!)

HINTS:

- If the kicking team has to ask for the ten yards, you probably haven't done your job. Laws XIII IBD2 and Law XVII require that players retreat, and they cannot be allowed to waste time.

- If you stand over the ball and try to move the wall, you are preventing a kick and inviting the defense to defy your own estimate of ten yards.

- Be careful about using your whistle to move the wall. You may be whistling when your back is turned on the ball, and some enterprising attacker has sent the ball on the way to the goal. Use your voice.

THE WALL

Closely allied with the "ten yards" ritual is the wall itself, always set up to prevent an easy shot at goal. Most important is the concept of the advantages which accrue to the attacking team. The attacking team may:

- Take the kick at any time, unless they have asked for ten yards.
- Station players within the defensive wall, if space allows.
- Form their own wall, in front of the "ten yard" wall.
- Ask for "ten yards" from the Referee.
- Delay the taking of the kick for a reasonable period of time in order to confuse the defense.

The well-prepared Referee must expect the unexpected when a free-kick is awarded near goal. The most common abuses are:

Defensive

(a) Players standing over or near the ball to delay.

Remedy: As already stated, move them back quickly, with a firm voice. Don't threaten them, but caution them if you must.

(b) All the players in the wall refuse to retreat the proper distance.

Remedy: Stop the taking of the kick, if you are convinced that the offense will not be disrupted. Caution the nearest defensive player who has not moved. As you caution, announce loudly that the next player will be treated the same unless the wall moves. It will move! You may also want to stop time. If you do so, make sure they know that these tactics will serve no good, for time is out.

(c) Players rush at the kicker (the ball) as he moves to kick, and before the ball is in play.

Remedy: Whistle immediately, before the ball is in play, and then caution. If whistle is late (after the kick), caution, and have the kick taken from the spot where the infraction occurred. If ball goes directly in goal following offender's action, allow goal (provided that you haven't whistled), then caution.

Offensive

(a) Occasionally more than one player "runs over" the ball in an attempt to confuse the defense. You may feel this is ungentlemanly conduct. Generally, Referees let this go, but remember the offense does not have unlimited advantages for the taking of the free-kick.

(b) Players try to force their way into a wall. A linking of arms by the defense seems fair, and is generally done to prevent the ball going through the wall. Players on the offense in a defensive wall will invariably cause elbowing, pushing, and striking. Discourage it.

61

FURTHER HINTS:

- Off-side sometimes occurs directly from a free-kick, when both teams are within a wall. The attacking players must move forward just prior to the kick to avoid the possibility of being called for off-side.

- If an indirect free-kick is taken within 10 yards of the opponent's goal, the Referee should say, "Defense, ten yards away or on the goal-line." It is not necessary to add that players, if on the goal-line, should be between the goal posts. If an infringement occurs, deal with it on an individual basis. *Both feet* must be on the goal-line.

- Young players under 14 have little concept of the wall and of tactics. Show them what is right, and they will comply.

- Most problems in the wall can be anticipated. Be ahead of the players in your thinking, and take care of problesm before they happen.

L.A. Aztecs

The wall continually poses problems for Referees. Here, the Referee has made the players comply with the 9.15 meters, and he is holding up play and turning his back in order to run into position for the taking of the free-kick. Can you see the offensive player in the wall? What do you think the players in white will do when the Referee has turned his back?

CHEAPSKATER

Make it two coats Fred —
this uniform has got to
last me for three weeks.

* Borrows a Timex from one of the spectators.

* Carries one card; yellow on one side and red on the other.

* Tapes up socks with roll of adhesive tape 'obtained' from a team trainer four months ago.

* Has his flip-coin attached to a chain.

* Collects discarded screw-in cleats laying in the vicinity of the field.

* Uses 15 year old Acme Thunderer which hangs on a shoelace lanyard.

* Uses Xerox copy of Referee Data Card contained in *Fair or Foul.*

* Asks team manager if he has cash, instead of a check.

* Sun has caused shoulder and seat of pants area to turn brown.

* Comes to game carrying Referee gear in paper Safeway bag.

* Gives wife worn out soccer shoes for use as she does the yard work.

The 1974 World Cup (Italy vs Haiti) had its moments of agony.

INJURIES

Soccer is not without its injuries, and they may result by means which are fair or foul, sometimes through inexperience and clumsiness, and sometimes through deviousness and premeditation.

The problem facing the Referee is how to stop the game at the proper time when an injury occurs in the field of play. A slight injury deserves only token notice by the Referee until a natural stoppage occurs, at which time he may stop the game. A more serious injury normally deserves immediate attention and the game should be stopped without delay. However, if the injury occurs at a place where there is no longer game activity and to a player who is not involved in the play when the injury is noticed, the game should be stopped only when the ball is out of play *or* when the player or his team is suddenly at a disadvantage through the injury. This is especially important when the goalkeeper is incapacitated and the play is suddenly shifted in his direction.

HINTS TO REFEREES

1. When the Referee stops play due to an injury, he must give a drop-ball at the point of play when the game was stopped. (High school — if one team has clear possession of the ball, give them an indirect-free-kick.)

    Drop-balls within the penalty-area are to be avoided, if possible. Stop play for an injury after the goalkeeper has made his clearing move.

2. Try to avoid touching a player. If he is injured and in need of medical attention, signal for help from a club trainer or coach.

3. Do not allow teams to group and refresh themselves during an injury timeout. Make every effort to have the injured player(s) removed from the field so that play may resume.

4. Do not allow the team trainer or coach on the field unless you suspect that the injured player cannot attend to himself.

5. Do not allow players from either team to crowd around an injured player.

6. Do not answer players' queries about the game during this stoppage of play.

7. An opponent who lifts a player from the ground to humiliate him and to minimize his injuries must be cautioned for ungentlemanly conduct.

8. Soccer injuries, as with ski injuries, are more frequent later in the day, when muscles become tired and reactions slow. Players also will sometimes feign injuries at this time to regain strength and wind.

9. In youth soccer the Referee should consider the age of the player in stopping play for injury. Generally, the younger the player, the quicker the game should be stopped.

Horst Müller

Circumstances surrounding injuries are as varied as the injuries themselves. Bad luck, player inadequacy, fatigue, or player intention can all be a part of what leads up to the drama of the game stoppage for injury. In a World Cup game (top), the Referee chooses to signal for the trainer. In a youth game (below), the Referee, though lacking somewhat in perfect dress, wisely decides to stop the game immediately and attend to a player who was hit in the nose by the ball. If a Referee has seen what caused the injury, he is better able to determine at what point to stop play.

WHAT TO DO AT HALFTIME

Law VII states that halftime shall not exceed five minutes, except by consent of the Referee. If, due to special circumstances, the Referee deems it necessary to extend the halftime period beyond five minutes, he will probably meet with little resistance, for this period usually lasts ten to fifteen minutes.

Some experienced Referees have the habit of announcing, upon the period's end, that "Time is up ... five minutes between halves." They will then immediately start timing this interval, and will reconvene the players four minutes later, allowing a minute for re-assembly and organization of the two teams. All of the above is advisable, for it establishes the Referee's authority even during halftime, and allows no extra time for rest.

The Referee should be seen only with his two neutral linesmen at halftime. They shall not accept refreshment from either team, nor shall they be seen discussing the game with managers, players, coaches, or spectators. This valuable time is to be spent exchanging mutual constructive criticisms on the progress of the game.

Probably the singlemost important topic at halftime should be a discussion of players' behavior and play. If there are problems or anticipated problems, (the second half invariably presents more of a challenge than the first), they should be brought out. Warnings, cautions, and ejections should be discussed in detail. Often Referees are seen at halftime with seemingly little to discuss. Two topics should be in mind: (1) "What did we do in the first half?" and (2) "How are we going to do in the second half?"

HINTS ON WHAT TO DO AT HALFTIME

1. Always retain the game ball at halftime, for you are responsible for the ball until game's end.

2. During the five minute interval, warm up again by running from one goal to the other as you re-inspect the nets, which may have become loose with halftime activities.

3. Never be afraid to ask a fellow Referee at half time if he is noticing things on the field that you are not seeing. If he is, it is his duty to report them to you.

4. If a Linesman is doing his job, he should be complimented at halftime by the Referee. If he is not, the Referee should try to be constructive in his approach to him. The Referee needs his support, for an uncooperative Linesman can destroy the efforts of the best Referee.

5. Be extra alert during the opening minutes of each half. This is the time when players will test your alertness and your strict enforcement of the rules of the game.

6. Never smoke within view of players or spectators.

"Don't just stand there, say something."
Experienced FIFA Referee John Davies of San Francisco knows when to turn it off.

V

Don't
Just Do Something..
Stand There

THE ADVANTAGE CLAUSE

"It must be clear, immediate, and effective."

The advantage clause is a very effective tool for the Referee, for it allows him to ignore the whistle for the good of the game.

Law V states that "a Referee may refrain from penalizing in cases where he is satisfied that by doing so he would give an advantage to the offending team."

The advantage clause is self-explanatory. Contrary to the "no harm, no foul" situation in basketball, there can indeed be harm, but as long as the offended player or team will retain the advantage, or have more of an advantage by retaining the ball without game stoppage, no foul is called.

The correct application of this clause within Law V is most difficult for the inexperienced Referee, and real understanding of its meaning will come only through extensive game experience. The new Referee should know here that he can only *assume* what *might* happen if he allows play to go on, and that he is always technically right by ignoring the clause and whistling for all violations, regardless of the position of the offended. Most qualified referees admit that in cases where extreme discipline problems prevail and when a player may retaliate for an unpunished offense, it is always better to call the foul and ignore the clause.

Generally speaking, the more advanced the level of the game, the more the advantage clause will be applied, for the players will expect it. In lower levels of soccer such as youth competition, the official should endeavor to teach the players that all fouls are unfair, and must be penalized.

"Play On."

Horst Muller

70

HINTS TO REFEREES

1. In applying the advantage, it is always advisable to acknowledge having seen a foul. Recommended signals are either raising an arm, or waving arms and hands at waist level with a verbal indication of "Advantage, Play On." This will indicate to both players and spectators that you have noticed the foul.

2. Once you have elected to apply the advantage, you may not change your decision, even though a player may stop play, lose his own advantage, and ask for a whistle.

3. When in doubt, do not use the advantage. The player must have clear possession and the clear advantage that he had before the infraction.

4. Early in the game, apply the advantage only when a direct scoring chance is evident, but not at midfield. After the authority of the Referee has been established, a more liberal application of advantage may be used.

5. In a hard fought game where extreme contact is frequent, it is often advisable to neglect the advantage as a preventive measure to keep the game in control.

6. If the advantage is applied, the Referee must wait until the ball is out of play to caution or eject.

7. The advantage is also applied when a player is fouled but a teammate obtains or retains control of the ball.

8. On a foul that takes place in the penalty-area, the Referee should apply the advantage clause only if he is almost certain that a goal will be scored. The biggest advantage is at the penalty-mark.

9. The Referee must be more concerned about the effect of an illegal act than about the act itself.

10. Do not be confused by the wording of the advantage clause. Although it mentions only the "offending" team, think of it this way: If you take the advantage (through the foul or infraction) away from the offending team (by the whistle) you give it to the "offended" team. If you don't whistle, they have gained nothing by their foul.

CONCACAF RECOMMENDED EXCEPTIONS TO THE ADVANTAGE

1. No advantage if a clear off-side.

2. No advantage during dangerous play.

3. No advantage if kicked deliberately.

☆ ★ ☆ ★ ☆ ★ ☆ ★ ☆ ★ ☆ ★ ☆ ★ ☆ ★ ☆ ★ ☆ ★ ☆ ★ ☆ ★ ☆ ★

"The response to soccer has changed from total ignorance to pure cliche without passing through acquaintance and appreciation."

—M. G. Cooke, New Republic 1977

☆ ★ ☆ ★ ☆ ★ ☆ ★ ☆ ★ ☆ ★ ☆ ★ ☆ ★ ☆ ★ ☆ ★ ☆ ★ ☆ ★ ☆ ★

THE OTHER ADVANTAGE

The advantage clause says that the Referee should . . .

"Refrain from penalizing in cases where he is satisfied that, by doing so, he would be giving an advantage to the offending team."

The "other" advantage has to do with a practical game flow, but most of all with good common sense.

Law V IBD 8 says,

"The laws of the game are intended to provide that games should be played with as little interference as possible, and in this view it is the duty of the Referees to penalize only deliberate breaches of the law. Constant whistling for trifling and doubtful breaches produces bad feeling and loss of temper on the part of the players and spoils the pleasure of the spectators."

The common interpretation tends to be to not whistle so many 'ticky-tack' fouls. This in part is a correct interpretation, however it is often used as carte blanche for doing nothing. This occasionally results in chaos.

V-8 is the hardest of all to implement properly. It is ten times more difficult than the advantage clause, and even that is a concept not fully comprehended by most Referees.

It is the feel and flow of the game, and as it goes, so goes your game control. It, like the advantage, takes on more importance as you officiate the older and more experienced player. V-8 can't be taught. It comes only with a continued awareness of it . . . and much experience. There are certain ancillary aspects of V-8 that lend themselves as practical hints in this section. A better title might be . . .

- Flow with the game or drown or
- Delay leads to decay or
- Things which annoy Referee Assessors.

SIGNALING A FOUL WITH REPEATED BLASTS OF THE WHISTLE

Everyone's attention is drawn toward you. It distracts the players' concentration. It often brings the game to a halt. One of the worst things it does is to diminish the effect of the whistle when it is really needed.

Law VIII   Every player shall be in his own half of the field and not less than 10 yards from the ball until the ball is kicked off.

Ask yourself as a Referee, "Is an advantage being gained?" If not, then call the kick back only if the encroachment is blatant. This is only done because it might cause your credibility as a Referee to be questioned.

Law XVII   The whole of the ball shall be placed within the quarter circle.

Is a player gaining an advantage because the ball is not 100% within the area? If you think so, then don't allow the kick until the situation is rectified. The main thing is that you don't require the letter of the law just because you are aware of its existence.

Law XVI   The ball is to be kicked from a point within that half of the goal-area that is nearest to where it crossed the line.

If 1 or 2 yards more or less from the middle of the goal, don't make a big deal about it. Let the defensive player go to the side that is closest for him. It means more playing time for the players and does away with another unnecessary delay. Of course, if you are asked by the defense or you perceive dissention about to creep in, then by all means quickly render your irrevocable decision.

Law XII   If the goalkeeper takes more than 4 steps when holding, etc. . . .

The purpose is to prevent the goalkeeper from wasting time. As long as this is complied with don't count stutter steps or be overly pickey about the number of steps taken . . . unless your Referee credibility can be seriously questioned. When did you last see a professional Referee call steps on a goalkeeper?

Your fellow official makes a non-serious mistake.

If possible, do not correct it until halftime or at game's end. For example,

• Your linesman points in a possibly incorrect direction.

• Your partner in a multiple Referee system forces a player to put the ball in the exact corner of the goal-area for a goal-kick.

If the players, coaches, or spectators don't make a big deal out of it . . . why should you? On the spot overrulings should only be done for a reason . . . and not merely to assert your authority or law knowledge.

Law XI   Off-side position, but goalkeeper can easily reach the ball first.

This has to be used carefully. Although CONCACAF recommends no type of an advantage on an off-side, many Referees feel that it aids game flow. If the Referee discovers that he made a mistake by not calling the off-side, he may still redeem himself with the late whistle . . . because the moment of judgment extends until the next moment of judgment.

"I said ten centimeters to the left."

Probably the most notable aspect of the 'other' advantage is the . . .

EXACT BLADE OF GRASS SYNDROME!!

Law XII   A free-kick is awarded to the opposing team from the place where the offense occurred.

How many times have you seen an over-zealous Referee run over to a spot and *demand* the ball be placed at that exact location? How many times have you seen him require that the ball be meaninglessly moved a yard or so to comply with the Referees' requirement? If an off-side occurred around the 30 yard line, who cares if the ball is placed 5-6 yards forward or back? Who cares if the ball is displaced laterally by 10-15 yards as long as no advantage is being gained? Only the officious Referee.

There are instances, however, not to be casual about —

- Defenders usually would prefer that the ball be placed just outside of the penalty-area as opposed to within. Don't compromise. If the foul was committed within the area, have the free-kick taken from inside the area.
- Don't ever let an off-side near the halfway-line result in the ball being kicked from within the offender's own half of the field.
- If one player is off-side and another player is merely in an off-side position, make sure that the ball is placed in the immediate vicinity of the player who was whistled for being off-side. If not, you will be chipping away at your own credibility.
- The closer to the goal that a foul is committed, the tighter the Referee should become regarding ball placement.

The foul that is committed near midfield or by the attacking team in the defender's territory should be given the same latitude as the routine off-side.

Law XV   The ball shall be thrown in from the point where it crossed the line.

Does the thrower's team gain an unfair advantage? If he 'crabs' 5-10 yards in either direction . . . .

- at midfield? . . . . . . NO
- close to the opponent's goal? . . . . . . YES, if in the direction of the opponent's goal (an unfair advantage). Otherwise, NO.
- close to his own goal? . . . . . . YES if it puts him within throwing range of his own goalkeeper (an unfair advantage). Otherwise, NO.

There are two questions you must ask yourself.

1. Is a team being taken advantage of? This you should not allow.
2. Am I being taken advantage of? We make outselves look bad enough without having to be helped along by the players. Don't be officious, but don't let them do a number on you either.

"ALLOW THEM TO CHEAT . . . . . . BUT NOT TO STEAL!!!!!"

—Joe Reed
National Federation Baseball Rules Committee

75

Antonio Marques (Brazil), one of the world's finest Referees, exerts his authority in a 1974 World Cup Game.

VI

Really Knowing
Fair From Foul

REFEREE COMPOSITION

If Mecca is proper field execution, perhaps now is the time to reflect upon our strong and weak points.

The diagram below depicts that there are five major ingredients necessary for the fully prepared Referee. The largest barrier for the Referee who wishes to successfully implement these tools is, of course, attitude. It totally encloses proper field execution. Attitude colors, distorts, and enhances all that we do on the field.

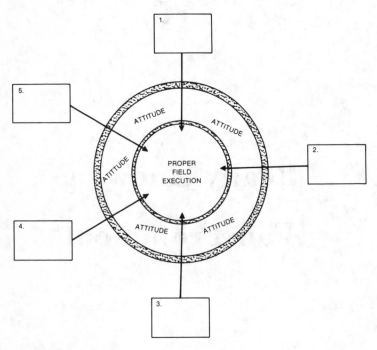

Review the following attitudinal points regularly. They are every bit as important as the rules contained within FIFA Law.

THE TEN COMMANDMENTS OF ATTITUDE

1. **Thou shalt have a good image** – What do we convey to the players, coaches, and spectators? . . . . Do we look the part? . . . . Are cards hanging out of our pockets? . . . . Socks at half-mast? . . . . Ill-fitting uniform? . . . . Are you viewed as a little Ceasar or a Casper Milktoast?

2. **Thou shalt have rapport with fellow officials** – How do you appear to your partner(s)? Are you capable of relaxing them? Do you bring out the best in them? If you don't, it's usually *your* fault.

3. *Thou shalt concentrate* — Are you able to sustain concentration throughout the game? Do you totally dedicate yourself to the task at hand for a full 90 minutes or do you occasionally find yourself standing around just watching play? How successful are you in fighting off mental fatigue. Both authors find that to do more than two (sometimes one) game in a day results in not staying sharp. When doing multiple games, are you with it or just a body putting in time? Don't accept too heavy a load. It does the game a disservice. If you must do it in a tournament... try to pace yourself.

4. *Thou shalt be emotionally stable* — We have all seen the unstable symptoms on the field. The Referee who appeared in house slippers to officiate a college game. He told a coach at halftime that he would beat him up if he received a bad rating (an interesting switch).... The Referee who received 7 unsatisfactory ratings out of 10.... The local Referee who was red-lined ("Do not assign") by all six of the schools within a particular high school league because he was so abrasive.... The Referee who gets players and coaches mad even before the game has started. The unstable Referee is not disciplined.

5. *Thou shalt be self-disciplined* — Can you control yourself on the field? Do you overreact to the abuse that is often heaped upon you? Do you intelligently apply the laws in a calm, professional manner?.... or do your glands take over?

6. *Thou shalt have confidence in self* — Do you think well of yourself? Do you like you?.... Don't overdo it though, the flipside of the coin is being pompous on an ego trip. Do you emulate a field general by wearing more than one Referee patch? If so, you have a poor self-image. People measure your ability by deeds on the field, not by how many badges you display. The confident Referee is not defensive.

7. *Thou shalt be non-defensive* — Are you able to be self-effacing? Can you admit your mistakes? (Where, when, how, and to whom is another matter).... or is it always 'them' (players, coaches, spectators, or partner(s))? The non-defensive Referee by his very actions, exudes confidence.

8. *Thou shalt be motivated* — Are you motivated to give your very best effort? If not, don't work the game.... even if you are donating your time on a 'freebie' basis.

9. *Thou shalt be flexible* — Do you have the ability to modify your behavior?.... or are you rigid, being unable to adapt to each new and unexpected situation as it occurs?

10. *Thou shalt not use the name of the Referee in vain* — How badly do you chew up the Referee when you are functioning as a coach or a spectator? Do you discretely keep it to yourself or only for the ears of a close companion? Some Referees are the most venomous critics imaginable. Why is this done?... Insecurity!!! It's usually the weakest Referees that chip away. Normally the louder and more vicious they are, the poorer is their own officiating. To openly criticize is to drive nails into your own coffin.... and into those of all the other men in black.

79

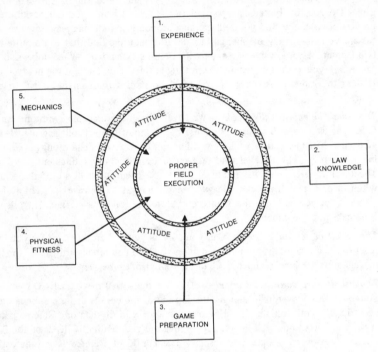

THE FIVE MAJOR INGREDIENTS (See diagram above)

1. **Experience** is the **most important** ingredient. Unfortunately it only comes so quickly.
    It takes much time to assimilate all that you have been exposed to. Often your very
    assignments are restrictive. You can't mature as an official if you never have tough or
    challenging games. Seek out the potentially difficult games. It may be painful, but
    with the proper attitude, it will cause you to grow. Vicarious experience can be
    gained from watching other Referees in action. Empathize with them during the
    game. What can you learn from them? What could they have learned from you?

2. **Law Knowledge** links up very closely with experience in order to be effective. You
    can't be a quality Referee without knowing the laws cold. You can however, know
    the laws inside and out and be quite ineffective on the field. A frequently heard
    put-down of a Referee by a fellow official is: "He is no good because he is a book
    Referee." Although this statement is often true, it seems to always come from a
    speaker who is attempting to absolve *his* less than adequate knowledge of the laws.
    The same parallel can be drawn between him and the Referee who screams at the
    ineptness of another official. The 'book Referee' statement is particularly offensive
    because it demeans one's knowledge of the laws of the game . . . . and that knowledge
    is essential.

3. *Game Preparation* – Do you psych up for all your games? Billy Cooke, ASL Referee, spends most of his day prior to his officiating assignment just thinking and concentrating upon his upcoming game. Do you just walk onto the field and slide into the match? It's no problem if the game doesn't test you, but if it does, you could be in hot water.

4. *Physical Fitness* is the **least important** of the five components for proper field execution. How many times have you seen a Referee who could not make it physically? One out of 50? Many Referees seem unfit, but it is because of their attitude. It is of course important to be in tip-top shape . . . . but you can only perform up to your physiological potential. Being in just 'average' shape is probably adequate for your officiating better than 95% of the time. Being lazy or 'dogging it' is prevalent, but only by Referees who are breaking many of the attitude commandments.

There is something other than experience that is a bit more important than law knowledge. It requires only about 1/20th of the effort to master as compared with a complete knowledge of the rules, and its practical impact is greater. That something is . . .

5. *Mechanics* – A well-known Referee assessor recently said, "Of all the sports I've observed, soccer officials are worse in mechanics than any other group of officials." Unfortunately, he is right!! The importance of mechanics has been recognized by various local high school officials' associations. Football and basketball tests have 25-30% of their test items devoted to mechanics. The baseball association allocates approximately 35% of its qualification exam to this important area. Mechanics should be learned so that it becomes reflexive in nature. Deviation from the 'accepted' is fine as long as you have a very good reason for doing so . . . . other than being lazy or having a lack of mental concentration.

Mechanics is the link between 'pure academia' and game control.

There is absolutely no excuse for having deficiencies in either law knowledge or mechanics because they can be studied out of a book . . . anytime . . . anyplace you desire. They are at *your* beck and call. Wouldn't it be nice if we could gain experience in the same manner?

Perhaps it seems that mechanics is being overstated a bit . . . but chances are that if you asked the question, "How can I gain a noticeable improvement in my soccer officiating skills in the shortest period of time?" . . . the answer for the majority would be . . . STUDY MECHANICS!!!

The concentration of the Referee must exceed that of the players.

CONCENTRATION

"There's nothing that concentrates a man's mind more than the knowledge that he's going to be hanged the next morning."

—Samuel Johnson

Concentration is usually something that is learned, like the law. Unlike the player, whose concentration usually breaks when his team loses the ball, the Referee can briefly relax only when the ball is not in play. And, like players, concentration diminishes when fatigue sets in. If you cannot keep up with play physically, you can't keep up mentally.

The "warming up" period for players should be used constructively by the Referee. You can learn much from the players at this time: Do they seem well-disciplined; Are they self-motivated, or responding to a leader or the coach? (highly important) How skilled are they? Merely asking these questions to yourself will cause you to think about the task at hand, and the accumulated bits of information will serve you in the game. It is all part of the "mental rehearsal" that Tom Tutko, noted sports psychologist, talks about in his book, *Sports Psyching* (J. B. Tarcher, 1976). While Tutko explains what is necessary for the athlete, his words fit the Referee as well.

Concentration really begins when you imagine what will happen on the field . . . what kinds of fouls are most likely to happen . . . . what is the best position for calling them . . . . . what are the most difficult situations for this age group and level . . . . what must I do to properly assess an "advantage" situation?

Of course, you are not to anticipate what is going to happen, but you must anticipate what *can* happen. Unfortunately, most Referees go into a game the way some people get behind the wheel of a car . . . . "I won't think about events and demands upon me until they happen." The Referee who thinks about refereeing only on the day of the game will seldom improve, and the Referee who thinks about his game only when it is being played is also less likely to advance.

Your concentration on all matters of play will lead to confidence. You are to lead the game at all times. The concentration takes many forms. Very quickly you are able to assess the weak and strong players, conditions of field, support you may expect from fellow officials, influence of crowd upon players, and how you are going to fare in the first stressful moment.

Look carefully for that first foul. How and when you see it and how you handle it will make a difference for the remainder of the game. You should be the first one on the field to anticipate that foul. If you referee like Gordon Hill, you will know a lot about fouls before they happen. Once Hill even stopped an important match because he *knew* what a player was *thinking* of doing.

It is possible to hear all, yet respond only to those stimuli which aid you. If a coach says, "Time's up, Ref!", don't take a glance at your watch at that moment. Wait, then when the coach is no longer looking at you (he'll not look at you unless you respond immediately), check your watch. It is possible that time IS up, but immediate response to such a command is a sign of weakness. Concentrate also on what is said and done on the sideline. It may help you.

Finally, try to think of the game as thousands of related "happenings" on which you should focus your attention. If you focus on each tiny segment of the game, you will not allow your mind to wander, and you will find that you are able to forget about how well (or poorly) you are doing. When you do, you will attain the level of awareness of Dick Giebner, former FIFA Referee: "When I'm out there I forget all my aches and pains, all of my personal problems. It's the only time I can forget everything and concentrate on one thing, my officiating."

☆ ★ ☆ ★ ☆ ★ ☆ ★ ☆ ★ ☆ ★ ☆ ★ ☆ ★ ☆ ★ ☆ ★ ☆ ★ ☆ ★ ☆ ★

Dr. William Beausay has developed "The Attention Concentration Test," which has been used in evaluating many officials in America.

The test can measure, with a great deal of accuracy, a Referee's ability to concentrate upon and to react to, situations. For more information on this test, write to him at 544 South Westwood, Toledo, Ohio 43609.

☆ ★ ☆ ★ ☆ ★ ☆ ★ ☆ ★ ☆ ★ ☆ ★ ☆ ★ ☆ ★ ☆ ★ ☆ ★ ☆ ★ ☆ ★

SPECTATOR

* If he had one more eye, he would be a cyclops.

* Never sees the fouls that the coaches and the spectators do.

"Sorry, but I can't start the match until you put more air in this game ball."

* Often can't find the field.

* Pulls the ball outside from six yards within the Penalty-Area.

* Can't find his car in the parking lot.

* Books his fellow official by mistake.

* When observed reading *Fair or Foul*, the book is upside-down.

* Always points in the wrong direction.

* Knows there is a God out there somewhere but has yet to see the light.

* Can't find his wife.

Which came first, the hold or the hand ball?

86

THE TEN MOST DIFFICULT DECISIONS

There are certain calls (or lack of calls) that have continually plagued Referees. In this section we present our view of the 'top ten'. The judging of the fair tackle, the intentional hand ball, and endangering the goalkeeper are not to be ignored because these, too, are difficult. We feel that the following present the Referee with an even more difficult challenge.

LETTING THE GAME FLOW

This is the 'uncall'. (See 'The Other Advantage' in Chapter V.) "Referee, is thy name nit-picker?" Do you always insist on ball placement for a free-kick on that exact spot? How tolerant are you of a reflexive outcry of a four letter word overheard by only a few and directed at no one in particular? Does every centimeter of the ball have to be within the quarter-circle on a corner-kick? Do you allow a reasonable amount of 'crabbing' along the touch-line for a throw-in? Do you whistle every niggling little foul? Do you react to every dissenting word? Remember, it is often wise to look the other way. Can you successfully make the distinction between letting the game flow and the discipline that is needed for game control? The majority of us have trouble, for this is *the* most difficult decision of all. "ALLOW THEM TO CHEAT, BUT NOT TO STEAL."

APPLYING THE ADVANTAGE

The advantage must be immediate, clear, and effective. Once you give it you may not change your mind. If you have doubt as to giving it . . . . don't!! Very rarely should it be given deep in one's own territory. The advantage often does not exist at the beginning of a period. The experienced Referee has the advantage on a string. He lets it out gradually as the players demonstrate they can handle it and immediately reels it in when nastiness or immaturity is exhibited. When it is applied there should be a verbal "advantage" to the players accompanied by a signal to both players and spectators that he has noticed the infraction and has chosen to let it pass.

THE 2ND CAUTION

How often have you ejected a player when he commits a second cautionable offense? Now ask yourself how often you have done it *prior* to consulting your Referee Data Card during the booking process. Your mind as well as your notebook should contain the names of cautioned players. Many players exploit the fact that they have a caution because they sense the psychological pressures that are brought to bear upon the Referee. To them, the caution doesn't say, "Cool it." It says, "Push the bounds a little bit further." They feel a certain immunity because the typical Referee is reluctant to eject unless the action is of a violent nature and can at least be marginally identified as such by players, coaches, and spectators alike.

THE DOUBLE STANDARD

Almost all of us are guilty of this. When we are, we are allowing defenders to control the game. What is a foul at midfield is often acceptable when committed within the penalty-area. It is a combination of being prudent and lacking the necessary intestinal fortitude. How often have you seen an attacker get 'heel nipped' in the penalty-area which is just enough to destroy his timing causing him to shoot wide or not to shoot at all? Have you ever given a penalty-kick for it? Do the players take advantage of you and their opponents when they are within the penalty-area? We have to strive more for consistency. There is no secret formula. Each Referee must introspect and make the decision for himself. It is axiomatic that more fouls called in the penalty-area means fewer fouls.

OFF-SIDE, IF PARTICIPATES

Since our last edition we have officiated with many experienced and respected Referees. More of them than we would like to admit appear to have a very limited practical grasp of the off-side law. They whistle it too often. The direct shot on goal that scores. It is so hard that no one can lay a finger on it. How many times has that goal been disallowed because a player was merely in an off-side position? Even the classical case of the non-participating wing, far away from play, why is he sanctioned? Rule of thumb: *Could* the player in question get to the ball first? If not, don't penalize.

OFF-SIDE AND THE 'KEEPER'

The goalkeeper is normally the last defender, but occasionally he will come off the line, bringing opponents into an off-side position. This play is always very quick to develop, and not anticipated, except by the most aware Referee. Is the goalkeeper adventurous and daring? If so, you should be particularly aware of this fact. If you miss this call probably no one will ever notice, for players, too, expect the goalkeeper to remain on the line.

THE CHARGE

Is it fair or foul? Were both players playing the ball? Where was the ball? Many officials incorrectly penalize the fair charge. If a big guy and a little guy go after the ball, the smaller one may very well be knocked on his wallet. If a player looks at the opponent just prior to charging him, then it is very likely going to be a foul charge. When judging the charge, 'read' intent in the eyes and face and look for non-shoulder contact.

DANGEROUS PLAY

Dangerous play is any action that creates a potential or an actual danger to an opponent, a teammate, or to oneself. It most often involves the 'high kick'. Just the act of raising the foot to chest level or higher does not make it dangerous. It must pose a real threat. The 'bicycle kick' is usually dangerous when it is done in close quarters. The real 'guts call' however, is when a player *puts himself* in jeopardy by putting his head down at waist or lower levels close to a player who is attempting to kick the ball How will you call it?

OBSTRUCTION

The players who think they are semi-sophisticated about the laws (usually between 16 and 19 years of age) will give you more flak about real or imagined obstructions than even the accursed hand ball. The player may legally obstruct when the ball is within playing distance. The laws say that obstruction must be intentional. The experienced Referee often determines intent by looking at the eyes and facial expression of the player in question. A common occurrence of the 'uncalled obstruction', particularly with adult players, is the defender who attempts to 'protect his goalkeeper'. In basketball the 'pick' and 'screen' are intentional and are allowed. If you see it in a soccer match that you are officiating, call it and give an IFK.

DANGEROUS PLAY OR OBSTRUCTION?

How often in one of your games has a player fallen to the gound, partially withholding the ball from play? It is very likely unintentional and he is thrashing about trying to kick it away. At the same time an opponent is also trying to kick the ball. Is it obstruction on the player on the ground? Is he guilty of dangerous play because he is putting himself in jeopardy? Is it dangerous play on the part of the opponent? Should a drop-ball be given? Sometimes the situation takes care of itself. Often it doesn't, and you become painfully aware that something must be done. Who gets the IFK? Whatever you do, do it quickly. Fans and players will be off your back and better yet, no one will be hurt.

Bill Smith

When is this considered dangerous?

89

12k . . . . HAVE YOU FORGOTTEN IT?

The "intelligent and gifted" player will develop talents and skills to the fullest, exploiting the opponents' weaknesses as well. The "crafty" or "smart" competitor may also be tempted to exploit the laws for his own benefit, sometimes taking advantage of the Referee.

There are players who, from the opening whistle, are on the fringes of being warned or cautioned. Some, when cautioned, know that Referees lack the courage to eject. They are therefore "protected," and allowed more freedom than the player who never receives the caution.

You are expected to judge the intent of all players. This expectation must be carried one step further: You must judge when a player is deliberately and persistently infringing on the laws. When this happens, you must invoke the most commonly forgotten aspect of LAW XII: SECTION K. "A player shall be cautioned if he persistently infringes on the Laws of the Game."

It is your duty to stop the player who fouls as a defensive tactic, and who really has lost nothing through the foul. Stopping an opponent at all costs is a tactic which ruins the game for spectators and causes injury and ill-feeling. The free-kick dutifully awarded is not enough!

REMEMBER: The violations do not have to be the same. (i.e., a tripping foul or two plus an intentional hand ball and an unfair charge by one player may be all you need. Don't you agree that a player who commits these three violations in a fairly short period of time is persistently infringing on the laws of the game?)

☆ ★ ☆ ★ ☆ ★ ☆ ★ ☆ ★ ☆ ★ ☆ ★ ☆ ★ ☆ ★ ☆ ★ ☆ ★ ☆ ★ ☆ ★ ☆ ★ ☆ ★ ☆ ★

Have you ever officiated a perfect game?

Comment: If you feel you have, tell others about it, for some Referees have been struggling for the perfect game for more than 20 years. There is always something to be learned from little mistakes, a wrong move or a wrong gesture which was ill-timed. Some experienced top officials make a large number of mistakes, but they are usually inconsequential to the control of the game.

☆ ★ ☆ ★ ☆ ★ ☆ ★ ☆ ★ ☆ ★ ☆ ★ ☆ ★ ☆ ★ ☆ ★ ☆ ★ ☆ ★ ☆ ★ ☆ ★ ☆ ★ ☆ ★

"YOU'VE GOT TO FEEL THE FOUL"

The argument goes on. Some Referees who are new to the game immediately grasp the essence of play, while others experienced in the game make poor officials. Conversely, some Referees place undue emphasis on laws too early, and never make it, and others who have played can identify with the "fair charge," the "sliding tackle," or the unfair tactic of the goalkeeper. Thus the argument: "What is the best background for training?"

Generalities are not particularly helpful here, but one fact remains: A Referee who has played, however modestly, can improve skills of officiating and understanding of play. If you've felt a foul, or know what an extended foot can do to a shin or ankle, you'll look for them in games. If you know how easy it is to be playing the ball and to honestly stumble into someone, you may have reached a new level. If you've taken a throw-in and raised your foot just after doing so, you'll know what the split-second means. If you've struggled, as a goalkeeper, to keep feet and arms still for the taking of a penalty, you may not call an inconsequential, minor infraction.

A Referee's field training should not be confined to the business end of the whistle. If you commiserate and compete in friendly games on the field with other Referees, you'll develop a more sensitive attitude toward all that goes on. Play, but remember to keep it safe! You're needed for your games!

"If you will kindly spit him out and give him his shirt back, I'll restart the game with a drop-ball."

FOULS THAT MEAN TROUBLE FOR YOU

Most of the play in your games is safe, fairly easy to follow, and without incident. However, you will sometimes see players committing fouls that are intentional, dangerous, and which will lead to hard feelings. Many of the most common ones are pictured here. Think about them, be ready for them, and be prepared to deal with them before they happen in your games.

The tackle from the side, with the leg crossing over the opponent's.

The foot kicking "over the ball," onto an opponent's shin. Variation: In an exaggerated manner, the player follows through after kicking the ball.

The tackle from behind, where the foot hits the opponent in the Achilles area.

The two-footed tackle, where the player "jumps in" to get the ball.

The goalkeeper jumping in at an opponent, presumably to protect himself as he makes the save.

92

The sliding tackle which misses the ball and catches the opponent in the lower leg or knee.

The late tackle from the side, where the opponent is hit in the thigh. This usually results from a bouncing ball that is not being perfectly controlled by the opponent.

A knee in the thigh from behind, in a feigned attempt to play the ball.

"Making a back" (stopping) in front of an opponent. Sometimes a player will lean down behind an opponent who is moving backward to play a ball.

The sliding tackle from behind, usually causing damage to the opponent's ankle, and sometimes to oneself.

THE BIG GAMES AND TELEVISION

Soccer's success at the gate has brought money to the game and the game to many who have not previously enjoyed it. Young players are practicing moves they see on the screen and on the stadium field, and are increasing their understanding of "total soccer."

Television, and the big games, unfortunately work against the Referee, particularly the new official who is trying to learn from the best. They work against good refereeing for the following reasons:

1. Commentators, with few exceptions, may know about the laws but know very little about refereeing.

2. Top Referees officiate top games. In an effort to keep games going, the advantage is sometimes applied to an extreme. The fouls that *are* called are usually tactically blatant, and the intent is obvious. The Referee's real challenge is to keep control of high-strung professionals who seek every advantage over the opponent.

3. Players know that Referees must keep the game going, and they expect fewer fouls to be called.

4. Player frustrations are often taken out on the Referee, and, depending on the sensitivity and personality of the Referee, they will usually be ignored. Consider Pele's words, from his autobiography, *My Life and the Beautiful Game*: "Losing your temper with a Referee is more allowable (than with an opponent) if one watches one's language. A sharp protest at a poor ruling may make the Referee more careful when the situation is more difficult."

5. The ten yards for a wall is usually violated. Referees and players are content with eight. Encroachment is allowed, with the kick never retaken.

6. The enormity of a penalty-kick is recognized, and is therefore seldom awarded.

7. Goalkeepers are allowed privileges with their steps.

8. Cautions and ejections seldom come early.

9. Players with cautions are allowed more freedom with the caution than they had without it, and they know it.

10. Many Referees refuse to give signals for the fouls they call.

All of this cannot be blamed on the officials, for they are doing a professional job for professionals. While these men are models of what a Referee should be, they have their own pressures in conformity to what the league thinks is right for spectators and the game. What the Referee thinks is right may not be important. At the highest levels, the laws are stretched by Referee, coach, and player. Don't join the ranks of lesser Referees who openly criticize Referees in top soccer.

Ron Davies (above) has created the "Referee Personalities" which appear throughout **Fair or Foul.** *Ron himself was a victim of one of the bad fouls of the game, just as he completed his work for the book. The opponent created a large gash in Ron's knee, in a very vicious tackle. The Referee did nothing except examine the player's cleats! When Ron is not nursing his wounds, he plays for the Los Angeles Aztecs in the North American Soccer League.*

J. Greenwood

"How can you possibly get a good shot of me way over there?"

Meetings, evaluations, and reports all come under one specific area of concern: The duties and responsibilities of the Referee.

VII

After It's Over..
Before It Begins Again

REFEREE MEETINGS

"Criticism will come from coaches if it doesn't first come from our own ranks."

The word "meeting" does not exactly conjure up squeals of delight, whether a person be a businessman, teacher, union member, churchgoer, or Referee. Unfortunately to a soccer official it is often that time when Referees get together to air grievances, boast about top assignments that were handled with ease, complain about the deterioration of play and conduct of players and to quibble about their *own* interpretations of the Laws of the Game. (Without a rule book, of course.) Another sad fact is that too many Referees are too set in their ways, and their own learning process terminated years ago.

To any serious observer of the game, there is something new to be learned from each contest. Moreover, the good Referee will realize that even a seasoned veteran of international matches will make mistakes, and that the only substantive difference among Referees is often the degree and frequency of these mistakes. If a group of Referees openly admit that their Referee Association meetings can provide a vehicle for freely admitting mistakes and correcting ingorance, they will find their field efforts improved, and jealousies will dwindle.

The Referee's privileged position in the game must not be taken lightly. His never-ending education is gained through the study of the Laws of the Game, his observation of other Referees, game experience, and in communication with fellow Referees. Our objectives here is to offer some suggestions as to how this communication process can be effected through group meetings.

SUGGESTED ACTIVITIES FOR REFEREE MEETINGS
(exclusive of training sessions for new Referees)

1. A *written test,* such as the one contained in this book, is an excellent method for initiating rules discussion. Since time is valuable, tests should be taken individually and brought to the meeting, having been corrected by the Referee. Test score totals need not be discussed. Each item should be discussed individually, and new items may be added for future tests.

2. A *review of certain laws of the game* is advisable, particularly at the beginning of the season. Law XII, Fouls and Misconduct, and Law XI, Off-Side, are the most obvious for generating lively discussion.

3. *Audio-visual material* such as movies will aid in clarifying the certain points of disagreement. The movies need not necessarily be on the laws, and may not be directed toward referees, but could be game movies which can be studied from the standpoint of game control and law application.

4. *Reviews of Books.* A few books now exist on refereeing, and can be reported upon by a member. FIFA News now carries interesting and timely information on rule interpretations, and this should be regularly brought to the attention of the association.

5. *Outside Speakers.* These people may have distinguished themselves in areas outside of refereeing. An accomplished Referee or umpire in another sport may also bring new insights into game-control Referee education.

6. *Game Situations.* Each meeting should have at least a short period devoted to recent situations on the field.

7. *Referee Evaluation – On Field.* If time and conditions permit, the group should observe a senior Referee in a game, and his performance should be evaluated.

8. *Individual Contributions by Member Referees.* In order for maximum efficiency to be achieved within the association, each member must participate actively at least once during the year. Each member should be given a topic for presentation, either in writing or as an instructional device at a meeting. A list of topics for presentation could include:

    a. Referee-Linesman cooperation
    b. Pre-game instructions to players
    c. Pre-game instructions from a Referee to his Linesmen
    d. Dealing with injuries
    e. How to handle club Linesmen
    f. Administering a caution
    g. When to make up time
    h. Writing disciplinary reports
    i. When is a charge a fair charge?
    j. Fundamental differences among the three systems of control
    k. How to evaluate a fellow official

HINTS

1. Many times an individual with limited or non-existent refereeing experience can best run your meetings. Like any administrator, he should be able to organize, delegate authority, and bring out the best in the membership.

2. Newsletters provide the needed communication during the offseason.

3. Try to include at least one social event each year in your calendar of activities. The sacrificing soccer wife should certainly be included.

4. Some Referee groups award an annual trophy or award to an outstandingly sportsmanlike player, team, or coach.

5. Coaches, players, and other administrators should be invited to attend meetings. For obvious reasons, game mistakes and game situations are not to be discussed in their presence.

COACHES' REFEREE EVALUATION

Certain leagues and Referee associations require periodic Referee evaluation. However, this is done in a haphazard manner, and often the methods are open to question. Since few organizations in soccer can afford Referee evaluators, Referees will have to rely on fellow Referees on the field and on coaches for constructive criticism. The criticism leveled at a fellow Referee is often misinterpreted, and can lead to a lack of cooperation on his part. The natural reaction of most Referees is to defend themselves when suggestions are made. Each Referee must decide if and how to ask for criticism and how to respond to it.

Coaches within Southern California are provided the opportunity to evaluate high school and college Referees every game during the season. The coach rates each Referee on a 5-point scale (see form on the opposite page). He may also make comments if he chooses (they are required whenever an unsatisfactory rating is given).

This information is then weighted and tabulated. Each Referee receives an evaluation package upon completion of the season. It contains all the specific ratings, by Referee as well as by school. All comments, good, bad, and otherwise are also printed. A Referee not only receives feedback regarding his assignments but also for every other Referee as well. This peer pressure, in many cases, has provided the impetus for improving one's performance on the field. Other times, unfortunately, it is rationalized away.

Sometimes a coach's comment on a card tickled our funny bone. Listed below are some of these comments which were extracted from several thousand rating cards. They combine both humor and pathos. All comments are verbatim . . . including spelling.

- _____ was 20 minutes late — Underwear hung beneath his shorts. His shirt was unbuttoned to the *waste*. He could not see fouls. Let the game get out of hand. Why not assign people who know soccer?

- There was a Ref. named Mr. Bliss, A lot of calls he did miss.

- Had a name-calling contest with the players. He is well known for his name-calling. My name is not S.O.B. crazy.

- Seems inconsistent — 'ticky-tacky' to 'blind' . . .

- . . . He *thinks* he is *good*, which makes matters worse . . . and a giant ego . . .

- . . . Have you ever seen an official roll the ball from 3 yards away for a drop ball?

- . . . . . . wore what appeared to be house slippers . . .

- . . . used a crackerjack whistle

- He said, "No offside because your team put him off-side on purpose, so it doesn't count."

- 1,783 calls went against us and one was for us.

- He refused to *due* the JV game

- I probably should protest however the man's a priest so what can I say?

SOUTHERN CALIFORNIA SOCCER OFFICIALS ASSOCIATION

COACHES' EVALUATION OF REFEREES

DATE: _____

GAME: _____ ( ) AT _____ ( )
(VISITOR)　　　　　SCORE　　　　　(HOME)　　　　　SCORE

OVERALL RATING*

NAME OF OFFICIAL	OUT-STANDING	GOOD	AVERAGE	WEAK	UNSATIS-FACTORY
A.					
B.					

NOTE: EXPLANATIONS ARE *REQUIRED* ON ALL UNSATISFACTORY RATINGS

*USE THIS CHECKLIST AS A GUIDE IN DETERMINING OVERALL RATING.

5 - OUTSTANDING　　　4 - GOOD　　　3 - AVERAGE　　　2 - WEAK　　　1 - UNSATISFACTORY

	A	B
GAME CONTROL	____	____
RULE APPLICATION	____	____
DECISIVENESS	____	____
IMPARTIALITY	____	____
PROFESSIONALISM	____	____
HUSTLE	____	____
SIGNALS	____	____
TOTALS –	[ ]	[ ]

IF POINT TOTALS ARE:

32-35 = OUTSTANDING

25-31 = GOOD

18-24 = AVERAGE

11-17 = WEAK

7-10 = UNSATISFACTORY

CONSTRUCTIVE COMMENTS: _____

_____

_____

_____

_____

_____

_____

_____

PLEASE COMPLETE AND RETURN TO:　　　　　SIGNED: _____

SCSOA – COMMISSIONER OF CERTIFICATION　　TITLE: _____
1217 3rd ST.
MANHATTAN BEACH, CA 90266　　　　　　　　SCHOOL: _____

101

- Should refrain from engaging in a discourse with each offending player to share with him many years of soccer experience.

- He calls what he sees, but I don't thing that he sees well.

- Despite the rain and mud, Mr._____ rose to new levels of incompetence.

- When I told my player to lay down, he gave me a yellow card.

- Made uncalled for remarks about the sexual gender of the JV coach.

- He walked away laughing after the other Ref. made a penalty call.

- Must have had a competition with the other Ref. to see who could blow his whistle the most.

- He is also *arogant* . . . nothing personal.

- He claimed he had a flat 2 weeks in a row. With the money he makes from coming late he should invest in some tires.

The Robert C. Niven Referee Award is presented to Bob Hill for excellence in officiating. Bill Mason, first recipient, presents the award. Referees should be recognized for their contributions to the game.

FACILITATOR

* Calls fouls commensurate with the level of play.

* Is respected by the coaches.

* Covers every inch of grass on the field if necessary.

   * Is flexible.

   * Quotes *Fair or Foul.*

   * Compliments and complements his fellow officials.

* Prevents problems before they occur.

* Is aware of God.

* Communicates with wife.

"Pat Smith of Kettering, Ohio has made great contributions to soccer refereeing. Players felt they were being treated fair when Pat whistled.

WRITING GAME REPORTS

"The game report is a very important part of Referee makeup. The average soccer Referee does not render a good report. It is perhaps the most neglected aspect of Referee training."

—Pat Smith, former Chief Referee
American Soccer League

The writing of game reports for both Referees and linesmen needs standardization. Referee groups and leagues should provide their own guidelines for the preparation of these "Word Pictures" which must serve the reviewer, who usually was not present at the game in question.

The form below is the Misconduct Report for the North American Soccer League. No such form exists in most leagues. We know of no report requirements in any high school or college league.

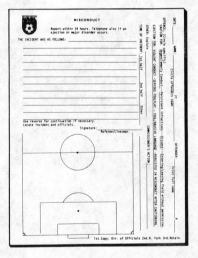

Pat Smith has said that Howard Krollfeifer, an American Referee who began whistling youth games in 1966, consistently writes the most concise and effective game reports in the American Soccer League. Krollfeifer is not a writer, and his reports deal not so much with detail, but with all that is needed for an intelligent judgment. His attitude is best expressed in the following: "I do not follow up on my game reports to find out what action was taken as I do feel that is not a part of a Referee's duties, and I am of the opinion that that knowledge might tend to prejudice a Referee if the full results of the game were known to him."

Sample reports from Krollfeifer's file appear here as models of clear, unemotional reporting of incidents. Only the names of players and teams have been changed to protect future Referees from the less-than-innocent!

105

The Referee is a record-keeper. Don't forget the importance of the game report.

Game: San Francisco vs New York

Date: June 5, 1977

I arrived at the 20th Century Field approximately 45 minutes prior to game time to inspect the field. I noted that the penalty-area at one one of the field was only 36 yards rather than 44; this was corrected by the home team manager prior to commencement of the game. The goal posts at both ends were sagging and wood straps were on the front of the posts presenting an uneven surface; it was not dangerous to the players, however the goal posts do leave alot to be desired.

The corner flags were only about 3 feet high and do not conform with regulations. The field contained a lot of rocks and broken glass and the entire field is not enclosed as required by the league, i.e., spectators can come onto the field without the fences restraining them.

I requested that both team captains wear arm bands in accordance with league rules; the San Francisco captain complied while the N.Y. captain declined.

At the 33rd minute of play, N.Y. player Don Lawrence (Jersey #14) was cautioned (yellow card displayed) for persistent infringement of the rules after he attempted to score a goal with his hand. He had previously committed two other hand ball violations and was warned by me to refrain from such actions. He conducted himself properly during the remainder of the game.

At the 62nd minute of play San Francisco player Frank Troeger (Jersey #10) prevented the opposing team from attack by jumping in the air and catching the ball with both hands and holding it after I stopped the game to afford a free-kick. Inasmuch as his actions were contrary to the rules and tends to build the game into disreputation, he was cautioned (yellow card displayed) for ungentlemanly conduct. He conducted himself properly during the remainder of the game.

H. Krollfeifer, Jr.
U.S.S.F., Referee

League: American Soccer League

Game: Astros vs Dynamos

Date: June 8, 1977

Timely commencement of the game was delayed for the following reasons:

1. Introduction of and opening comments from League Commissioner, Mr. R. Cousy

2. Pre-game ceremonies: presentation of flowers, etc.

At the 34th minute of play, Dynamos player, Denny Hamilton (Jersey #9) pulled the jersey of Astros player D. Perrin (Jersey #7) while the latter player, on a partial break away, was proceeding with the ball. Hamilton's foul pulled Perrin away from the ball and spun him around, but did not throw him to the ground. Play was immediately stopped and Hamilton was cautioned (yellow card displayed) for ungentlemanly conduct, (Law XII (M)).

While play was stopped, Astros player, G. Tanasale (Jersey #8) attempted to confront Hamilton. Both players were approximately five yards apart when I interceded and prevented Tanasale from taking any action. As I prepared to put the ball in play, Dynamo player, M. Noyes (Jersey #6) punched Tanasale in the face. Tanasale immediately fell to the ground with a bit of obvious overacting. Inasmuch as I observed the punching violation, I immediately ejected Noyes (red card displayed) for violent conduct, (Law XII (N)). Before play was recommenced, I consulted with my linesman, H. Baldwin, who was approximately fifteen yards from the incident, and was advised by him that the punch incident was not precipitated by Tanasale. It is to be noted that Noyes did not protest the ejection and immediately left the field. He remained on the Dynamos bench throughout the game, and conducted himself in a genlemanly manner. Play was recommenced with a direct free-kick awarded to Astros because of the aforementioned holding violation.

At the 78th minute of play, Dynamos player, A. Tatis (Jersey #20) committed the third, in a series of violations involving pushing and holding. He was immediately cautioned (yellow card displayed) for persistent infringement (Law XII (K)). Play recommenced with a direct free-kick awarded to Astros.

At the 123rd minute of play (fifth overtime period), Astros player M. Millea (Jersey #4) was cleanly tackled by Dynamos player, I. Tatis (Jersey #16). While the latter player was proceeding with the ball, Millea attempted to strike him from behind. Play was immediately stopped, and Millea was cautioned (yellow card displayed) for ungenlemanly conduct (Law XII (M)). Inasmuch as Millea did not make body contact with Tatis, I elected to administer a caution rather than an ejection for violent conduct.

At the 146th minute of play (seventh overtime period), an Astros player kicked the ball over the Dynamos goal-line which resulted in a goal-kick awarded to Dynamos. The ball boy immediately retrieved the ball and threw it to the Dynamos goal-keeper, E. Badre (Jersey #1) who deliberately headed the ball away from the field and over the fence and running track. Inasmuch as Badre's action was a deliberate attempt to delay the game, and he had been previously verbally warned by me, I delayed the goal-kick and administered a caution (yellow card displayed) for delay of game, (Law V — Advice to Referees).

108

At the conclusion of the eighth overtime period, my linesman H. Baldwin, signalled me to the sideline and advised me of a violation committed by Dynamos player and Captain, C. Miller (Jersey #15). According to Mr. Baldwin, Miller used his head to butt an Astros player. Mr. Baldwin indicated that the action was not serious enough to warrant ejection; therefore, he was cautioned (yellow card displayed) for ungentlemanly conduct (Law XII (M)).

H. Krollfeifer, Jr.
USSF Referee

HINTS FOR REFEREES

1. Misconduct of officials and spectators are to be reported, as well as players.

2. Do not rely on your memory on the field. Record the time of the incident, as well as any words that were spoken to you at the time of the incident.

3. The Referee must act upon the testimony of his neutral Linesman, even though the Referee may not have seen the incident.

4. Incidents must not be discussed after the match, even with other Referees. Reports on other Referees or Linesmen must be filed separately, as soon as possible.

5. All cautions and ejections must be reported.

6. The Referee's report must include all incidents on and off the field, and must contain only the facts.

7. When the Referee's report has been made and submitted, the job has been completed.

"Many a top Referee from the Senior Leagues has found himself sadly lacking the sentiment essential for working youth games."

—Ken Mullen, Referee Instructor

☆ ★ ☆ ★ ☆ ★ ☆ ★ ☆ ★ ☆ ★ ☆ ★ ☆ ★ ☆ ★ ☆ ★ ☆ ★ ☆ ★

Sculptor: Silvio Gazzaniga
Producer: Beroni-Milano

THE FIFA CUP, emblematic of supremacy in the world game.

VIII

The World Cup

WORLD CUP FACILITATORS . . . . . SINCE THE BEGINNING

The history of the World Cup has been chronicled many times, in books, reports, and countless stories. This remarkable series of games, however, has never been told from the viewpoint of the Referee, at least not any report which brings us back to the first competition in 1930. Istvan Somos of Budapest, Hungary has exclusively written for FAIR OR FOUL "The Great Moments", and has also supplied photographs of those ten honored Referees who have whistled in the most prestigious event in all of sport. Not a word has been changed from Mr. Somos, a man who is the world's expert on World Cup Referees.

Horst Muller

In a 1974 World Cup game, the captain of Holland, Cruyff, appeals to Referee Werner Winsemann for an explanation of a foul. A short word or two may result, but the game will proceed with a minimum of talk. Winsemann is one of North America's top referees, and was again selected to officiate in the World Cup.

112

THE GREAT MOMENTS IN THE HISTORY OF FOOTBALL
WHO WILL BE ON THE ELEVENTH?

Ten pictures, ten moments. The difference can hardly be noticed at first sight. Handshake here, handshake there. Handshake right here. Handshake over there. The gestures do not eternize a great goal, no special feeling is expressed by the movements.

On all the pictures, however, the following is common: in the background of the handshakes stands a person dressed in black; the referee of the match; as the reader can presume from the ball, the dresses, and from other things, the photoreporters took snapshots at the first moments of the match. The photos could be simple moments of everyday life, moments of matches which do not throw into a fever hundreds of thousand, but here there is question of more. We could even say of the most, as the photos show the most amical moments of the ten World Cup finals played up to now, these greatest tournaments of football.

We said: the most amical moments. Yes, look only: on these photos nobody is angry with the referees, here even the referees smile at the players and the lens of the photo machines, as well as at king Gustav Adolf of Sweden, etc.

If the players and referees had stood in the middle of the ground after the match, for recalling the picture, the faces would have been different. And this is natural. One team became world champion, while the other one lost.

What matches can the reader remember seeing these pictures!

What can these faces relate looking back for many years?

And from the take the referee cannot be absent! How much could beat the pulse of the players and referees in these historical moments of football?

The pictures do not disclose much from the discordance in the background.

The pictures don't show the 22 players.

The pictures don't betray: it started like this. Three, four, five, six persons among them one-one conductor dressed in black greet each other and, thus, together in one society they greet all of us, who are waiting now for the eleventh final.

It is a mere chance that on the past ten World Cup finals European referees blew the whistle? This series will not get broken now? The captains of which teams will stand around the referees?

One question after another.

Looking at the ten photos we can play with our thoughts, as we like.

This compilation serves this purpose, as well.

When the whistle is blown, playing can begin. . .

*1930.VII.30. Final of the first World Cup played in the Centenario Stadium of Monte-
video; /Uruguay-Argentine 4:2 solumn exchange of flags before the match. From left to
right, Nasazzi, captain of the "Uru" team, in the middle John Langenus Belgian FIFA
referee in breeches, Ferrira captain of the Argentine team, Sacuedo, Bolivian linesman.*

*1934.VI.10. Before the Italy-Czechoslovakia final /2:1/ played in the Olympic Stadium
of Rome. Combi, captain of the Italian and Planicka, captain of the Czechoslovak team
greet each other with amical handshake. In the middle: Ivan Eklind Swedish FIFA-
referee of the final.*

114

1938.VI.10. Before the Italy-Hungary final /4:2/ Waited for with much interest and played in the Colombes Stadium of Paris, the two captains Meazza and dr. Sarosi greet each other. In the middle: M. Capdeville, French referee of the final.

1950.VII.16. Before the Uruguay-Brasil final /Uruguay won to 2:1/ played before 200,000 spectators in the world known Maracana Stadium of Rio de Janeiro /from right to left/, Friaca, captain of the Brasilian team and Varela, captain of Uruguay's team greet each other and exchange the flags. In the middle: Georg Raeder, English FIFA referee of the match.

1954.VII.4. The two captains of the final played by the German Federal Republic and Hungary /3:2/ in the Wanckdorf Stadium of Bern. /from left to right/ Fritz Walter and Ferenc Puskas. In the middle W. Ling, English FIFA referee of the final and the two linesmen, the Italian Orlandini and B. M. Griffiths from Wales, who died since this time.

1958.VI.29. Before the Brasil-Sweden World Cup final /5:2/ played in the Rasunda Stadium of Stockholm, Maurice Guigue, French referee of the match, from him to the right Dusch /German Federal Republic/, Gardeazabal Spanish linesman, who died in the meantime and Bellini, captain of the Brasilian team get presented to Gustav Adolf, king of Sweden.

1962.VI.17. Final played by Brasil and Czechloslovakia / 3:1/ in the Estadio Nacional of Santiago de Chile; in the middle Nyikolaj G. Latisev / Soviet-Union/ referee of the match, calls with his whistle the two teams to the ground. From left, with the ball under his arm, the Dutch Leo Horn, from the right the Scotch Davidson, linesmen of the match.

1966.VII.30. Before the final played by England and German Federal Republic in the Wembley Stadium of London: Uwe Seeler /German Federal Republic/ from the left and Bobby Moore /England/ from the right, exchange as captain of the teams the flags. In the middle: Gottfried Dienst, Swiss FIFA referee and his two linesmen: Bahramov /Soviet/ and dr. Galba /Czech/.

117

1970.VI.21. Before the World Cup final /4:1/ played by Brasil and Italy in the Aztec Stadium of Mexico, Giacinto Facchetti /Italian/ and Carlos Alberto /Brasilian/ captain exchange the flags and shake hands. In the middle: Rudi Glockner, FIFA referee of the German Democratic Republic. (From left: Scheurer /Swiss/, from right /Corerezza /Argentine/ linesmen.

1974.VII.7. Final played by the German Federal Republic and Holland /2:1/ before 79,000 spectators in the Olympic Stadium of Munich. /From left to right/ Johan Cruyff captain of the Dutch team, and Franz Beckenbauer captain of the German team solemnly exchange the flags. In the middle: John Keith Taylor, English FIFA referee of the match. /From left /Barreto /Uruguay/, /from right/ Archundia /Mexico/, linesmen.

Exclusive By Istvan Somos /Budapest/

118

REFEREEING AT THE WORLD CUP

With most sports, officiating at the Olympics is considered the highest honor. In soccer, however, the Olympics comes second to the World Cup, for both players and Referees. As the game grows, so has the status of the World Cup Referee. The 1978 World Cup included 32 Referees/Linesmen from 32 different countries, with three home-country officials who work only as Linesmen. Six back-up Referees form the full complement of officials for the three week competition. The complete list is as follows:

Referees and/or Linesmen

Argentina	Angel Coerezza
Austria	Erich Linemayr
Belgium	Francis Rion
Brazil	Arnaldo Coelho
Canada	Werner Winsemann
Chile	Juan Silvagno
England	Patrick Partridge
Ethiopia	Gebreyesus Tesfaye
France	Robert Wurtz
German DR	Adolf Prokop
Germany FR	Ferdinand Biwersi
Hungary	Karoly Palotai
Iran	Jafar Namdar
Israel	Abraham Klein
Italy	Sergio Gonella
Mexico	Alfonso Archundia
Netherlands	Charles Corver
Peru	Cesar Orozco
Poland	Alojzy Jarguz
Portugal	Antonio Jose da Silva Garrido
Rumania	Nicolae Rainea
Scotland	John Gordon
Senegal	Youssou N'Diaye
Spain	Angel Franco Martinez
Sweden	Ulf Eriksson
Switzerland	Jean Dubach
Syria	Farouk Bouzo
Tunisia	Hedi Seoudi
Uruguay	Ramon Barreto Ruiz
USSR	Anatoli Ivanov
Wales	Clive Thomas
Yugoslavia	Dusan Maksimovic

Linesmen

Argentina
Miguel Comesana
Arturo Ithurralde
Luis Pestarino

Reserves

Austria	Franz Woehrer
Belgium	Alfred Delcourt
Brazil	Romualdo Arppi Filho
France	Michel Kitabdjian
Germany FR	Heinz Aldinger
Italy	Alberto Michelotti

These officials all wear the FIFA badge, the most coveted badge in soccer. It is worn by fewer than 700 Referees in the 143 FIFA member countries. These men have risen to the top of their avocation through long years of officiating at club, semi-pro, and professional levels. They are originally recommended for the FIFA list by their home countries.

FIFA is not obliged to accept referee nominations for the international list, but they usually do. Every country may nominate up to seven referees whether they have 50,000 or 50 referees in the national association. After the Referee has officiated two Class "A" international matches, he has won his badge. Therefore, some qualify but never receive full recognition.

FIFA appoints Referees and Linesmen only for World Cup and Olympic Games, both the preliminary and final rounds of games. For all other matches of an international nature, whether at the club or national level, the appointments are made by the country or Federation concerned, or by an agreement between the two countries, if a match is a friendly one. In each game of the final tournament of the World Cup and Olympic Games, the three match officials are selected from different neutral countries. In all other cases, the three officials come from the same neutral country, though an exception can be made in the preliminary matches of the Olympic Games where countries can mutually agree on Linesmen from a nearer country.

FIFA Referees receive no payment for officiating in an international match. All travel and living expenses are paid. None of these men make a living officiating, although they are probably the most professional group of sports Referees in the world. They are constantly scrutinized by Referee "Inspectors" or "Assessors," but are not subjected to written tests. Their field performance and physical fitness is the main concern of the inspector, and detailed reports on most FIFA Referees are kept in Zurich. From these reports are drawn the lists for World Cup and Olympic Games competitions.

Due to the nature of the game, its worldwide popularity, the unusual rules calling for one man maintaining complete control over the game and its timing and record-keeping, certainly the most demanding neutral position in all of sports officiating falls on the shoulders of the FIFA Referee.

The seven FIFA Referees currently on the list in the United States are:

Gino D'Ippolitto	New York
Toros Kibritjian	California
Henry Landauer	California
Anthony Nobile	New York
James Ross	Pennsylvania
David Socha	Massachusetts
Michael Wuertz	Wisconsin

"I made it, I'm one of the seven."

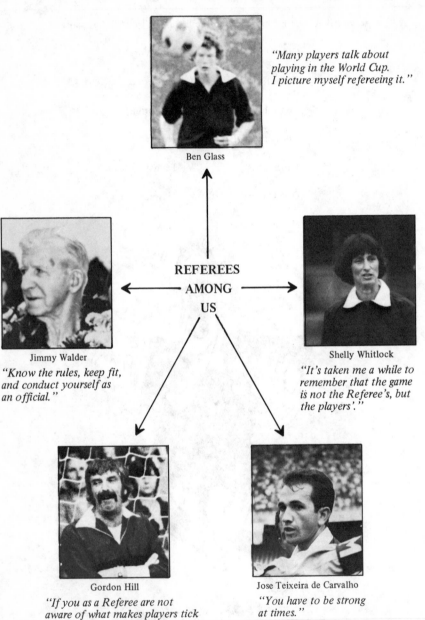

Ben Glass

*"Many players talk about
playing in the World Cup.
I picture myself refereeing it."*

**REFEREES
AMONG
US**

Jimmy Walder

*"Know the rules, keep fit,
and conduct yourself as
an official."*

Shelly Whitlock

*"It's taken me a while to
remember that the game
is not the Referee's, but
the players'."*

Gordon Hill

*"If you as a Referee are not
aware of what makes players tick
and how they perform, you
shouldn't be refereeing."*

Jose Teixeira de Carvalho

*"You have to be strong
at times."*

IX

You Meet
The Greatest People

BEN GLASS . . . A Young Referee Who Started Very Early

"Many players talk about playing in the World Cup. I picture myself refereeing it." . . . Ben Glass III

One of the first things you notice about Ben Glass is his intense interest in officiating. He has read the books, officiated hundreds of games while still a teenager, organized Referees in the Williamsburg (VA) Youth League, and attended clinics by some of the top lecturers in North America.

While in the eighth grade, Ben started by whistling some scrimmages of his Dad's team. Now, with an intimate knowledge of the laws and a sensitive understanding of players and their needs, Ben is one of the most promising young Referees in America.

A growing majority of Referee organizers have been speaking of players and the contribution they can make as officials. Ben, a member of a National Junior Cup championship team, plays well, and knows the problems of players and Referees:

- "I tell the players that if there is anything they want to know during the game and if they ask politely, they will get an answer."

- "Honesty with players leads to respect. If you tell a player that the next time he tackles from behind without a chance of winning the ball, you're going to caution him, you must do it. Otherwise, you've lost his respect and that of the other players."

In thirteen years of playing soccer, Ben has never been sent off the field. No doubt his attitude toward Referees has helped him as a player, where he could concentrate on his game and ignore the incidents which upset lesser players. Working with people in soccer is Ben's priority, and it is almost certain that someday he will be seen working international games and providing a new kind of inspiration. Ben Glass, of Annandale, Virginia. A player, also in the middle headed for the top.

Ben Glass follows the play closely and is in excellent condition to keep up with play.

125

SHELLY WHITLOCK . . . A Woman Getting Near the Top

The recruiting of Referees is a challenge without end, and with the growth of girls' and women's soccer has come greater need for more officials. In the search for Referees, girls and women are often overlooked. They are needed for all of soccer, not just competitions involving their own sex.

Among those who already referee, a few have made great progress, and should be an inspiration to others who will follow. Shelly Whitlock of Garland, Texas is an example of an aggressive, serious Referee who enjoys the game and everyone in it. "I've been accepted at all levels because of my enthusiasm and interest," she says. "It's taken me a while to remember that the game is not the Referee's, but the players'.

Shelly, who officiated a final game in 1977 at an international youth tournament in Sweden, started officiating in girls' games, where fouls and incidents are typically less frequent. She also "ran line" in boys' games, where she could observe experienced Referees from close-in. Foul recognition came easier.

Many women feel that since they've never played the game, they would have great difficulty in controlling play. Shelly feels otherwise. "Most of all you must have a sensitivity and a feeling for people. If you relax and enjoy the game, law application is easier and it will all fall into place."

Women officials do have their problems, and Shelly is trying to help them overcome those which are most common. First, women are not used to sprinting, and have a tendency to be behind play. Another problem is that they feel they inhibit men by their presence in a men's game, and may be sensitive to certain language on the field. Still others have said that they find difficulty in making firm and timely decisions. But it is generally felt that the problems that men Referees face are no different, and that refereeing tends to be a matter of personality, and not of sex.

Shelly Whitlock officiates each game as if it were a championship match. Above all, she brings a willingness to learn and to improve.

Shelly Whitlock is now comfortable in the middle, and players accept her authority. Here she officiates a game of under 19 boys, Norway vs Sweden.

GORDON HILL . . . Profile of a Referee Personality

Players seldom mention the memorable qualities in an official. The Referee is known for his decisions alone, and little attention is paid to those personality traits that are unique.

An exception would be Gordon Hill. Recently retired from refereeing in the North American Soccer League, Hill is still known as an articulate, memorable, controversial, and unorthodox individual. Whether it was the style of his socks or his method of dealing with the unruly, Gordon placed his stamp on a match, and enjoyed being noticed. The game was better for it, and players usually felt that they were fairly treated.

Hill was so involved in his game that once he was even seen applauding an exceptional move by a player. His philosophy was one of understanding the player and the game, helping everyone to increase their enjoyment. "Referees create a mood for the game," he said in his popular book, *Give a Little Whistle*. Hill's popularity extended to players, coaches, and spectators alike. After being recognized in England by being chosen to referee the Cup Final, Hill came to the United States, and whistled the final of the North American Soccer League play-offs.

The example and success of a Gordon Hill is an inspiration for those who mistakenly feel that refereeing is mechanical and routine. There is no limit to the potential growth of the Referee, and the personality must emerge with each game.

Some thoughts from Hill, from his book:

- "If you as a Referee are not aware of what makes players tick and how they perform, you shouldn't be refereeing."

- "I honestly feel that any person who is emotionally involved in what he's doing cannot help showing dissent. It occurs in all walks of life . . . nobody can feel totally satisfied with what's going on around him."

- "No Referee is perfect; there isn't a match where a Referee can look back and say: 'I was faultless.' "

- "What happens when a Referee is having a bad game is that there's a steady wearing down of your confidence, with players becoming suspicious of your competence and deciding to take action themselves."

- "Players never respect a Referee who is easy going, a pushover."

- "You get a certain excitement through knowing that the violent or ungentlemanly conduct is lying just beneath the surface and must be controlled if it erupts."

Gordon Hill was known for his earthy "banter" with the players. Most players liked him for it.

JOSE TEIXEIRA DE CARVALHO . . . Experience Comes to America

Many of the great soccer legends come from Brazil: Maracana, the largest stadium, Pele, the most goals, and the World Cup, returned there after being won in 1958, 1962, and 1970.

At the highest levels, the Referee in Brazil is full-time, and is paid well. Refereeing is not the province of retired players. Jose Teixeira de Carvalho, now 37 and living in Los Angeles, is testimony to that. He began his career at 17, and was a full-time professional before 21. For more than 10 years he operated in world-class soccer, in an atmosphere of tension, excitement, and pressure. "In Brazil, many people like soccer *too much*," Jose says. "They become very mad when their team loses."

Referees in Brazil are well-known, and are reported and evaluated even by newspapers and magazines. Several soccer publications have their "All-Star" picks, and included in the list is the "Referee of the Year," a distinction that many would value. Also, tradition gives way to comfort, as Referees wear yellow shirts during the heat of the day games.

One of Jose's more vivid memories was the expulsion of Pele during October 1965. With his team leading 3-0 and only 10 minutes remaining, Pele committed a "bad foul." It was the first time he had been ejected in a league game, and few Referees would want the distinction of making the decision. "He made a bad foul, and it was nothing big to me," said the veteran of 50 Pele games. He's like any other player. We are friends." Understandably, the incident drew much attention from the Brazilian press, but Jose felt what he did was right. Pele missed his next game.

What are the problems of whistling in such a charged atmosphere? Jose is guarded in his comparison with soccer in America. "It is more difficult in Brazil, because a player keeps the ball longer, inviting tackles and dangerous play. Everyone wants the Referee to blow the whistle, and sometimes you must do it because of retaliation."

Jose is a true professional. One is impressed with his intensity as he discusses game control. There is no doubt that he feels all Referees should take their appointments more seriously, to the point of allowing the game to triumph, even though it means expelling the world's leading attraction!

Jose Teixeira de Carvalho was quite a celebrity among Referees in his native Brazil. Here he is being interviewed before a game.

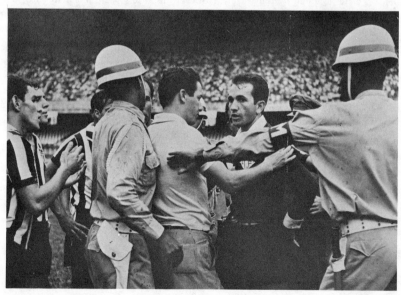

After the game he sometimes needed the help of everyone. However, he was never assaulted by a player.

JIMMY WALDER ... A Giant Among Referees

There is probably no one in America who would challenge the title which has been given James A. Walder of Philadelphia, Pennsylvania: "Dean of Referees." Walder whistled his first game in 1909 when he filled in at a local youth game. He was soon taken up by the magic and challenge of the whistle, quickly laying aside plans to continue playing. The career extended through seven decades, and he last appeared as a Referee at the age of 84 on October 31, 1969 at Christopher Dock High School in Landsdale, Pennsylvania. Appropriately, he was feted by members of both teams, coaches, parents, and students.

Walder's soccer biography directly touched more than 50,000 players in his 4500 games. The 30,000 miles he ran on the field, the million miles he travelled in behalf of the game, the thousands of Referees he counseled at halftime . . . all were a part of a selfless desire to keep the game alive and to allow people to play and enjoy the sport. Walder was a FIFA Referee who officiated without a patch. These emblems were simply not awarded then, but he did conduct 30 top-level professional international games. His contact with the college game began in 1913, and ended in 1965, when he was 78, and able to keep up with men one quarter his age.

The Dual Referee System was conceived and first implemented during the post-World War II era when games were officiated by a single Referee without the help of linesmen, thanks to Walder and his longtime friend, Harry Rodgers, who at the age of 75 is still refereeing. Even then, these men suffered the agonies of the visionaries, and their ideas were accepted by only a few. However, dissenters could not help but listen, since these two Referees were so respected in the soccer world. Eventually, the system won out, and was accepted in colleges.

Jimmy, who still goes to games, helped form the United States Referees' Association in 1913. He lived through the rule changes, the use of goal judges, the dark days of common violence on the amateur and professional playing fields, and finally has observed the emergence of the game through the schools and youth organizations. At 94, his dream has come true, one which was voiced many times to the press: "One of these days, the game will catch the fancy of the American youngster." To all Referees, he has this advice: "Know the rules, keep fit, and conduct yourself as an official."

Jimmy Walder (second from right), is presented with the game ball and a garland of flowers following his final game as a Referee on October 31, 1969. His longtime friend and partner, Harry Rodgers, whistled the game with Jimmy. While there are few Referees who could hope to be as dedicated to officiating, his example has been followed by many.

Raff Frano

It has been said that some Referees learn the rules by Rote.

X

The
Rules Almanac

Oto Maxmilian

A ball sitting on the goal-line, a nemesis for the Referee who is out of position. Where must the Referee or Linesman be to judge whether or not this goal is valid?

Hidden and implied rules, International Board Decisions, Referee Commission interpretations, and other bits and pieces of information about the Laws of the Game are hard
to find. While some of the materials in this synopsis section may be found in other parts
of the book, it is offered here in basic summary fashion as an adjunct to the Laws.

Important information from the seventeen Laws of the Game is summarized in order,
and may be referred to accordingly. An effort has been made to be concise yet complete
in our examination of these Laws. For the new or for the experienced Referee, it is best
read and studied after reviewing the Laws. It will then serve as a refresher, and an understanding of the synopsis is an important prelude to the taking of the two soccer tests in
Chapter XI.

Law I   THE FIELD OF PLAY
            The Field of Play
            Conversions
            (Yards/Meters)
Law II   THE BALL
            The Ball
Law III   THE NUMBER OF PLAYERS
            Players
            Substitutions
            Illness/Injury
            The Goalkeeper
Law IV   PLAYERS' EQUIPMENT
            Equipment/Apparel
Law V   REFEREES
            Referee
            Advantage Clause
            Termination of Game
Law VI   LINESMEN (See Chapter III)
Law VII   DURATION OF THE GAME
            Timing
Law VIII   THE START OF PLAY
            Kick-Off
            Drop-Ball
            Outside Agent
Law IX   BALL IN AND OUT OF PLAY
            In/Out of Play

Law X   METHOD OF SCORING
            Scoring
Law XI   OFF-SIDE
            Off-Side
Law XII   FOULS AND MISCONDUCT
            Fouls and Misconduct
            Warnings
            Cautions
            Ejections
            Entering/Leaving the Field
Law XIII   FREE-KICK
            Free-Kicks — General
            Indirect Free-Kick
            Misconduct
            Dangerous Play
            Direct Free-Kick
            Charging
Law XIV   PENALTY-KICK
            Penalty-Kick
Law XV   THROW-IN
            Throw-In
Law XVI   GOAL-KICK
            Goal-Kick
Law XVII   CORNER-KICK
            Corner-Kick and
            Corner-Post

FIELD OF PLAY

(ALL UNDESIGNATED DISTANCES IN YARDS)

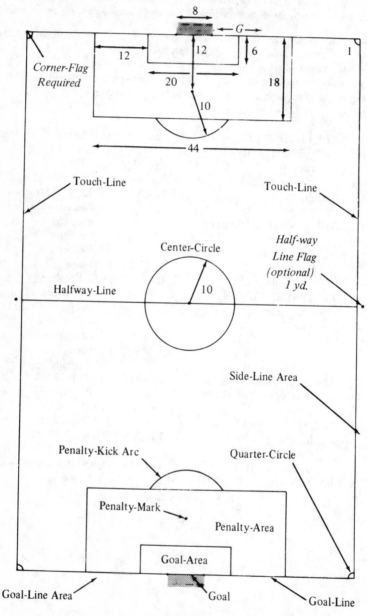

Field of Play

AREAS

GOAL	8 Yards—Wide 8 Feet—Height	• Length and height are inside measurements. • Width and depth of posts and cross-bars (which should be white) are a maximum of 5 inches. • A rope is not a satisfactory substitute for a cross-bar when played under competitive rules. • A net, if used, should extend not less than 5 feet beyond the goal-line. • Posts and bars are made of wood, metal, or other approved material.
GOAL-AREA	20 Yards—Wide 6 Yards—Deep	• The space within the inside areas of the field of play includes the width of the lines marking those areas.
PENALTY-AREA	44 Yards—Wide 18 Yards—Deep	
CORNER-AREA	1 Yard Radius from corner	
PENALTY-MARK	12 Yards from Goal-Line	• From front of goal-area. or • From front of penalty-area. } 6 Yards — • Mark = 9 inch diameter spot (approx.) is conventional • College and High School uses a penalty-kick line (2 ft long).
CENTER-CIRCLE	10 Yard Radius	

Lines — Maximum of 5 inches in width — Part of the areas they limit (2-1/2 to 3 inches advised). Goal-lines must be the same width as the goal-posts and cross-bar. Touch-lines and goal-lines belong to the field of play.

	FIFA	INTERNATIONAL MATCHES	HIGH SCHOOL	COLLEGE
TOUCH-LINE	100 yards minimum 130 yards maximum	110 Yards 120 Yards	100 Yards 120 Yards	110 Yards 120 Yards
GOAL-LINE	50 yards minimum 100 yards maximum	70 Yards 80 Yards	65 Yards 75 Yards	65 Yards 75 Yards

(The field of play shall be rectangular)

OLYMPIC FINALS AND WORLD CUP   115 x 64 Yards   (105 x 68 Meters)

FLAGS

CORNER	5 feet high (minimum) — Blunted end. (High School — Football style corner-flags are acceptable)
HALFWAY-LINE (Optional)	1 yard (minimum) from the touch-line at midfield.

Protests for irregularities in measurement must be made in writing prior to the start of the game. If the irregularity did not occur prior to the start of the match, the protest cannot be accepted.

HESITATOR

* Stands back with hands on hips and watches play.

* Refuses to caution coach for fear of low rating.

* Whistle goes up to his mouth but he never blows it.

* Has never called a penalty-kick.

* Calls players "gentlemen" even when they are maiming one another.

* Has diarrhea before and after each game.

* Whispers "Play On."

* Is afraid of God.

* Hides from wife.

* Keeps *Fair or Foul* hidden inside a plain brown cover.

CONVERSIONS

Yards to Meters
(National Bureau of Standards)

	Meters
1 inch	.0254 (2-1/2 cm)
5 inches	.127 (12-1/2 cm)
1 foot	.3048 (30-1/2 cm)
1 yard	.9144
5 yards	4.57
10 yards	9.14
50 yards	45.72
100 yards	91.44

Meters to Yards

Meters	Yards	Feet	Inches
1	1		3-1/2
5	5	1	5
10	10	2	9.7 (393.7 inches)
50	54	2	1/2
100	109	1	1

"The time for inspecting the ball is before the game, not as it's coming at you."

THE BALL

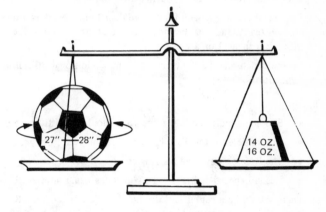

Pressure —
9-10.5 psi at sea level.

Hand pressure should dent the ball's surface 1/4 to 1/2 inch.

College — Ball must bounce between 60-65" when dropped onto a cement floor from 100 inches.

Diameter is 8-3/4"

Youth

26.5-28"	13 yrs. & older	14-16 oz.	A size 5 ball
15-16.5"	9-12 yrs. old	12-14 oz.	A size 4 ball
13.5-15"	8 yrs. & younger	10-12 oz.	A size 3 ball

Outer Casing — Leather or other approved material. *College* — must be made of leather.

Color — None specified.

A minimum of two balls are required. *College* — Ball must be of the same make. Professional games require three balls.

If the game is played on a neutral field, each team must supply at least two balls in good condition. Captains select one of two balls.

The ball shall not be changed during the game unless authorized by the Referee.

Variations of size or weight during the game is not enough to consider the ball unfit because it was official at the start of the game, unless the Referee considers it otherwise.

If the ball bursts or becomes deflated during the course of a match, the game shall be stopped and restarted with a drop-ball.

If this happens during a stoppage of the game, the game shall be restarted accordingly.

PLAYERS

(A player is one who is currently participating in the game.)

Two teams are comprised of not more than 11 nor less than 7 players (recommended) on each team. One must be the goalkeeper. (High School — the game can't be started with fewer than 11 on a side.)

On the bench may be the coach, trainer, 1 additional official of the team and up to 5 substitutes.

Captain

- Should be indicated in the line-up as should a substitute captain.
- Responsible for the discipline of his teammates.
- The Referee may need his assistance.
- Has no special rights ... This includes being allowed to talk to the Referee.

There should be a captain on the field. If there is none, the Referee appoints one. If he refuses, the game could be terminated.

An ineligible player on the opposing team should be protested in writing before the game starts.

Horst Müller

The pause for substitution does not have to be a somber affair.

144

SUBSTITUTIONS

(To substitute is to bring in a player from the bench.)

A substitute is considered as being a player.

Substitution is:

- Done during a play stoppage.
- The Referee must be informed before the change is made.
- The player being substituted for must leave the field before his replacement enters.
- Substitutes are to enter at the halfway-line.

A player who has been substituted for can take no further part in the game.

A player who has been ordered off the field after the starting kick-off may not be substituted for.

A player who has been ordered off the field *before play begins* may be substituted for.

A player who has been ordered off the field after the starting kick-off may not be substituted for.

Number of Substitutes

FIFA = 2 of possible 5

Youth = 4

High School = No limit. Substitution is the same as college plus the team in possession of the ball may substitute on a throw-in.

College = Up to 7. May substitute on a Goal-Kick, Corner-Kick, Goal, between periods, and during an injury or the administering of a caution/ejection. (Opponents can substitute a like number if there is a substitution for a caution, ejection, or injury.

Goalkeeper Substitution

See Goalkeeper (this chapter).

ILLNESS/INJURY

1. Stop the game if a player has been seriously injured. Restart with a drop-ball. (*High School* — IFK if there is clear possession.)

2. If a player other than the GK is slightly injured, play shall not be stopped until the ball has ceased to be in play.

3. A player who is able to reach the side-line area under his own power shall not be treated on the field.

4. No person may enter the field to help an injured player unless permission has been granted by the Referee.

5. Time allowances are made for injuries.

6. If the GK is injured or passed out — Immediately whistle. Play is resumed with a drop-ball. No score can be allowed.

Oto Maxmilian

Play must be immediately stopped when a goalkeeper is injured.

146

Horst Müller

"Let's drag him over there."

"We have lots of real 'personalities' among the Referees, and they tend to go their own way. By putting themselves in the foreground they make it much more difficult to reach uniformity. This is why the aim of every Referee's meeting, of every conference and discussion must be to try to reach uniformity in the interpretation of the soccer laws."

–Frederich Seipelt
European Referee Instructor

There is enough competition on the field. Referees do not need to compete with each other or with players for attention.

GOALKEEPER

Possession

To have the ball within his hands or cradled within his arms.

Possession is also a finger, hand, arm or leg on a stationary ball brought under the control of the GK.

Steps

If more than 4 steps are taken — IFK (Steps taken to regain balance do not count.)

ACTION WITH BALL	POSSESSION	COUNT STEPS	
HOLDING IT	YES	YES	
BOUNCING IT	NO (H.S./COL. = YES)	YES	
THROWING IT UP AND CATCHING IT	NO (H.S. = YES)	YES	
ROLLING IT	NO	*SOMETIMES YES SOMETIMES NO	

*If the goalkeeper rolls the ball out so it can be safely played by another player then one step is counted each time he picks the ball up or stops it with his hand.

If the goalkeeper rolls the ball along close to his body in a manner so that it cannot be safely played by another player, then *each step* is counted.

Delaying Tactics

- He only has the time necessary to put the ball back into play.
- Holds the ball too long (even if injured).
- Baits an opponent by withholding the ball from play.
- Repeatedly kicks the ball back and forth with another player.
- Dribbles the ball with his feet around the penalty-area.
- Associated with PK (see section on Penalty-Kick — this chapter).

Charging (See also Charging — this chapter.)

He may be charged:

LOCATION	HE OBSTRUCTS	HAS POSSESSION OF BALL	DOES NOT HAVE POSSESSION OF BALL
WITHIN THE GOAL-AREA			CAN *NOT* BE CHARGED — IFK
IN ALL OTHER PORTIONS OF THE PENALTY-AREA			

Unintentional body contact is not to be penalized.

- Youth, High School, College — GK may not be charged inside the penalty-area.

	COLLEGE AND H.S.	YOUTH
INTENTIONAL CHARGING	EJECT AND DIRECT	CAUTION AND DIRECT
_UN_INTENTIONAL CHARGING	DIRECT	IFK

Changing/Substitution

Must be done when ball is not in play.

May be substituted for whenever there is a stoppage in play including:

- When a PK has been awarded to the opposing team.
- If a PK is retaken.

Referee must be notified. A change of jersey does not constitute official notification (but the player wearing the jersey is the GK and has all the GK privileges).

If a GK is substituted without notifying the Referee:

- If he *changes places* with another player – caution both players when ball is out of play.
- If replaced by a *substitute* – the GK is cautioned and if the Referee stopped play exclusively to administer this caution then IFK is given where the ball was when the game was stopped.

College – IFK for replacement by any teammate.

High School – IFK when ball handled by non-reporting GK.

Referee may signal GK change to the other official(s) by patting the top of his own head if he has been duly notifed. (*Fair or Foul* recommendation.)

Ungentlemanly Conduct – Caution and IFK

Hits ball with an object held in the hand.

Holds onto upright or cross-bar to gain an unfair advantage.

Leans on shoulders of teammate to gain an unfair advantage.

Lying down in front of his goal as a contemptuous gesture in a very one-sided game.

Miscellaneous

GK shall wear colors which distinguish him from the other players (including the other GK) and the Referee.

A GK may score in opponent's goal by throwing or making a clearing kick, provided he is within his own PA.

If GK is injured or passes out – immediately stop play. Resume with a drop-ball. No score can be allowed.

EQUIPMENT/APPAREL

The Referee should inspect player equipment prior to the start of the game.

A player may wear glasses (at his own risk). It is up to the Referee as to whether restraining straps are necessary. No metal bracelets, wrist watches or any object that may be dangerous to himself or to the other players.

A player should not play without a jersey. (If the Referee allows it, it must be reported.

Shirt numbers are not to be changed except when substituting or changing places with the goalkeeper. If changed — CAUTION, require them to change back and IFK if the game was in progress.

Players can't take part in a game without shoes (one or both) unless none of the players have them. A goal counts, however, even if scored by a player who has lost his shoe(s). No goal is allowed if a flying shoe distracted the GK.

Any Referee who is asked to examine a player's shoes should always do so.

Shoes

	MATERIAL	MINIMUM DIAMETER	MAXIMUM PROTRUSION	
STUDS (Screw-In)	LEATHER RUBBER ALUMINUM PLASTIC	1/2 inch	3/4 inch	● Must be solid
STUDS (Moulded)	RUBBER PLASTIC POLYURETHANE	1/2 inch (if less than 10 studs) otherwise, 3/8 inch		
BARS	LEATHER RUBBER			● Must extend the total width of the sole.

American football shoes having a distinctive screw-in toe cleat are not allowed.

Shoes with metal posts extending from the soles upon which a threaded stud is screwed onto, are illegal.

NO ☝ ☝ YES

The Referee is authorized to order jerseys changed if similarity of colors impairs the control of the game. Home team should change.

A cast is not permitted if the Referee decides it is dangerous to the other players. (High School and Youth — Casts, even if padded, are not allowed.)

ROTTENTATOR

* Always needs a shave.

* B.O. causes players and coaches to stay away from him.

* Is chronically late for every game.

* Wears stolen FIFA patch.

* Never washes his uniform.

Tells people that he wrote *Fair or Foul.*

* Shrugs shoulders when other official makes an unpopular call.

* Leaves after game saying he will shower at home.

* Blames God for everything.

* Wife avoids him.

REFEREE

1. The Referee's authority commences as soon as he is in the vicinity of the field of play.

2. Players (including the captain) do not have the right to address the Referee. If any do . . . the Referee is within his right to CAUTION and IFK.

3. A Referee can only reverse his decision as long as the game has not been restarted.

4. The Referee has no authority to declare a winner in a game he terminates. He must however, make a detailed report to the proper authority. (*High School and College* — He may declare a forfeit.)

5. If he is late and the game is in progress, he may not take over.

   Club Game — If the Referee doesn't show, a substitute Referee may officiate provided both captains agree in writing.

6. The Referee may not start the game using the diagonal system of control if a Linesman is missing.

7. The Referee may name a substitute Linesman to replace one who did not show up, who may act until the designated Linesman arrives. Rather than have an unfamiliar Linesman, it is suggested that the Referee and Linesman utilize the Two Referee System. *(Fair or Foul)*

8. He has discretionary powers in regard to dangerous playing. He can punish it with a CAUTION and an IFK.

9. To terminate a game for bad visibility he can use as a suggested standard either not being able to see one goal while standing at the other, or not being able to see both goals from the center circle.

10. It is the duty of the Referee to act upon the information of a *neutral* Linesman with regard to incidents that do not come under the personal notice of the Referee.

    If an immediate decision is rendered, he may penalize, as appropriate. If, however, play had continued, all he can do is CAUTION or EJECT.

11. A Referee, not having seen a score, may not allow the goal if reported by a *non-neutral* Linesman.

12. He must not allow both Linesmen to place themselves on the same touch-line. (Reference System — used in Russia.)

13. Coaching from the boundary lines is not allowed (FIFA) — First WARN, then CAUTION, then EJECT.

14. The Referee should not allow players to waste time. The law requires that players retreat the required 10 yards. The Referee must assert his personality and apply the laws of the game.

ADVANTAGE CLAUSE (LAW V) *See Chapter V – Advantage.*

(It is a clause, not a law.)

The Referee shall refrain from penalizing when it would be an advantage to the offending team. — ADVANTAGE CLAUSE

If the Referee has decided to apply the advantage clause and to let the game proceed, he cannot revoke his decision if the presumed advantage has not been realized, even though he has not, by any gesture, indicated his decision.

In order to justify the decision for applying the advantage clause, the advantage should be evident, clear, and immediate.

The advantage clause . . .

● Should almost never be applied in the defensive 1/3 of the field.

● Is infrequently applied at midfield.

● Is most often applied in the attacking 1/3 of the field (excluding the PA).

The advantage clause should only be awarded within the penalty-area if the Referee is almost positive that a goal will be scored.

The advantage may not be awarded during the process of putting the ball back into play, (e.g., throw-in, kick-off) until *after* it actually is in play.

TERMINATION OF GAME

When may the Referee terminate a game?

1. When he considers that he will not be able to exert complete vigilance over the game.

2. If one team has less than seven players. (A recommendation.)

3. If the Referee cannot see one goal while standing at the other or he can't see both goals while standing in the center circle. (A recommendation.)

4. When the field is invaded by spectators or players, and the official feels that he cannot restore order.

5. When a player refuses to leave the game, and play cannot be continued.

6. If the field is no longer properly marked, through rain or other elements and cannot be remarked.

7. If there are no more game balls that are acceptable to the Referee.

8. When the Referee is incapacitated, and cannot continue, unless a neutral Linesman replaces him. (We recommend that the Two Referee System be instituted under such circumstances.)

9. When the ground becomes so wet that the ball will not bounce.

10. If a wind condition will not allow a stationary ball to remain so.

11. When smog prevails to the extent that the players' health is endangered.

TIMING

Playing time begins from the moment the ball is legally put into play (travels its circumference in a forward direction), not on the sounding of the whistle. There is a running clock, and time is stopped only at the Referee's discretion.

Time Allowance

- Treatment of injuries when a player cannot be safely removed from the field.
- Lost (or not easily recovered) ball or one in need of replacement.
- Time wasting by either team.
- Extension of time for penalty-kick.

High school and college soccer . . . the clock is stopped after a goal and for the taking of a penalty-kick and for cautions/ejections.

If, at the end of a period, an error in timing (shortage) is noted, and called to the Referee's attention by a neutral Linesman and acknowledged, the players must be called back onto the field and play must continue for the duration of the shortage.

Time losses occurring in the one period may not be added to another.

The duration of the game can't be protested.

Game Time

FIFA and College	High School	Youth
Two equal periods of 45 minutes each	Two periods of 45 minutes each or Four quarters of 20 minutes each	Division 1 – Two periods of 40 minutes each Division 2 – Boys – Two periods of 35 minutes each Division 2 – Girls Division 3 – Boys – Two periods of 30 minutes each Division 3 – Girls Division 4, 5 – Boys – Two periods of 25 minutes each Division 4 – Girls Division 6 – Boys – Two periods of 20 minutes each

Halftime

FIFA	High School	Youth	College
5 minutes (May be extended to not more than 15 minutes)	10 minutes (2 minutes between quarters)	Minimum – 5 minutes Maximum – 10 minutes	Maximum of 10 minutes

Captains of both teams *may not* agree to forego the half-time interval if any player objects.

If Necessary to Establish a Winner (Overtime)

FIFA	High School	College
Two periods of 15 minutes each (Generally accepted) 5 minutes between regulation period and overtime is recommended.	Two periods of 5 minutes each.	Two periods of 10 minutes each.

154

KICK-OFF

WHEN TAKEN		• To start the game. • To re-start after half-time and over-time periods. • After a team scores a goal.
WHERE TAKEN	Center of the field	• Each player must be in his own half of the field. A player having one foot in each half of the field is not in his own half of the field – RETAKE
IN-PLAY	CIRCUMFERENCE and into opponent's half of play.	• If travels along the center-line and goes out of bounds, RETAKE because ball must be kicked forward. • If teammate of kicker or any player touches the ball before it is in play – RETAKE
PLAYS BALL TWICE IN SUCCESSION	IFK	
SCORE DIRECTLY?	NO	• Opponent's goal – GOAL-KICK. • Own goal – RETAKE – Not in play.
DISTANCE AWAY	Opponent's = 10 Yards	

If there is successive encroachment or the ball isn't kicked into the opponent's half of play . . .

- 1st time – WARN and RETAKE
- 2nd time – CAUTION and RETAKE
- 3rd time – EJECT and RETAKE

The home team captain normally flips the coin. The captain of the visiting team calls the toss. The winner of the coin toss has the choice of kick-off or side. If side is chosen, the other team must kick-off. After the captain winning the flip has made his decision, he may not change his mind.

At half-time, sides are changed and the opposite team kicks-off. Note that this kick-off is in the same direction as it was to begin the game.

If there is overtime, a coin toss will again prevail.

DROP-BALL

WHEN TAKEN?	*	
HOW TAKEN?	Dropped, not thrown	• Drop from waist height of the players.
WHERE TAKEN?	Where ball was when play was stopped	(College, High School, Youth — No drop balls in the penalty-area.)
IN PLAY	When touches the ground.	• If goes over goal/touch-line before touched by any player — RETAKE. • If played before touches ground . . . 1st time WARN and RETAKE 2nd time CAUTION and RETAKE (High School — IFK but no caution) • 3rd time EJECT and RETAKE
OFF-SIDE DIRECTLY?	No	• This pertains only to the *first* player to play the ball.
DISTANCE AWAY	No prescribed distance that players must be away from the ball.	• Players may not interfere with the dropping of the ball.

If, during a DROP-BALL, but before the ball is actually dropped, a foul is committed — Referee can CAUTION or EJECT but can't award a free-kick because the ball isn't in play.

*When taken . . .

- Temporary suspension not covered elsewhere in soccer laws.

- Ball out of bounds — Referee unable to identify the player who last played it.

- Ball out of bounds after simultaneously coming off of 2 opponents.

- Player(s) accidentally falls on ball and play is stopped before it becomes dangerous.

- After stoppage for illness/injury.

- Ball hits a corner-post or an upright and breaks it.

- Ball strikes an outside agent or the outside agent causes interference.

- Simultaneous fouls of the same gravity. (This is a rarity.)

- When the ball bursts or becomes deflated during the course of a match. (If the ball bursts or becomes deflated as the game is being restarted and *before the ball has been played or touched by a player* — RETAKE . . . even if it hits a foreign object. Exception: The ball bursts on the cross-bar when taking a Penalty-Kick = DROP-BALL.)

- If the Referee mistakenly whistles.
- If the Referee prematurely awards a goal.
- The instant the Referee notices the inside of the goal is altered, if done prior to the ball going into the goal (other than GK moving the cross-bar).

The Drop Ball

1. The Ball is to be dropped at that place where the ball was positioned when the play was stopped. (College, High School and Youth – Ball is not dropped within the Penalty-Area.)

2. It is often advisable to quickly say "Drop-ball," and to drop it immediately. Both opponents do not have to be present. This is particularly the case when one or both teams delay in positioning themselves for the drop.

3. When the ball is to be dropped within the Penalty-Area, be sure that a defender is present.

4. The Referee may require that players face a certain direction. This is important for a drop-ball near the goal-line, for they should be facing the touch-line rather than the goal-line. This limits the possibility of a goal being scored directly.

5. If a drop-ball is taken near the goal-line, hits a rock, and then goes directly into the goal without being played by any player – RETAKE.

6. To give a drop-ball when two players simultaneously kick a ball out of bounds (as indicated by Law VIII) tends to indicate Referee indecision. Most experienced Referees will award the throw-in or the goal-kick to the defensive team should this situation occur. If a drop-ball is given, it should be done at the point it left the field of play.

7. When using the diagonal system with neutral linesmen, always face one of your linesmen when dropping the ball.

8. A goalkeeper within the PA may pick up a drop-ball directly after it hits the ground, for the ball is in play. (High School – The GK cannot be one of the players involved in the drop.)

9. The player who first plays the ball may play it twice in succession.

POTENTATOR

* Expects players and coaches to cater to him.
* Autographs copies of the rule book.
* Wears presidential fitness patch on his uniform.
* Is oblivious to calls made by his fellow official.
* Kign of the center circle.
* Runs the short diagonal and calls most fouls from 50 yards away.
* Claims to have been the prime consultant for the writing of *Fair or Foul.*
* Talks only to God.
* Has two wives.

OUTSIDE AGENT (FOREIGN OBJECTS)

If a spectator, animal, reserve-ball, or any other object enters the field of play —
Referee, if necessary, will stop play and will award a DROP-BALL.

A limb of a tree would be considered a foreign object if it overhung into the field and
was touched by an in play ball.

The bodies of the Referees and Linesmen are not considered foreign objects. They
are neutral objects and are part of the field if they are within the field of play.

A goal can't be awarded in any case if the ball has been prevented by some outside
agent from passing over the goal-line, or if the agent touched the ball.

Following a restart, if the ball is in play and touches a foreign object prior to any
other player having touched it . . .

- If a penalty-kick — RETAKE
- All other situations — DROP-BALL
  (Kick-off, goal-kick, corner-kick, etc.)

Substitutes are not to be considered outside agents. They are considered as players
for the purpose of this law.

Ejected players are outside agents.

Oto Maxmilian

"Don't worry, Gentlemen, I'll take care of this outside agent."

159

IN/OUT OF PLAY

It is the position of the ball that is important, not the position of the player.

Ball in Play	After . . .
KICK-OFF	Circumference and into opponent's half of the field.
GOAL-KICK	Clears the penalty-area.
FREE-KICK	Circumference.
FREE-KICK (taken inside own penalty-area)	Circumference and clears the penalty-area.
PENALTY-KICK	Circumference and forward.
THROW-IN	Has been released and enters the field of play (touches or passes the outside edge of the touch-line).
CORNER-KICK	Circumference.
DROP-BALL	Touches ground.
Ball Out of Play	
Wholly crosses the touch or goal-line (ground or air).	If the ball completely crosses the boundary lines in the air, but, because of the wind, returns to the field of play, it shall be considered out of bounds.
When game has been stopped by the Referee.	Temporary suspension not covered elsewhere in soccer laws – DROP-BALL.

Ball is in play at all other times including:

- If it rebounds from a goal-post, cross bar, or corner flag into the field of play.
- If it rebounds off of a Referee or linesman who is in the field of play.
- An infringement of the laws until the whistle is sounded.

SCORING

A goal is scored when the *whole* of the ball has completely passed over the back edge of the goal-line between the goal-posts and under the cross-bar.

A goal scored immedittely after an infraction is noticed by the Referee does not count unless he has applied the Advantage Clause.

If the GK is injured or passes out, no subsequent score is allowed. After the GK has recovered or has been replaced, resume play with a DROP-BALL.

A Referee having not seen a score may allow the goal only if reported by a neutral linesman.

The score of a forfeit is 1-0. (College and High School)

Advantage

If a 'hand ball' on a defensive player goes into his own goal, the score shall count. (Advantage Clause)

Premature Awarding of a Score

If a score is awarded prematurely by the Referee, which the goalkeeper managed to stop on or near the goal-line, a DROP-BALL must be given where the ball was when the Referee whistled. For High School, College and Youth, a DROP-BALL may not be given within the penalty-area.

Outside Agent

A goal cannot be awarded in any case if the ball has been prevented by some outside agent from passing over the goal-line or if it crosses the goal-line after having contacted an outside agent.

Alteration of Goal

Whenever the goal has been altered . . .

- If noticed before a goal was scored – DROP-BALL
- If noticed after the goal was scored – GOAL.

Field Entry/Exit Without Permission

- Unauthorized entry
  - If score in own goal = GOAL and CAUTION
  - If score in opponent's goal = NO GOAL, CAUTION, INDIRECT
- 12th player entry followed by the scoring of a goal . . . . .
  - *If play has not been resumed* – NO GOAL. Have captain send one player off the field. Resume play with IFK from where the ball was played into the goal.
  - *If play has been resumed* -- GOAL. Have captain send one player off the field. Resume play with IFK from where the ball was when play was stopped.

Whenever the identity of the 12th player is known – CAUTION him.

OFF-SIDE

A player is in an off-side position if he is nearer the opponent's goal-line than THE BALL (Diagram 1=D1) at the *moment* the ball is played (D3) unless . . .

Two opponents are nearer their goal-line than he is. (D2)(D3)	Being in line with an opponent means that the opponent (whole or part) *is not* between the player and the goal-line. (D5)

Receives the ball directly from a . . .
 	
  GOAL-KICK
  CORNER-KICK   (D7)
  THROW-IN
  DROP-BALL   (D9)
	This protection ends when a teammate plays the ball. (D8)
	
	A player may be penalized for being off-side when directly playing the ball from a free-kick or a penalty-kick.

The ball was last played by an opponent. (D11)	He is on-side if he receives the ball only because it was deflected (to slow down or change direction) by a defender). A player who is in an off-side position must be judged off-side if he receives the ball directly from a rebound from the up-right or cross-bar as opposed to having last been deflected by a defender.
He is in his own half of the field of play. (D10)	A player with one foot in each half of the field is not considered as being in his own half of the field. The halfway-line is considered to be part of both halves of the field, and a player with both feet on and/or behind this line can't be off-side.

The player is not off-side if the ball was last played by himself (e.g., player with the ball falls and ball goes behind him. He may get back up, go back and retrieve the ball).

It is not off-side if he is in line with the ball (D6).

When a defensive wall is formed on the goal-line and an offensive player is part of that wall, the offensive player is in an off-side position the moment the ball is played, unless he moves on-side before the ball is played.

The off-side is called if the player is in an off-side position and he:

Takes advantage of his position . . .
Participates in play . . .
Influences or interferes with play . . .
Trys to gain an (effective) advantage.

RULE OF THUMB

If the player in the off-side position has *no* chance of reaching the ball before anyone else, then he is not to be penalized for being off-side.

An off-side is occasionally called if the player is in an off-side position and he:

Interferes with the play or with an opponent	A player who advances toward an opponent or the ball may be deemed as influencing the course of the game.
Distracts an opposing player	• Standing in front of the GK may affect his line of vision and concentration. • A close-by attacker may be taking advantage of his position if the GK has to allow for his presence. — It could be considered GK distraction if the opponent is inside the goal area. — It shouldn't be considered GK distraction if the opponent is outside the penalty area.

HINTS

If the Referee is positive a defensive player will intercept a pass he may not give the off-side. (CONCACAF however, says no advantage shall be given on an off-side.)

A player in an off-side position can't put himself on-side as long as he was judged to be in an off-side position when the ball was played. (D4)

The moment of judgment is one thing, the moment you may penalize may be a different time.

Participation is judged until the next movement of judgment. (The next time the ball is played.)

A player may step off of the field in order to *avoid* an off-side (D13). But a player may not step off the field in order to *cause* an off-side (D14).

If a player's momentum carries him into the goal itself, he may remain without being penalized as long as he does not distract the GK. (D12)

Be aware of a team's employment of the 'off-side trap.' (Defenses move up in unison before the ball is played in order to put an attacker in an off-side position.)

DIAGRAMS

1. RELATIONSHIP TO THE BALL

A passes the ball. **B** runs from position 1 to position 2 and kicks the ball into the net. *Not offside* because even though there were not 2 opponents between **B** and the goal-line, he was *behind* (not ahead) of the ball.

2. OFF-SIDE PASS

A passes to **B** who is off-side because he is ahead of the ball at the moment it is played by a teammate and there aren't two opponents between him and the goal-line when the ball was passed.

3. MOMENT OF PASS

A runs the ball up and passes the ball. **B** then runs from position 1 to position 2. **B** is not off-side because *at the moment of the pass* he had two opponents between him and the goal-line. *Not off-side.*

4. CAN'T GET BACK ON-SIDE

A passes toward **B** who is in an off-side position. **B** comes back to get the ball but is whistled off-side because he can't put himself on-side.

5. BEING 'IN-LINE' WITH A DEFENDER

A passes the ball to **B** who is 'in line' with his opponent. **B** is *off-side* because only the goal-keeper is between him and the goal-line.

6. BEING 'IN-LINE' WITH THE BALL

A passes the ball **B** then runs from position 1 to position 2. Although **B** did not have 2 opponents between him and the goal-line, he is *not off-side* because he was not ahead (he was in-line) of the ball.

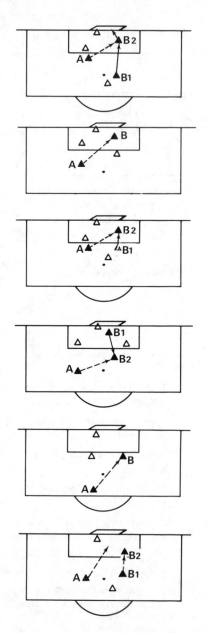

164

7. DIRECTLY FROM A CORNER-KICK

A kicks the corner-kick to **B** who heads it into the goal. *Not off-side* because the ball was received directly from a corner-kick.

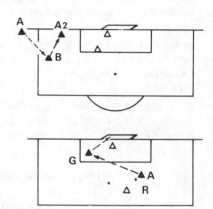

8. *AFTER* A CORNER-KICK

A kicks the corner-kick to **B** who passes to **A** at position 2. **B** received the ball directly and is not off-side.

C was in front of the ball and didn't have two opponents between himself and the goal-line so is off-side the instant **B** plays the ball. **A** is *off-side* at position 2 because there are not two defensive players between him and the goal-line.

9. RESUMING PLAY WITH A DROP-BALL

The Referee (**R**) drops the ball and **A** kicks the ball directly to **B** who shoots and scores. **A** is not off-side as he played the ball directly from the drop, but **B** is off-side because immunity from being in an off-side position was removed as soon as the ball was touched by another player.

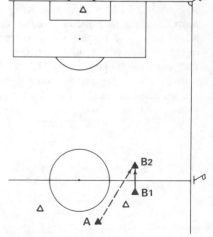

10. OWN HALF OF FIELD

A passes the ball. **B** then goes from position 1 to position 2. **B** is not off-side because he was within his half of the field at the moment of the pass.

11. GOALKEEPER DEFLECTION AND NON-PARTICIPATION

A kicks toward the goal. The ball is deflected by the goalkeeper to **B** who kicks the ball into the goal.

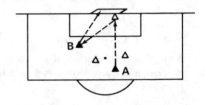

Although **B** is in an off-side position he is not to be penalized because the ball was last played by opponent and he was judged too far out of play to be participating at the moment of the shot.

If, however, the Referee feels that **B** would have been able to get to the ball before the GK deflection, then the off-side would have been called.

If the ball had been deflected by a cross-bar instead of an opponent, it would be off-side becaue there weren't two opponents between him and the goal-line.

INFREQUENTLY OCCURRING SITUATIONS

12. OFFENSIVE PLAYER GOES INSIDE GOAL

A runs the ball to position 1 and passes to **B**. **A**, realizing he is in an off-side position, runs into the goal and remains there passively. *Not off-side* because **A** was not interfering in play nor was he interfering with the opponents. If, at any time, the Referee feels that **A2** is actively distracting the goalkeeper, (mere presence is not sufficient), then he shall call off-side. Play would be resumed with an IFK on the goal-line, even though the infraction occurred outside the field of play.

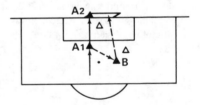

13. INTO THE SIDE-LINE AREA TO AVOID THE OFF-SIDE POSITION

While **A** passes to **B**, **C** sees that he is off-side and runs off the field toward position 2. He continues trotting down the side-line area and enters the field at position 3. He has removed himself from the off-side position.

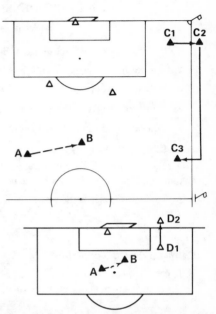

14. DEFENSE MAY NOT PUT MAN OFF-SIDE BY LEAVING THE FIELD

Defensive player **D** moves from position 1 to position 2 in an attempt to put **B** off-side. This is not allowed. *Not off-side.*

MISCONDUCT – CAUTION

Sometimes at midfield an incorrectly placed ball will show you don't know the laws of the game. If the kick is going to the right, and the infraction was for off-side, how important is it for the ball to be correctly placed?

CONDENSED OFF-SIDE
(See diagram ⟶)

I. To be off-side is to take advantage of being in an off-side position.

Taking advantage means the same as writers and lecturers who say . . .

- "Participates in play" . . . .
- "Influences play" . . . .
- "Seeks to gain an (effective) advantage" . . . .
- "Interferes with play"

A rule of thumb that we often use is the question, "When the ball is played, do you think that the player in the off-side position *might* be able to get to it first?

A "yes" answer means the whistle is blown and an off-side is called.

II. *What is the Off-Side position?*

It is being *ahead* of the ball . . . not even or behind the ball, but ahead. The player is closer to the opponents' goal-line than the ball is . . . .

WHEN?

. . . the moment the ball is played. This is the moment of judgment, and it lasts until the next moment of judgment, which is of course, the *next* time the ball is played.

UNLESS . . . .

III. There are various ways of escaping from this off-side position, any of which give the player immunity from being in an off-side position. They are highlighted by four bullets in the diagram on the opposing page.

When the ball is received directly from the Corner-Kick, Goal-Kick, Throw-In, or Drop Ball, it is significant to note that no one can be in an off-side position until the ball is played.

PLAYER *TAKES ADVANTAGE*
OF BEING IN AN OFF-SIDE *POSITION*

OFF-SIDE POSITION

WHAT: PLAYER IS CLOSER TO THE OPPONENTS
GOAL-LINE THAN THE *BALL* IS.

WHEN: THE *MOMENT* THE BALL IS PLAYED.

ESCAPE?

- Two defenders nearer own goal-line than the player.

- Ball last played by an opponent.

- Player in own half of field.

- Receive the ball *directly* from a:
    - Corner-kick
    - Throw-in
    - Goal-kick
    - Drop ball

169

George Tiedemann

Anticipating the foul . . . . . . professional style.

170

FOULS AND MISCONDUCT

1. An offense or attempted offense *is committed at the place where the player concerned initiated the action.*

2. An unintentional hand ball, trip, push, kick, or charge from behind — no infringement. Intention comprises as much of the foul as the contact itself. Sometimes seemingly violent play is not penalized because there is no intention. This is often due to the players not knowing how to play the game, which often results in dangerous play.

3. An offense normally punishable by a free-kick or a penalty-kick, if committed while play is suspended, can result only in a warning, caution or ejection.

4. An offense occurring outside a Referee's field of vision is indicated by a neutral linesman. The Referee can award a free-kick or a penalty-kick, if done via an immediate decision.

5. Substitute players will be treated in all respects the same as the 11 players on the field. If the substitute fouls, punishment remains the same. (IFK, DIRECT, PENALTY)

6. If a player outside the field strikes or trips someone who is inside the field — Penalize as appropriate (Direct, Penalty, etc.).

7. Two *opposing* players *outside the boundary* of the field of play and one intentionally commits misconduct or violent conduct upon the other, stop the game, caution or eject and resume with DROP-BALL.

8. Retaliation when fouled is not permitted. A player shall not retaliate in any way.

9. If two infractions of a different nature are committed at the same time, the Referee will punish the more serious offense.

10. Two players on the same team simultaneously commit offenses having comparable priority against members of the opposite team. Award the opposition that which gives them the greatest knowledge.

11. Two players on the same team commit offenses upon one another. Caution or eject, then restart play with an IFK in favor of the opponents.

12. Hard or particularly dangerous fouls are left up to the Referee's discretion as to whether he administers a caution or not.

13. The captain is responsible for the conduct of his team. (See Players — this chapter.)

14. Do not accept (either caution or eject) any foul that is committed:

    - Off the ball.
    - With malice aforethought.
    - By going over the ball.

15. In the Penalty-Area — to do nothing is better than to compromise with a lessor foul (an IFK).

16. Never 'pull' the ball out of the Penalty-Area if you are convinced that the foul occurred there.

INTENTIONAL VS DELIBERATE

1. There is a rather fine line to be drawn between the intentional foul (as mentioned in Law XII) and one that is done deliberately. The deliberate foul should be penalized at least with a caution and quite often an ejection.

The intentional foul — The player determines to act in a certain way.

The deliberate foul — It is intentionally committed with careful and thorough consideration. It is characterized by ***awareness of the consequences.*** More conscious will is involved with the deliberate foul.

WARNINGS OR "SOFT CAUTIONS"

Warn the first time a . . .

- *Kick-off* — is intentionally not played into opponent's half of the field or is subject to encroachment. RETAKE

- *Corner-Kick* — has defensive encroachment. RETAKE or ADVANTAGE CLAUSE

- *Goal-Kick* or *Free-Kick (within own Penalty-Area)* — intentionally not kicked beyond Penalty-Area or an opposing player encroaches, or any player touches the ball within the Penalty-Area.

- *Free-Kick* — has defensive encroachment. RETAKE (more often results in a caution)

- *Drop-Ball* — is touched or played before hitting the ground. RETAKE

CAUTIONS (YELLOW CARD)

Cause . . .	Action If Ball in Play	
Ungentlemanly conduct	IFK	● See 'Ungentlemanly Conduct' – this chapter.
Constantly infringes the laws of the game	(As per offense)	
Dissent	IFK	● Shows by word or movements of the body.
Field entry or exit without permission	IFK	● Apply advantage clause if applicable.
Deliberately fouling	(As per offense)	● Deliberately catching the ball to prevent an attack from developing.
Dangerous play (if Referee desires)	IFK	● See 'Dangerous Play'.
Player (other than the goalie changes shirt numbers.	IFK	● Require them to change back.
Delaying the taking of a free-kick. (Defensive player wasting time getting back 10 yards from the ball.	RETAKE	● The law requires that the players get back. The Referee must assert his personality and apply the laws of the game.
Coaching from the side-line.	DROP-BALL	

Caution during a penalty-kick if there is an encroachment, the wrong person kicks, or any distraction either to or by the GK

Upon receiving his third caution during a season, the player is required to appear before a Referees' commission regarding possible suspension. (FIFA)

Caution the Second Time in Succession a . . .

- *Kick-Off* – is intentionally not played into opponent's half of the field or is subject to encroachment. RETAKE

- *Corner-Kick* – has defensive encroachment. RETAKE or ADVANTAGE CLAUSE

- *Goal-Kick* or *Free-Kick (within own penalty-area)* – is intentionally not kicked beyond penalty-area or an opposing player encroaches, or any player touches the ball within the penalty-area.

- *Drop-Ball* – is touched or played before hitting the ground. RETAKE

☆ ★ ☆ ★ ☆ ★ ☆ ★ ☆ ★ ☆ ★ ☆ ★ ☆ ★ ☆ ★ ☆ ★ ☆ ★ ☆

"If you have to use the yellow card to control the game, something's wrong."

—Joe Cassisi, Coaching Commissioner
California Youth Soccer Association, North

☆ ★ ☆ ★ ☆ ★ ☆ ★ ☆ ★ ☆ ★ ☆ ★ ☆ ★ ☆ ★ ☆ ★ ☆

EJECTION (RED CARD)

Condition

VIOLENT CONDUCT OR SERIOUS FOUL PLAY	If player strikes an opponent far away from play, if the advantage is applicable, do not eject until first stoppage of play.
Maliciously strikes or attempts to strike.	
Maliciously kicks or attempts to kick.	Two teammates fighting with one another.
Spitting at.	Throwing any object at any player.
Persists in misconduct after having received a caution.	NOTE: A player is never given a second caution.
Foul or abusive language and/or gestures.	The same applies to foul language coming from outside the field of play.

The game is restarted with a DIRECT FREE-KICK if the strike or kick offenses are committed against an opponent. It is restarted with an IFK in all other situations when the infraction is committed on the field of play. (Striking or kicking a Referee, Linesman, spectator or teammate — even if in the Penalty-Area.)

If a Player is Ejected . . .

- Before game starts — he can be replaced by a named substitute.
- Any time after play has started — he cannot be replaced.

If ejected, a player may not occupy the side-line or goal-line area. He must leave the general area of play.

An ejected player is considered as being an outside agent.

Miscellaneous Ejections

- If a player starts to go after another player in a violent manner instead of the ball.
- Intentional charging of the goalkeeper (youth/high school/college).

Oto Maxmilian

Many have said that soccer's future is in the hands of competent officials. Hopefully, incidents like this, where a player is ejected, will be less and less frequent as the game matures.

174

ENTERING/LEAVING THE FIELD

Left the Field	Comment
Equipment Adjustment	Must present himself to the Referee for inspection prior to re-entry.
Injury	May return after the Referee signals.
Without permission	CAUTION AND IFK May be allowed to re-enter. Also when abandoned due to disagreements with teammates or if sent off by his captain.

If Ordered Off the Field . . .	Replacement
Before play starts	May be replaced by a named substitute
After play begins	May not be replaced
At Half time	

Player Entry Without Permission . . .	Goal?	Action
Entry without scoring	– – –	CAUTION AND IFK
If he scores in opponent's goal	NO GOAL	
If he scores in own goal	GOAL	CAUTION

If a goal was scored and if it is then determined that there were 12 players on the field, have the captain send 1 player off the field and . . .

> . . . If play has *not* been restarted – NO GOAL. Resume play from where the ball was kicked or headed into the goal.

> . . . If play has been restarted – GOAL. Resume play with an IFK from where the ball was when it was noticed that there were 12 players.

FREE-KICKS – GENERAL (NON PENALTY-KICK)

Conditions	Kick, in relation to own penalty-area		
	OUTSIDE	INSIDE	
Where is kick taken?	At the point of infraction		• Taken by any player and in any direction. The ball must be stationary. • Player taking the kick may step outside the boundary lines.
In play	Circumference	Circumference and outside the penalty-area.	• If taken on or near the boundary lines and goes out of bounds before traveling its own circumference – RETAKE.
Plays ball a second time	IFK	RETAKE (if hasn't passed penalty-area) Otherwise – IFK	
Opponent's distance from ball is until it is in play.	10 Yards	10 Yards and outside the penalty-area	• Player taking the kick may voluntarily renounce the distance advantage allowed him. • If an offensive player requests 10 yards and then kicks the ball while the Referee is establishing the wall . . . you may apply the advantage, or CAUTION and RETAKE. • If a free-kick is taken within 10 yards from the defending team's goal, the defending players may be on the goal-line between the goal-posts. They must however, have both feet on the goal-line.
Opponent encroachment and Referee stops play before kick is taken.	DELAY KICK		
Opponent encroachment and Referee unable to stop play before kick is taken.	CAUTION AND RETAKE		• Encroachment only applies to defensive players.
Goes directly into one's own goal.	CORNER	RETAKE	• Kick taken from within own penalty-area goes outside of the penalty-area and for some reason comes back and goes directly into own goal (e.g., wind) – CORNER.
Score goal directly against an opponent	DIRECT – Yes IFK – No – GOAL-KICK		
Can teammate be directly off-side?	YES		
Ball is kicked back to goalkeeper who takes it into his hands within his own penalty-area.	O.K.	RETAKE	

INDIRECT FREE-KICK (IFK)

A goal cannot be scored unless the ball has been played or touched by a player from either team other than the kicker before passing into the goal.

Referee signals by raising his arm. He keeps it raised until the kick is taken. (If the Referee fails to do so and a goal is scored directly, he should have the kick RETAKEN.) It is recommended that he keep his arm aloft until the outcome of the kick is determined.

The following results in an INDIRECT FREE-KICK . . .

After putting the ball into play, plays ball twice in succession.	If done during the taking of a kick-off, throw-in, free-kick, corner-kick, penalty-kick, or goal-kick going outside the PA.
Off-side	
Ungentlemanly conduct	CAUTION – See the next page.
Dangerous play (see this chapter)	The Referee sometimes cautions.
Goalkeeper takes more than 4 steps with ball. (See 'Goal-keeper' in Chapter IV)	The 4 Step Rule applies throughout until the ball has been played by someone else. While holding, bouncing, or throwing the ball and catching it again.
Fair charges at the wrong moment.	• When no obstruction or ball wasn't within playing distance. • Charging the GK is allowed *except* when . . . – He is not in possession of the ball within his goal-area. • Youth, High School & College – Goalie can never be charged within his own penalty-area.
Dissent with decision by . . . • Throws ball away (GL) • Leaves field • Other	Usually CAUTION – Sometimes EJECTION . . . it depends upon intensity.
Obstruction	If done intentionally and not within playing distance. *(Hint* – Look at the players eyes and facial expression if possible. • Using his body as an obstacle • With or without the ball, he backs into an opponent. • If occurs when the ball is not within playing distance of the 2 players involved. • After corner-kick, if opponent then stands in front of the GK, making no attempt to play the ball. • Running across an opponents path to retard his progress. • Attempting to prevent the goalkeeper from putting the ball into play (e.g., player standing directly in front of the GK).
Changing numbers (non-goalkeeper)	CAUTION – For ungentlemanly conduct. Require the players to change back.
Restarting game after violent conduct directed against non-opponents. • Referee • Linesman • Spectators • One's own teammates	• Hitting • Kicking EJECT • Foul language and/or gestures • Insult (includes spitting)

If an IFK is taken on the opponent's goal-line, the ball must be kicked backwards or to the side because the ball could never be in play if it was kicked forward.

UNGENTLEMANLY CONDUCT (ALSO CAUTION)

Basic

Restart with an IFK unless the occurrence is when the ball is out of play.

Ungentlemanly conduct applies when directed toward opposing players, teammates, Referees, linesmen and spectators. It occurs when the game is brought into disrepute by unexpected or unprecedented behavior. It offends against the spirit of the game. (e.g., A defender within his penalty-area fists a ball out of the goal. He should be cautioned. Even if the penalty-kick is converted, the defender has lost his reputation as a sportsman and the whole game is the poorer.)

Deliberate Hand Ball

- To prevent a goal from being scored.
- To prevent an attack from developing.
- To put the game into disrepute.

Delaying Tactics

To delay taking a kick (GK has only the time necessary to put the ball back into play).

When in possession of the ball, GK baits opponent by withholding the ball from play.

Holding ball — GK holds too long or any player holds the ball with his legs, or lies on the ball for an unreasonable length of time.

GK and another player kicking the ball repeatedly back and forth.

GK wastes time by dribbling the ball with his feet around the penalty-area.

Defenders not retreating 10 yards for a free-kick or a corner-kick.

- Do not leave or too slow in retiring.
- Stand on or in front of the ball.

Harassment

Distracting opponents by dancing about gesticulating, shouting or other actions. (Opponents moving back and forth — even if 10 yards away.)

Jumping in front of a player taking a corner, free-kick, or throw-in.

Worrying or obstructing GK. To interfere or attempt to interfere with his clearing move. (May warn on first offense if not blatant.)

Most attempts to prevent the GK from putting the ball into play (e.g, offensive player sticks out his leg to inhibit the kick).

Adopting a threatening attitude toward another.

Field Entry/Exit

Coming onto or going off the field without the Referee's permission.

After having received the Referee's permission to leave the field but before having actually left, playing the ball. It is alright as long as the player was not trying to achieve a position of illegal advantage.

Injury

Opponent pulling an injured player from the field in order to humiliate him or to minimize his injury.

Faking an injury.

Penalty-Kick

Goalkeeper swings his hands about.

Player other than the one who is designated, kicks the ball.

The kicker fakes a kick to get the GK to move his feet.

Objects

GK (within his penalty-area) hits the ball with an object in his hand.

Throwing an object at the ball.

Hiding a dangerous object upon his person (this may also result in an ejection).

Leverage Used Unfairly

Leaning on shoulders of teammate.

Holds onto uprights or to the crossbar to gain an unfair advantage. Steadies himself to kick the ball or in order to jump higher.)

Miscellaneous

To keep playing the ball after hearing the whistle.

Making any reference to the religion or morals of any individual.

GK lying down near his goal as a contempt-showing action when the game is very one-sided.

Lighting a cigarette.

Fullback going behind his goal-line to create an off-side.

Defender rushes forward from a wall before the ball is kicked.

After asking for 10 yards, kicking the ball before the Referee has given the signal. (Apply the advantage if applicable.)

Two players carrying on a conversation which indirectly dissents with the decision of a Referee 'Over his head.'

Even if these two players were teammates, a foul should be called for dangerous play.

DANGEROUS PLAY

(Cautions are frequently administered. It is up to the Referee if he chooses to use his discretionary powers.)

1. Restart with INDIRECT unless occurrence is when ball is out of play.

2. The Referee has discretionary powers regarding a negligent action associated with dangerous play.

   a. Player comes to the ball in a manner which is dangerous to another player.

   b. Whenever a player puts himself in danger (e.g., head down at waist level or lower (normally OK for GK)).

   c. Scissors-kick (bicycle, double kick), if it causes another player to move away. If he kicks the opponent – still an IFK because it wasn't intentional.

   d. Sliding tackle if ball is played but contact is first made with an opponent.

   e. High kicking or knee at head level.

   f. Kicking ball or at ball when in possession by the GK.

   g. Heading ball when held aloft by GK is almost always dangerous play.

   h. Goalkeeper or field player lifting knee or leg to fend off an opponent.

   i. Stretching out a leg toward the opponent when it could be dangerous to the opponent.

   j. Accidentally jumping at an opponent.

3. Dangerous play does not have to be committed against an opponent. It can be dangerous even if done against a teammate.

DIRECT FREE-KICK

Kicking
(Show red card)

Tripping
(No red card)

Jumping at

Pushing

Holding

Charging Violently
Charging from Behind

Striking

Handling Ball

182

DIRECT FREE-KICK

A goal can be scored 'directly' into the opponent's goal.

A direct free kick results from any of the following *intentionally* committed offenses against an opponent:

Infraction	If Attempted	Comments
1. KICKING	X	EJECT, kicks must be directed only at the ball. 'Foot Over' (the ball) kick is considered kicking.
2. TRIPPING	X	No clear intention to play the ball. Sliding tackle – ball not played. Also stooping in front of or behind an opponent. Tackle from behind • If trip and ball is not played – DIRECT/PK • If ball is played, but in the process, contact is first made with an opponent, IFK (Dangerous Play) • If play ball first, followed by an unintentional trip – PLAY ON
3. JUMPING AT		• To play the ball is to jump "straight up." • To "accidentally" jump at an opponent is to be guilty of dangerous play.
4. CHARGING VIOLENTLY or dangerously		• Termed an unfair charge. • Hip action bumping.
5. CHARGING FROM BACK		• Unless fair charging an opponent who is obstructing. • If a player deliberately turns his back to an opponent when he is about to be tackled, he may be charged, but not in a dangerous manner.
6. STRIKING	X	EJECT • Also throwing an object including a ball at the player. • Throw-in violently at a player – Take kick from touch-line.
7. HOLDING 8. PUSHING		• Grabbing any part of clothing. • Leaning on opponent's shoulders. • Arm stretched across the chest which retards the opponent's progress. • Two teammates boxing in or fair charging an opponent simultaneously. • Resting hand on opponent while in pursuit of ball.
9. HANDLES THE BALL • Deliberately handling the ball in order to prevent an attack from developing on a goal – CAUTION. • Handling the ball before it is put into play is not considered a 'Hand-Ball.'		• Doesn't apply to goalkeeper in his penalty-area. • To fall and accidentally touch the ball is not a hand-ball. • The hand is taken to be the whole of the arm, from the shoulders down through the fingers. • It is intentional when a player extends his arms to present a larger target to the ball or intentionally moves his hands/arms toward the ball (hand striking the ball instead of ball striking the hand). • Instinctive movements of the hands or arms to protect against being hit in the face or groin (brest – women) shall not be considered as intent in handling the ball. The hands used 'palms-outward' is normally intent. If defensive player should score in his own goal with his hands, the score shall count – ADVANTAGE. • Holding an object is considered an extension of the hand.

This charge is violent, and from behind. The player (right) makes no attempt to play the ball.

CHARGING

In order for a charge to be made fairly, the player:

- May not have hands or arms extended away from the body.
- Must execute only with the shoulder against another shoulder; chest, arms, hands, and hips may not be used. A charge must not be made with or against the chest.
- Must have one or both feet in contact with the ground.

Fair Charge

Non-goalkeeper Not Playing the Ball	Obstruction	No Obstruction
FROM THE BACK	'Play on'	DIRECT
FROM THE FRONT	'Play on'	INDIRECT

If a player deliberately turns his back when about to be tackled, he may be charged in a non-dangerous manner (but only with the shoulder).

- To look at opponent as you charge him is not playing the ball.
- A fair charge doesn't have to be weak. It can be hard, but it may not be violent.

Goalkeeper

- He may be charged:

LOCATION	HE OBSTRUCTS	HAS POSSESSION OF BALL	DOES NOT HAVE POSSESSION OF BALL
WITHIN THE GOAL AREA	/////	/////	*CAN NOT* BE CHARGED IFK
IN ALL OTHER PORTIONS OF THE PENALTY AREA	/////	/////	/////

- If charged while corner-kick is in the air — IFK because he is within his own goal area and didn't have the ball.
- Unintentional body contact is not to be penalized.

Youth, High School, College — GK may not be charged within his own penalty-area.

	COLLEGE AND H.S.	YOUTH
INTENTIONAL CHARGING	EJECT AND DIRECT	CAUTION AND DIRECT
*UN*INTENTIONAL CHARGING	DIRECT	IFK

Unfair Charge

If charged violently, dangerously, or from behind (unless obstructing) — DIRECT.

185

IMITATOR

* Calls what the other official calls.

* Calls coach "Doctor" unless he knows his first name.

* Tries to please everyone.

* Calls off-side whenever defensive player throws up his hand.

* Emphasizes a foreign accent.

* Calls obstruction in the Penalty-Area instead of tripping.

* Agrees with God.

* Agrees with wife.

* Paid to have his name mentioned in the acknowledgment section of *Fair or Foul.*

PENALTY-KICK

Penalty-Kick
Point to penalty-spot

A penalty-kick results whenever one of the nine (9) infractions is committed by the defending team inside the penalty-area when the ball is in play regardless where the ball is, which would have resulted in a direct free-kick if committed outside the area. Taken from the penalty mark (spot) – (12 yards from the goal-line), the ball may not be placed elsewhere regardless of the condition of the spot.

Referee does not whistle for the beginning of the kick until all players are properly positioned. (This includes the GK having his feet on the goal-line.)

It is recommended that the Referee hand the ball to the kicker, allowing him to position it on the spot. This also serves to identify the kicker to the goalkeeper.

The Referee must verify that no player is outside the field of play.

Correct Positioning

All players except kicker and goalkeeper must be . . .	In the field of play.	• Kicker may step outside of the penalty-area or the 10 yard arc in order to gain momentum as long as it is not done prior to the whistle for the taking of the kick.
	At least 10 yards away from the penalty-spot.	
	Outside the penalty-area.	• See encroachment

Goalkeeper must stand on the goal-line between the goal-posts without moving his feet until the ball is kicked (circumference). If the GK gets into an improper position on the goal-line after the signal for the kick but before the ball is kicked, the Referee awaits the results of the kick. If no goal is scored – RETAKE.

A goalkeeper may be substituted for on a Penalty-Kick. (High School/College = Not from the bench.)

Any player may take the Penalty-Kick. (This includes their GK.)

If a penalty-kick is retaken, either the GK or the kicker may be changed.

This is an excellent position for viewing a penalty-kick . . . . but not for the Referee.

The Kick	Action	
If not in a forward direction	RETAKE	• After the ball is kicked in a forward direction, a teammate may run in from outside the penalty-area and kick the ball.
In play	CIRCUMFERENCE	
The ball is played by the kicker a second time in succession	IFK	
Player other than the one designated . . . kicks and . . .		• Referee must be informed as to who is taking the P.K. • GK may request that the kicker be identified to him.
• Scores.	CAUTION RETAKE	
• Doesn't score. Ball crosses goal-line.	CAUTION GOAL-KICK	
• Doesn't score. Ball rebounds into play.	CAUTION IFK	
• Rebounds off GK and goes over end-line.	CAUTION CORNER	
Distraction by shouting, making motions – ungentlemanly conduct.		• Normal body movements are OK, swinging hands are not.
• If before kick.	CAUTION	
• If goal.	CAUTION & GOAL	CAUTION RETAKE
• If no goal.	CAUTION & RETAKE	If distraction is directed against the goalkeeper
Ball crosses goal-line.		CAUTION GOAL-KICK
Ball rebounds into play.		CAUTION INDIRECT
OFF-SIDE	IFK	• If kicker plays the ball to a player who is in an off-side position. • Ball rebounds from goal-posts or cross-bar to a player who is judged to be in an off-side position. • If the ball is deflected to him by the GK, there is no off-side.
Ball touches an outside agent.		
• As goes toward goal.	RETAKE	
• As rebounds into play.	DROP-BALL	
Ball bursts directly on a goal-post or the cross-bar.	DROP-BALL	

The Penalty-Kick is considered an extension of the Direct Free-Kick. (e.g., A goal can't be scored directly against oneself – ball rebounds from cross-bar and goes directly into own goal.)

It is ungentlemanly conduct if the kicker fakes a kick to get the GK to move his feet.

ENCROACHMENT

A Caution is given for all encroachments. (Except for High School and College.)

After having whistled for the kick to be taken, the Referee does not intervene for an encroachment. He awaits the results of the kick.

Result	An Attacker	A Defender or GK Movement	Offense *and* Defense
GOAL	RETAKE	GOAL	
NO GOAL Save by GK or ball rebounds into play.	IFK		
Ball goes over the goal-line but not into the goal.	GOAL-KICK	RETAKE	RETAKE
GK touches the ball which goes over the goal-line but not into the goal.	CORNER		

(Column group header: Encroachment By ...)

Offensive encroachment in conjunction with the GK moving his feet — RETAKE whatever the result.

If, before the referee signals for the Penalty-Kick to be taken, an offensive player encroaches into the PA and kicks the ball — CAUTION and RETAKE.

HINT FOR REFEREES

Quite often a penalty kick situation results in protest and confusion on the field, and the Referee will have difficulty restoring order and may have to caution or eject players on the defensive team. It is advisable to pick up the ball immediately after whistling for the penalty, retaining possession until the players from both teams have cleared the area. The ball should then be given to the kicker for him to place on the penalty-mark in readiness for the kick. It is suggested that the kicker be identified to the goalkeeper. The Referee then positions himself, and after both kicker and goalkeeper are ready, he gives the signal for the kick to be taken.

TIME EXTENSION FOR PENALTY-KICK

(Referee should notify both captains prior to the taking of the kick that time has been extended.)

When a match is extended to allow a penalty-kick to be taken or retaken (be it at halftime or games end), the extension shall last until the moment when the penalty-kick has been completed. The players should be cleared out of the immediate vicinity to eliminate possible encroachment and other violations.

Ball

• Kicked out of bounds.
• Kicked toward goal and is clearly saved by the Goalkeeper
• Hits upright or cross-bar and . . .
    Goes out of bounds.
    Rebounds into play.
• Not kicked strongly enough to reach goal.
• Kicked toward teammate instead of towards goal.
• Hits upright or cross-bar and bursts.
	END OF PERIOD

• Ball goes directly into the goal. • Kicked toward goal, touched by GK, goes into the goal. • Hits upright or cross-bar and goes into the goal.	GOAL
• Ball touches an outside agent.	RETAKE

☆ ★ ☆ ★ ☆ ★ ☆ ★ ☆ ★ ☆ ★ ☆ ★ ☆ ★ ☆ ★ ☆ ★ ☆ ★ ☆ ★ ☆

"The worst thing about being a Referee is sitting in the packed stands surrounded by uninformed spectators."

—Ron Norris

☆ ★ ☆ ★ ☆ ★ ☆ ★ ☆ ★ ☆ ★ ☆ ★ ☆ ★ ☆ ★ ☆ ★ ☆ ★ ☆ ★ ☆

☆ ★ ☆ ★ ☆ ★ ☆ ★ ☆ ★ ☆ ★ ☆ ★ ☆ ★ ☆ ★ ☆ ★ ☆ ★ ☆ ★ ☆

The Referee who helps other Referees helps himself.

☆ ★ ☆ ★ ☆ ★ ☆ ★ ☆ ★ ☆ ★ ☆ ★ ☆ ★ ☆ ★ ☆ ★ ☆ ★ ☆ ★ ☆

FIFA Championships must not be decided by kicks from the penalty-mark. In the event that a non-championship game must be settled by kicks from penalty-mark, the following conditions must prevail.

1. The Referee shall choose the goal at which all of the kicks from the penalty-mark shall be taken.

2. The Referee shall toss a coin, and the team whose captain wins the toss must take the first kick.

3. Each team shall take five kicks from the penalty-mark. The kicks shall be taken alternately.

4. The team which scores the greater number of goals shall be declared the winner.

5. Only the players who are on the field at the end of the match, which shall mean at the end of extra time, insofar as a match in which extra time is authorized, is concerned, shall be eligible to take part in the kicking from the penalty-mark.

6. If,safter each team has taken five kicks, each has scored the same number of goals, the taking of penalty-kicks shall continue, in the same order (on a sudden death basis) until such time as each has taken the same number of kicks and one team has scored a goal more than the other. The kicks shall not continue after one team has scored a total of goals which establish them as winners.

7. Each kick shall be taken by a different player, and not until all eligible players of any team have taken a kick may a player of the same team have a second kick.

8. Any player who was on the field at the end of the match (see paragraph 5 above) may change places with his goalkeeper at any time during the taking of kicks from the penalty-mark.

9. Other than the player taking a kick, and the opposing goalkeeper, all players shall remain within the center circle while the taking of the kicks from the penalty-mark is in progress.

10. Unless stated to the contrary herein, the conditions of Laws X and XIV will apply in the taking of these kicks. The relevant paragraphs of the board decisions in relation to Law XIV shall be interpreted by analogy.

THROW-IN

BASIC	A member of the opposing team last touched the ball prior to it going completely out of bounds (air or ground) outside the touch-line.
WHERE DOES THROWN BALL ENTER THE FIELD OF PLAY?	At the point where it crossed the touch-line out of bounds. If at some other point . . . RETAKE.
IN PLAY	After it has been released — as soon as it passes or touches the outside edge of the touch-line in flight. (Considered to have entered the field of play.)
PLAY A SECOND TIME	IFK
SCORE A GOAL DIRECTLY?	NO — Throw directly into opponents goal — GOAL-KICK. Throw directly into own goal — CORNER-KICK.
OFF-SIDE DIRECTLY?	NO
DISTANCE AWAY	• Thrower must be allowed to deliver the ball properly. • If opponents dance about or gesticulate in a way calculated to distract or impede the thrower — CAUTION — ungentlemanly behavior.

The thrower, at the moment of delivery, must . . .

- Face the field of play with some part of the body.
- Have part of *each* foot on or outside the touch-line and on the ground. (If both heels are on the touch-line it quite often will result in a foul throw-in due to the player rising on his toes and losing contact with the ground.

    Feet may be apart.

    May not deliver the ball while running (both feet in motion).

    Taken within 1 meter of the touch-line.

- Use both hands and shall deliver the ball from behind and over his head.

    Ball must be delivered with equal force and simultaneously with both hands.

    It may not be delivered with one hand and directed with the other. (Very pronounced R-L or L-R spin is often penalized.)

- Throw-in is not allowed to be merely dropped, it must be thrown.

    If a continuous movement, it does not matter at what point it is released.

    A very 'gentle' throw is *not* considered to be a drop.

Miscellaneous

Takes throw-in improperly	Throw-in is TURNOVER to other team
Intentionally throws ball away from the field of play	CAUTION – RETAKE
Throw intentionally at Referee	EJECT – IFK
Throw ball at an opponent	
• If as a tactic	O.K. if done in a non-dangerous manner
• If violence against an opponent	EJECT – DIRECT from the touch-line
Throw-in hits Referee, Linesman or corner-flag.	
• Remains in play.	'PLAY ON' ·
• Goes out of bounds.	TURNOVER
Throw-in	
• Goes into opponent's goal.	GOAL-KICK
• Goes into own goal.	CORNER

● From point of contact.

The ball must be thrown into the field of play. If the ball hits the ground before it enters the field of play – RETAKE.

On the throw-in – If the ball is not played by any player and . . .

- It never was considered to have entered the field of play – RETAKE.
- It went in and out of the field of play – TURNOVER. (Any part of the ball touching or penetrating the outside edge of the touch-line following its release is considered to have entered the field of play.)

L.A. Aztecs Photo

A throw-in at midfield. What could be more insignificant? Even Elton John is spellbound.

GOAL-KICK

Goal-Kick
Point toward the halfway-line with one hand and
to the location of the kick with the other.

BASIC	Offense last played the whole of the ball over the goal-line (air or ground excluding going into the goal.	
WHERE TAKEN	Within that 1/2 of the goal-area nearest where it crossed the goal-line.	• In taking the kick, only some part of the ball or its projection need be within the proper half of the goal-area.
IN PLAY	Beyond the penalty-area.	• If doesn't go beyond penalty-area – RETAKE. • If crosses the goal-line . . . Inside the penalty-area – RETAKE. Outside the penalty-area – CORNER.
KICKER PLAYS BALL TWICE IN SUCCESSION	IFK	• If the ball is not yet in play (hasn't left P.A.) – RETAKE. • If takes kick properly and ball is returned by a strong wind and he plays it again – IFK.
SCORE GOAL DIRECTLY?	In opponents goal – GOAL-KICK. In own goal – RETAKE.	• Kick goes beyond penalty-area and for any reason comes back directly into one's own goal – CORNER. • If properly taken and it hits the Referee and goes into own goal – CORNER.
DIRECTLY OFF-SIDE?	NO	
DISTANCE AWAY (Opposition)	Outside of penalty-area until ball clears the penalty-area.	• If opponent is trying to leave the P.A., let the kick go, the opponent must be trying to gain an unfair advantage in order to be sanctioned.
(Teammates)	Any distance.	• May remain inside P.A.

The ball must be stationary, but it is quite in order for the GK to hold down the ball with one hand and simultaneously kick it in order to quickly put the ball into play.

If the ball is intentionally not kicked beyond the penalty-area, or an offensive player encroaches or any player touches ball before passing penalty-area . . .

- 1st time   – WARN
- 2nd time   – CAUTION   RETAKE
- 3rd time   – EJECT

CORNER-KICK AND CORNER-FLAG POST

Corner-Kick

BASIC		The defense last played the whole of the ball over the goal-line (air or ground) excluding going into the goal.	
WHERE IS KICK TAKEN?		The *whole* of the ball must be within the quarter circle at the nearest corner-flag post.	
		Youth — Under 9 years old. Kicks are taken from the intersection of the goal-line and the penalty-area.	
IN PLAY		CIRCUMFERENCE	
KICKER PLAYS THE BALL A SECOND TIME IN SUCCESSION		IFK	The kicker is not allowed to paly it a second time including if the corner-kick hits a goal-post, Referee, or Linesman.
SCORE A GOAL DIRECTLY?		YES	Even into your own goal.
OFF-SIDE DIRECTLY?		NO	
DISTANCE AWAY	Opponents	10 YARDS	If attacker places himself immediately in the way of the goalkeeper — this is O.K., however if the goalkeeper moves, the attacker may not follow him to interfere with him once the ball is kicked into play. To do so is to obstruct the goalkeeper — CAUTION.
	Teammates	ANY DISTANCE	Otherwise a player may occupy any location within the field. • If opponent encroaches . . . 1st time — WARN 2nd time — CAUTION RETAKE 3rd time — EJECT

Goalkeeper charged while the kick is in the air . . .

- Fair charge — IFK (Because goalkeeper was within own goal-area and didn't have the ball.)
- Charged violently — DIRECT

If the ball crosses over the middle of the cross-bar after having been last played by a defensive player, the Referee immediately signals from which corner it is to be taken.

Corner-Post

Corner flag-post must not be moved — WARN . . . then CAUTION. (To move means to alter from its stationary straight-up position.)

Ball hits corner flag-post and . . .

- Rebounds into field of play — IN PLAY.
- Breaks it — DROP BALL — Play is suspended until post is either mended, removed or replaced.
- Knocks down or tilts the corner-post away from the field of play in a non-dangerous manner — PLAY ON and refix at 1st opportunity.

If ball goes out of bounds by knocking down or going over the corner-flag . . .

- Last played by defense — GOAL-KICK
- Last played by defense — THROW-IN by offense.

The Referee appears 'cornered' by the field.

No matter how much you know about rules, things can still go wrong.

Referee Larry Harris who also umpires baseball, hit the dirt in this high school state championship game when his cletes came into contact with a rough spot on the field. He was running backwards at the time.

☆ ★ ☆ ★ ☆ ★ ☆ ★ ☆ ★ ☆ ★ ☆ ★ ☆ ★ ☆ ★ ☆ ★ ☆ ★ ☆ ★ ☆ ★

If you have never fallen down on a soccer field, then you probably do not run backwards as much as you should.

☆ ★ ☆ ★ ☆ ★ ☆ ★ ☆ ★ ☆ ★ ☆ ★ ☆ ★ ☆ ★ ☆ ★ ☆ ★ ☆ ★ ☆ ★

☆ ★ ☆ ★ ☆ ★ ☆ ★ ☆ ★ ☆ ★ ☆ ★ ☆ ★ ☆ ★ ☆ ★ ☆ ★ ☆ ★ ☆ ★ ☆ ★ ☆ ★

Have you studied officials in other sports?

Comment: You will notice several references in this book to sports and officials other than in soccer. If you referee other sports, you will find that it will help you immeasurably in your conduct of soccer games. If you referee only in soccer, study top officials in other sports. Your game control, mechanics, and conduct will improve.

☆ ★ ☆ ★ ☆ ★ ☆ ★ ☆ ★ ☆ ★ ☆ ★ ☆ ★ ☆ ★ ☆ ★ ☆ ★ ☆ ★ ☆ ★ ☆ ★ ☆ ★

XI

Testing

Your Knowledge

BASIC REFEREE'S TEST

There are 91 questions. Each one is worth 1.1 points.

Playing Area

Below are measurements as listed by FIFA, mostly from Law I – Field of Play. You are to fill in the most common purpose(s) each distance is used for. (Eg. 44 Yards = *Width* – *Penalty-Area)*

1. 130 Yards _____

   120 Yards _____

   110 Yards _____

2. 100 Yards (2 answers) _____ - _____

   80 Yards _____

   70 Yards _____

3. 50 Yards _____

   18 Yards _____

   12 Yards _____

4. 10 Yards (2 answers) _____ - _____

   8 Yards _____

   6 Yards _____

5. 1 Yard (2 answers) _____ - _____

   8 Feet _____

   5 Feet _____

6. 28 Inches _____

   27 Inches _____

   5 Inches (2 answers) _____ - _____

7. Area measurements are made from "inside to inside." True (T)_____ False (F)_____.

8. It is possible that the field of play *could* be a square. (T) _____ (F) _____.

Given the following field diagram:

9. Line 'A' is called the _____

10. 'B' is termed the _____ flag.

11. The flag at 'B' can be as close as _____ to line 'A'.

12. Line 'C' at the center of the field is termed the _____

13. 'D' is called the _____

14. 'E' is called the _____

15. Lines are part of their corresponding areas. (Circle the letter)   T   F

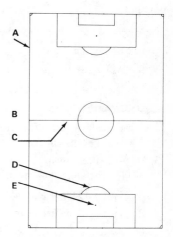

Equipment and Players

16. If a player experiences "shoe failure" of some type, during the match, he may complete the game minus either one or both of the shoes.   T   F

17. The outer casing of the ball must be made of leather.   T   F

18. Select the letter(s) of those objects which may not be worn during a match.

    A. Metal identification bracelets

    B. Glasses

    C. Cotton gloves

    D. Wrist watch

    E. Fur lined athletic supporter.

19. During a game, shirt numbers can be exchanged . . .

    A. For any player at any time.

    B. Only with a replacement for the goalkeeper.

    C. Only at half-time.

    D. For any player whenever the ball is not in play.

    E. Never.

20. A match should not be considered valid if a team fields fewer than _____ players. (How many?)

Referee

21. A Referee can reverse his decision . . .

    A. At any time.

    B. As long as the game has not been restarted.

    C. Only when the ball is in play.

    D. Never.

22. A player who is sent off the field before the kickoff which starts the
    game can be replaced.   T   F

23. When a soccer referee enters a stadium in the USA where there are in excess of
    50,000 spectators, how should he enter the field of play?

    A. Trot onto the field *in advance* of the two teams.

    B. Trot onto the field *with* the two teams.

    C. *Streak* onto the field with the two teams.

    D. Follow behind the two teams as they enter the field.

    E. With some apprehension. He is at an incorrect location. His 'Buster Brown'
       outfit will be out of place at this American football game.

24. Coaching from the boundary lines is not allowed.   T   F

25. When the Referee chooses to refrain from penalizing, he is most likely exercising the

    _____   _____. (Two words)

26. Dissent with the Referee's decision when the ball is in play results in . . . (Pick the
    letter(s) of your choice.)

    A. Nothing.

    B. Caution.

    C. Ejection.

    D. Indirect Free-Kick.

    E. Direct Free-Kick or Penalty-Kick

    F. Drop-Ball

27. In a "Diagonal System," a match may not begin or continue without
    both Linesmen being in position.   T   F

Timing, In/Out of Play, Resumption, and Miscellaneous

28. (Answer the bullet (●) which relates to your interests.) There are two equal periods of . . .

● _____ minutes for FIFA (or College)   ● Youth (Boys)

● _____ minutes for High School   _____ minutes for Division I.

_____ minutes for Division II.

_____ minutes for Division III.

_____ minutes for Division IV.

_____ minutes for Division V.

_____ minutes for Division VI.

29. Half-time lasts _____ minutes.

30. What action is taken by the Referee when the ball rebounds off of a Referee or Linesman who is in the field of play? _____

31. What happens when a ball last played by a defensive player hits the corner-flag post and rebounds back into the field of play?
    A. Goal-kick
    B. Corner-kick
    C. Throw-in for offensive team
    D. Drop-ball
    E. Ball in play

32. On a kick-off, playing time begins when the whistle blows.　　　　　　　T　　F

33. If the Referee prematurely awards a score which the goalkeeper managed to stop on the goal-line . . . What is the result if he immediately is aware of his mistake?
    A. A Goal
    B. A Drop-Ball at the place where the ball was when the Referee whistled.
    C. A Drop-Ball at the point where the ball was kicked or headed.
    D. Direct Free-Kick from the point where the ball was when the Referee whistled.
    E. Direct Free-Kick from the point where the ball was kicked or headed.
    F. A Drop-Ball at the closest point outside the Penalty-Area.

34. The goalkeeper with the ball in his possession, may take not more than _____ steps. (How many?)

Off-side

Name the four conditions when a player is not in an off-side position even though at the moment the ball was played, he was nearer the opponent's goal-line than the ball.

Condition No. 1 – As play is being restarted, he receives the ball directly from a (an) . . .

35. A. _____   36. C. _____

    B. _____   D. _____

37. *Condition No. 2* – _____

38. *Condition No. 3* – _____

39. *Condition No. 4* – _____

Given the following situations, indicate if the player should be sanctioned for being off-side or not.

	Off-Side	Not Off-Side		Off-Side	Not Off-Side
40.			44.		
41.			45.		
42.			46.		
43.			47.		

– – → Movement of the ball

——→ Movement of player (with or without the ball)

△ Defensive team

▲ Offensive team

40.

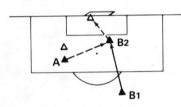

As A passes, B is at position 1. He then runs to position 2 and kicks the ball into the goal.

41.

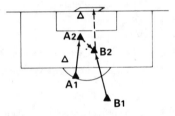

A runs the ball from position 1 to position 2 (while B is running from position 1 to position 2) and then passes back to B who kicks the ball into the goal.

42.

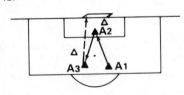

A runs the ball from position 1 to position 2 where he slips and falls with the ball rolling *behind* him. A gets up, goes back to get the ball at position 3, then kicks the ball into the goal.

43.

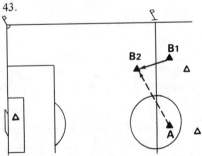

A passes, then B goes from position 1 to position 2.

44.

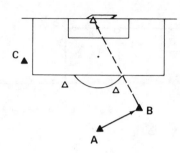

A passes to B who kicks the ball into the goal.

45.

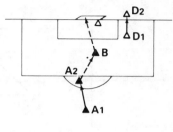

As A runs the ball from position 1 to position 2, D goes from position 1 to position 2. A then passes to B who kicks the ball into the goal.

46.

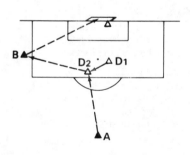

A kicks toward the goal as D goes from position 1 to position 2. He deflects the ball to B who kicks the ball into the goal.

47.

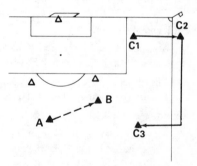

A passes to B. C realizes he is an off-side position at position 1, so he runs off of the field of play and continues without stopping through position 2 and arrives at position 3 which is behind B.

On a Penalty-Kick, A kicks the ball toward position 2. B then runs from position 1 to position 2 and kicks the ball into the goal.

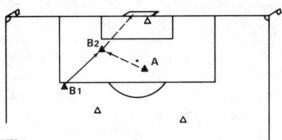

48. The results are:

   A. Off-side

   B. Goal counts

   C. Turn over to defense because the ball wasn't played straight ahead.

   D. Drop-ball

   E. Penalty-kick must be retaken.

49. A player could be sanctioned for being off-side even if he received the ball from the front as he is proceeding toward the opponent's goal.   T   F

Fouls and Misconduct

50. A player who attempts to kick the opposing goalkeeper as he is in possession of the ball, is ejected. Play is resumed with an Indirect Free-Kick.   T   F

51. The goalkeeper can never be charged in the Goal-Area or in the Penalty-Area whether he is in possession of the ball or not.   T   F

Regarding a Free-Kick

52. A player who is intentionally hit by an opponent may strike back only if he did not provoke the initial attack.   T   F

53. The player taking the kick may voluntarily renounce the distance advantage allowed him by not waiting for the opponent's getting the proper distance back.   T   F

54. The kick may be taken by any player and in any direction.   T   F

There are nine (9) offenses which are penalized by the awarding of a Direct Free-Kick if committed intentionally. Name them.

55.-56. _____   _____   _____

        _____   _____   _____

        _____   _____   _____

Given the four conditions in the following matrix (57 – 64), fill in both boxes to the right with the proper answer (if it is a question) or merely indicate the proper disposition.

Conditions relating to *all* free-kicks. (Both Direct and Indirect)	Kick is taken from . . .	
	Outside the Penalty-Area	10 yards from the goal-line *within the kicker's own* Penalty-Area
How far away must the opponents be until the ball is in play?	57.	58.
The kicker plays the ball a second time just after the ball has traveled its circumference.	59.	60.
Kick goes directly into one's own goal.	61.	62.
Ball is kicked to one's own goalkeeper (inside his own Penalty-Area) who takes it into his own hands.	63.	64.

Regarding a Penalty-Kick

65. After receiving the signal from the Referee and before making the Penalty-kick, the player taking the kick intentionally picks up the ball with his hands. This results in . . .

   A. Nothing

   B. Drop-Ball

   C. Indirect Free-Kick

   D. Direct Free-Kick

   E. Penalty-Kick against his team

66. If the Ball is kicked in a non-forward direction, the kick is retaken.   T   F

67. A teammate of the kicker may be sanctioned for being off-side.   T   F

68. A penalty-kick may result even if the infraction was committed outside of the goal-area.   T   F

Regarding a Kick-Off

69. Defensive encroachment results in an Indirect Free-Kick.   T   F

Regarding a Throw-in

70. A throw-in which goes directly into the opponent's goal after the ball brushes the goalkeeper's knee is a goal. T   F

71. The ball may be thrown at the back of an opponent if used as a tactic and done in a non-violent manner. T   F

Regarding a Goal-Kick

72. The ball may be placed just within the corner of the Penalty-Area provided the ball had crossed the Goal-Line on that side of the field. T   F

73. The kick need not be made in a forward direction. T   F

Regarding a Corner-Kick

74. The corner-flag post may be removed when taking the kick provided it is immediately replaced. T   F

75. Only part of the ball need be within the quarter circle. T   F

MATCHING

Using this list . . .

Code	Disposition
PK	Penalty-kick
DFK	Direct Free-Kick
IFK	Indirect Free-Kick
CK	Corner-Kick
GK	Goal-Kick
DB	Drop-Ball
TI	Throw-In — Taken by the opposing team
RETAKE	Retake — The kick, throw-in, or drop-ball
PO	Nothing . . . or . . . 'Play On'
Goal	The goal counts

. . . select the appropriate code which reflects the disposition of the following statements.

76. _____ Play is interrupted by a non-referee's whistle.

77. _____ Distracting an opponent by shouting or other actions.

78. _____ On Kick-off, the ball is kicked straight into one's own goal.

79. _____ On Kick-off, the ball is kicked down the line in the center of the field toward the sideline and goes out of bounds.

If the ball bursts at the moment of restarting the game (Kick-off, corner-kick, free-kick, etc.) . . . (80 and 81 only)

80. _____ . . . If no other player has touched it.

81. _____ . . . If it has already been touched.

82. _____ A drop-ball taken near the goal-line hits a rock and rolls directly into the goal.

208

83. _____ An unintentional hand ball at the middle of the field.

84. _____ Goalkeeper standing outside of his penalty-area, reaches inside it and touches the ball.

85. _____ A scissors-kick being considered dangerous play.

86. _____ When the Referee raises his arm prior to restarting play . . . What does it signal?

87. _____ On a goal-kick, the ball is played twice in succession by the same player with the ball not traveling beyond the penalty-area.

88. _____ On a goal-kick, there is opponent encroachment just after the ball has traveled its circumference.

89. _____ A player takes a throw-in which goes down the line into the field of play and then out again before anyone on either team touches or plays the ball.

90. The whole of the ball passes over the goal line (but not into the goal itself) after being last touched by a member of the . . .

_____ . . . Defensive team   _____ . . . Offensive team

91. A throw-in hits a Referee or Linesman who is in the field of play and the ball goes directly . . .

_____ into the opponent's goal   _____ into his own goal.

☆ ★ ☆ ★ ☆ ★ ☆ ★ ☆ ★ ☆ ★ ☆ ★ ☆ ★ ☆ ★ ☆ ★ ☆ ★ ☆ ★ ☆ ★ ☆ ★ ☆ ★ ☆ ★

What was your score on your last Referee's test?

Comment: After you've taken a test, insist on knowing the areas of your weakness. Presumably, you should make a perfect score the second time around. And, stop trying to defend all those wrong answers!

☆ ★ ☆ ★ ☆ ★ ☆ ★ ☆ ★ ☆ ★ ☆ ★ ☆ ★ ☆ ★ ☆ ★ ☆ ★ ☆ ★ ☆ ★ ☆ ★ ☆ ★ ☆ ★

KEY AND CRITIQUE

1. Maximum length of field
   Maximum length – International
   Minimum length – International
2. Maximum width, minimum length
   Maximum width – International
   Minimum width – International
3. Minimum width
   Penalty-Area – Depth
   Penalty-Mark distance from goal-line
4. Center-circle, penalty-kick arc
   Goal width
   Goal-area depth
5. Quarter-circle, halfway-line flag
   Goal height
   Minimum height corner-flag
6. Maximum circumference of ball
   Minimum circumference of ball
   Maximum width of lines, maximum width of post and cross-bar.
7. False . . . .   Just the goal. The space within the inside areas of the field of play includes the width of the lines marking these areas.
8. False . . . .   The length in all cases shall exceed the width.
9. Touch-line . . . .
10. Halfway-line . . . .
11. 1 Yard . . . .
12. Halfway-line . . . .
13. Penalty-kick arc . . . .
14. Penalty-mark . . . .   High School and College – Penalty-kick line (2 feet)
15. True . . . .
16. False . . . .
17. False . . . .   It may be made of leather or *any approved* substance.

18. A and D .... Glasses are allowed, because they are considered a part of the player's person. They are however, worn at his own risk.

19. B ....

20. 7 .... High School — May not initially field less than 11 players.

21. B ....

22. True ....

23. E .... The 'C' answer could also be considered correct.

24. True .... College, High School and Youth = False

25. Advantage Clause (Rule) ......

26. B & D ....

27. True ....

28. FIFA = 45 minutes ....
    High School = 40 minutes
    Youth — Division   I = 40 minutes   — Division IV = 25 minutes
         — Division II = 35 minutes   — Division V = 25 minutes
         — Division III = 30 minutes   — Division VI = 20 minutes

29. FIFA — Not more than 5 minutes
    College — 10 minutes
    High School — 10 minutes
    Youth — Not less than 5 minutes
            or more than 10 minutes

30. None — The ball is in play .....

31. E .... The ball having been last played by the offense or the defense has no bearing.

32. False .... Not until the ball is put into play.

33. B .... Youth, High school, and college is F.

34. 4 ....

35. Corner-kick, Goal-kick ⎫
                           ⎬ In any order
36. Throw-in, Drop Ball ... ⎭

37. In own half of field   ⎫
                                            ⎪
38. Two or more opponents between   ⎬ In any order
        him and the goal-line   ⎪
                                            ⎪
39. Ball last touched by an opponent   ⎭

40. NOT OFF-SIDE . . . . On side at moment of pass.

41. NOT OFF-SIDE . . . . 'A' was not participating in play.

42. NOT OFF-SIDE . . . . Ball last played by the player himself.

43. NOT OFF-SIDE . . . . Pass made when B in own half of field.

44. NOT OFF-SIDE . . . . B has 3 players between him and the goal-line. C is not influencing play or distracting the GK.

45. NOT OFF-SIDE . . . . Defensive player can't create an off-side position by leaving the field. He should be cautioned.

46. NOT OFF-SIDE . . . . B plays the ball after last touched by an opponent. B was not influencing play or distracting when A played the ball.

47. NOT OFF-SIDE . . . . An offensive player may leave the field of play in order to avoid being off-side.

48. B . . . . B was behind the ball when it was played in a forward direction.

49. True . . . . It could come toward him in an off-side position from a cross-bar, goal post, or as a result of the wind and screw.

50. False . . . . It should be a DIRECT FREE-KICK.

51. False (FIFA) . . . . He may be charged *unless* he does not have True (Youth, High School, possession of the ball and is within his goal and College) area.

52. False . . . . He may never strike back.

53. True . . . . Unless he has asked for the 10 yds.

54. True . . . . The only exception to this would be a free-kick taken within the ball's circumference of a goal-line or a touch-line.

55. Striking, kicking, tripping, ... ⎫ Any order. If miss one or two of the nine then
    pushing, holding, hand-ball ⎬ mark one question wrong. If miss three or more
56. Jumping at, violent charge, ⎭ of them then both are to be marked wrong.
    charge from behind

57. 10 Yards . . . .

58. 10 Yards *and* outside the penalty
    area.

212

59. INDIRECT 60. RETAKE . . . . .
61. CORNER 62. RETAKE . . . . . } All are retakes because the ball had not yet been put into play.
63. PLAY ON 64. RETAKE . . . . .

65. A . . . . Ball not yet in play.

66. True . . . .

67. True . . . . If he participates

68. True . . . . An infraction occuring within the *Penalty-Area*.

69. False . . . .

70. True . . . .

71. True . . . .

72. False . . . . It must be placed within the *Goal-Area*.

73. True . . . . The only requirement is that it clears the penalty-area.

74. False . . . .

75. False . . . . The *whole* of the ball must be within the corner-area.

76. PO . . . .

77. IFK . . . . Ungentlemanly conduct.

78. Retake . . . . It must go into the opponent's half of the field

79. Retake . . . . before it is considered in play.

80. Retake . . . .

81. DB . . . .

82. Retake . . . . It must be touched before a goal can be scored.

83. PO . . . .

84. PO . . . . It is the position of the ball, not the player.

85. IFK . . . .

86. IFK . . . . College and High School uses an underarm swing employing both arms

87. Retake . . . . } The ball must leave the penalty-area before it is
88. Retake . . . . } in play.

89. Throw-in by opposing team . . . . On a throw-in, the ball does not need to be played in order to be considered 'in play.'

90. CK . . . . . . GK . . . .

91. GK . . . . . . CK . . . .

THE ADVANCED REFEREE'S TEST

NOTE: The purpose of this test is to instruct, not to evaluate. It is quite difficult and is meant to be tricky in spots. Hopefully it will cause you to gain a few new insights into the laws.

There are 71 questions. Each one is worth 1.4 points.

Areas and Equipment

1. If a net is used, what is the minimum distance that it should extend behind the goal-line?

   A. 1 foot

   B. 3 feet

   C. 5 feet

   D. 8 feet

   E. 12 feet

State the number and the title of the law where you will find the following:

	Law #	Title
2. Basic about the drop-ball.		
Replaying a match in full.		
3. Cautions		
Photographers electronic flash are prohibited.		
4. Coaching from boundary lines.		
Injuries		
5. Player moves the corner-flag.		
Ball rebounds off of Referee.		

6. A goalkeeper must wear colors which distinguish him from the other goalkeeper.   T   F

Referee

7. A player who has abandoned the field as a protest against the Referee may not come back into the game until he receives the Referee's permission.   T   F

In/Out of Play, Resumption, and Miscellaneous

8. A goal-kick could be taken at the same exact spot within the goal-area regardless of where on the end-line the ball went of bounds.   T   F

9. Pick the letter(s) which represent possible Referee action(s) if a foul is committed during a drop-ball but before the ball is actually dropped.

A. Award a throw-in

B. Caution

C. Eject

D. IFK

E. Direct Free-Kick

F. Penalty-Kick

10. What happens when a ball last played by a *defensive* player hits the corner-flag, breaking off part of the post and then rebounds into the field of play?

A. Goal-kick

B. Corner-kick

C. Throw-in for offensive team

D. Drop-ball

E. Ball in play

11. During play the GK exchanges shirts with the FB without notifying the Referee. When the new GK touches the ball, what will happen?

A. Penalty-kick and caution

B. Direct and caution

C. IFK and caution

D. Both players are cautioned after the ball goes out of play.

E. The new GK is ejected.

12. The GK takes four steps with the ball in his possession. He then dribbles *outside* of his penalty-area and then back some 5 – 10 yards within his penalty-area. He picks up the ball, takes 3 steps and makes a clearing kick. This results in . . .

A. Nothing, ball is in play

B. Drop-ball

C. IFK

D. Direct free-kick

E. Penalty-kick

13. Within the penalty-area the GK catches the ball and takes 3 steps while rolling it along the ground with his hand so it could be safely played by an opponent. He intentionally picks it up, takes 2 steps and makes a clearing kick. This results in . . .

A. Nothing, ball is in play

B. Drop-ball

C. IFK

D. Direct free-kick

E. Penalty-kick

The ball goes out of bounds by knocking down or going over the corner-flag. What is the action taken if it was last played by:

14. An offensive player? _____

15. A defensive player? _____

A. Throw-in for offense
B. Throw-in for defense
C. Drop-ball
D. Goal-kick
E. Corner-kick

16. While the ball is in play, a player asks and receives the Referee's permission to leave the field. Just before he is about to cross the touch-line the ball unexpectedly comes to him and he shoots it into the opponent's goal. He was not off-side. It is . . .

A. A goal because he hadn't left the field yet.

B. A goal only because he had not, by asking permission to leave, attained a position of illegal advantage.

C. No goal. A caution is given and play is restarted with a drop-ball because he is considered an outside agent as soon as permission to leave the field is given.

D. No goal. A caution is given – Restart with an IFK.

E. No goal. A caution is given – Restart with a Direct Free-Kick.

17. Choose the situation(s) for which FIFA Law requires the use of the whistle.

A. The kick-off

B. Penalty-kick

C. Scoring of a goal

D. Game termination

E. None of the above

Fouls and Misconduct

18. A player who high kicks causing a *teammate* to move out of the way is sanctioned with an IFK against his team.   T   F

19. A charge, in order to be made fairly, must be done with the shoulder or hip and done against another shoulder or hip.   T   F

For the next 16 questions (20–35), place an 'X' in the appropriate column and then state how the game would be restarted. The ball is to be considered in play and the advantage clause is not applicable when the situation occurred. (If a free-kick, state which type.)

Situation		Eject	Caution	Nothing		How is game restarted?
Player intentionally stretches his arms, moving them up and down and steps from side to side in order to obstruct an opponent but doesn't make bodily contact.	20.				21.	
Inside his own Penalty-Area he spits at an opponent.	22.				23.	
Attempt to kick the Referee but doesn't actually make physical contact.	24.				25.	
Misconduct — The second time sanctioned.	26.				27.	
The third time in succession when a drop-ball is taken a player kicks the ball before it hits the ground.	28.				29.	
Using foul language at an opponent.	30.				31.	
Two teammates, fighting with each other within their own penalty-area.	32.				33.	
Player leans on the shoulders of a *teammate*.	34.				35.	

36. When an IFK is being taken in the middle of the opponent's Penalty-Area, the defenders may stand on or slightly behind the goal-line.   T   F

37. A defensive player who is outside his own Penalty-Area throws his shoe which hits an opponent inside this Penalty-Area. This results in a Direct Free-Kick being awarded.   T   F

Regarding a Penalty-Kick

38. If players from both sides encroach during the taking of the kick and *no goal* was scored . . .

    A. Goal-Kick

    B. Drop-ball

    C. Retake the kick

    D. IFK for the offense

    E. IFK for the defense

    F. Ball in play

39. If the kick rebounds into play, what does the Referee do that is different regarding . . .

    - Defensive encroachment

        . . . as opposed to . . .

    - The GK having moved his feet too soon?

---

40. If a game is being settled by kicks taken from the penalty-mark, all players other than the player taking the kick and the two goalkeepers . . .

    A. may be anywhere in the field of play.

    B. may be anywhere except within the Penalty-Area.

    C. shall remain within the Center Circle.

    D. must be off the field of play.

    E. are placed according to the discretion of the Referee.

41. After the Referee signals for the kick to be taken, the goalkeeper's feet must be on or slightly behind the goal-line and they may not be moved until after the kicker makes contact with the ball.   T   F

42. Defensive players (other than the GK) may place themselves anywhere as long as they are within the field of play and outside of the Penalty-Area.   T   F

43. All offensive and defensive encroachment results in a caution.   T   F

Regarding a Drop-Ball

44. Teammates of players involved must be a minimum of _____ yards away.

218

Regarding a Throw-In

45. After releasing the ball, there must be noticeable follow through in order that the throw be considered legal.   T   F

46. Even if the ball enters the field of play at the exact point it went out of bounds, the throw cannot be allowed if made from behind a crowd control rope.   T   F

47. It can be a legal throw-in when both feet are inside the playing field with only the heels on the boundary line.   T   F

48. The ball may cross the touch-line in flight at a point which is closer to the thrower's own goal than the actual point it went out of bounds.   T   F

Regarding an Off-Side

49. A player can't be in an off-side position if he is in line with the ball the moment it is played.   T   F

50. A player participating in a drop-ball, directly kicks the ball to a teammate in an off-side position. This should result in an off-side being whistled.   T   F

MATCHING

Using this list . . .

Code	Disposition
PK	Penalty-Kick
DFK	Direct Free-Kick
IFK	Indirect Free-Kick
CK	Corner-Kick
GK	Goal-Kick
DB	Drop-Ball
TI	Throw-In taken by the opposing team
Retake	Retake – The kick, throw-in, or drop-ball
PO	Nothing . . . or 'Play On'
Goal	The goal counts

. . . select the appropriate code which reflects the disposition of the following statements.

51. _____ Offensive encroachment on a penalty-kick. The ball is punched back over the top of the goal and out of play by the GK.

52. _____ Inside the penalty-area, a defender (non-GK) intentionally touches the ball with his hand. As it leaves his hand, an attacking player deliberately handles the ball and it then rolls into the goal.

53. _____ A player *attempts* to trip an opponent at midfield but doesn't make contact.

219

54. _____ Player taking a direct free-kick outside the opponent's penalty-area kicks the ball which rebounds off of the cross-bar. As he kicks the ball again, it caroms off of a defensive fullback's hands who lunged at the ball and dribbles into the goal.

55. _____ While play is in progress in the penalty-area, a defender crosses the goal-line and strikes a Linesman. You stop the game to eject the offending player. How do you restart?

56. _____ A GK, standing within his own Penalty-Area, throws the ball with the aid of a strong wind into his opponent's goal without any other player touching the ball.

57. _____ List the way(s) (if any) that a player could *directly* score a goal against *his team* as he is in the process of putting the ball back into play.

58. _____ In his own Penalty-Area, a GK takes off his shoe and hits the ball with it.

The next three questions are based upon a Goal-kick being taken which goes out of the Penalty-Area and is directly blown back due to a strong wind.

59. _____ On its way back, the ball bounces off of the Referee and rolls into the goal.

60. _____ GK takes the kick. On its way back he intentionally touches the ball with his hand and it rolls into the goal.

61. _____ Same question as #60, only the person involved is a FB.

62. _____ The ball, as a result of a corner-kick taken approximately one foot from the end-line boundary of the quarter circle goes off the side of the kicker's shoe and out of bounds over this line.

63. _____ Player attempts to kick the ball when held by the goalkeeper.

64. _____ As the GK jumps up and has legal possession of the ball over his head, the ball is headed out of his hands by an attacker.

65. _____ The defensive player involved in a drop-ball within his penalty-area plays the ball twice in succession.

66. _____ A non-goalkeeper attempts to handle the ball in his penalty-area.

67. _____ A player takes a Penalty-Kick. The ball hits the cross-bar and bursts, falling completely within the goal.

68. _____ On a throw-in, the ball is thrown from some distance behind the side-line. Just after it bounces and subsequently enters the field, the thrower runs into the field of play and kicks the ball into the opponent's goal.

69. _____ GK passes out due to the heat 2 seconds before the ball is kicked completely within his goal.

70. _____ A substitute replaces the GK without notifying the Referee. If the game was stopped when the new GK touches the ball in his Penalty-Area, how would you restart play?

71. _____ Within his own Penalty-Area, a defensive player goes after the ball via a tackle from behind. The player succeeds in playing the ball by kicking it away but he first touches the legs of the attacker who was in the process of dribbling the ball.

☆ ★ ☆ ★ ☆ ★ ☆ ★ ☆ ★ ☆ ★ ☆ ★ ☆ ★ ☆ ★ ☆ ★ ☆ ★ ☆ ★ ☆ ★ ☆ ★ ☆ ★ ☆ ★ ☆ ★ ☆ ★ ☆ ★

A MISTAKE THAT'S EASY TO MAKE

Some glaring errors are easily rectified. Others not so easily. The 1977 collegiate national championship game brought embarrassment to a Referee.

Player **A**, to the surprise of all, played the ball back to his own goalkeeper, at a time when it appeared that he would bring the ball up to start an attack. **B**, slow to move in defense, collected the pass back to the goalkeeper. The Referee (Dual System) whistled for off-side. The play stopped. **B** quickly pointed out that the defense last played the ball, but it was too late. The Referee gave a drop-ball, but the damage was done. Only concentration can prevent such mistakes in games, as the Referee must expect the unexpected.

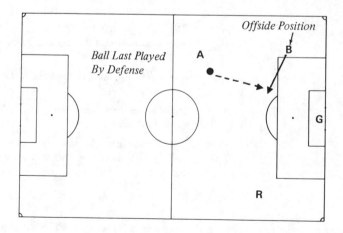

☆ ★ ☆ ★ ☆ ★ ☆ ★ ☆ ★ ☆ ★ ☆ ★ ☆ ★ ☆ ★ ☆ ★ ☆ ★ ☆ ★ ☆ ★ ☆ ★ ☆ ★ ☆ ★ ☆ ★ ☆ ★ ☆ ★

KEY AND CRITIQUE

1. C . . . .

2. 8 The Start of Play . . . .
   7 Duration of Game . . . .

3. 12 Fouls and Misconduct . . . . . .
   1 Field of play . . . .

4. 5 Referee . . . .
   5 Referee . . . .

5. 17 Corner-Kick . . . .
   9 Ball In and Out of Play . . . . .

6. True . . . .

7. False . . . .   He can't return in any case because he was ejected for his actions.

8. True . . . .   The ball can be placed along any part of the imaginary line which separates one half of the goal-area from the other.

9. B & C . . . .   No other action can be taken because the ball is not in play.

10. D . . . .   The reason for this is to not allow play to continue (for safety reasons) until the post has been replaced, repaired, or removed.

11. D . . . .   The answer could be 'C' if the GK changed with a *substitute*. (The FB was a *player*) High School and College = C.

12. C . . . .   The 4-step rule applies until the ball is played by another player.

13. A . . . .   Rolling the ball along the ground does not constitute possession.

14. D . . . .   The defense gets the benefit of doubt as to whether it went over the touch-line or the goal-line.

15. A . . . .

16. B . . . .

17. E None of the above . . . .   Only a signal is required. FIFA strongly recommends a whistle for A, B, and D.

18. True . . . .   Dangerous play knows no distinction between teammate or opponent. It must be sanctioned.

19. False . . . . Shoulder to shoulder is O.K. but not the hip.

20. CAUTION 21. IFK . . . .

22. EJECT 23. IFK . . . . Violent conduct.

24. EJECT 25. IFK . . . . Violent conduct directed at other than opponents.

26. EJECT 27. IFK . . . .

28. EJECT 29. RETAKE – Eject the 3rd time in succession an offense
　　　　　　　　DROP-BALL occurs which intially resulted in a warning and was followed by a caution.

30. EJECT 31. IFK . . . .

32. EJECT 33. IFK . . . . Violent conduct directed at other than opponents.

34. CAUTION 35. INDIRECT . . .

36. False . . . . Defending players must be within the field of play during a free-kick. They may be on, but not behind the goal-line.

37. True . . . . The offense is committed at the place where the player concerned *initiated* the action.

38. C . . . . Regardless of the result, the kick is retaken.

39. A *caution* is given for
the encroachment.

40. C . . . .

41. False . . . . Slightly behind is no good. Some part of both feet must remain stationary *on* the goal-line.

42. False . . . . They must also be at least 10 yards away from the kicker.

43. True . . . . Most Referees are not aware of this little known aspect of Law XIV (High School and college FALSE)

44. 0 . . . . They may be anywhere as long as they don't interfere with the drop-ball.

45. False . . . . As long as it is a throw and the motion is not broken prior to release.

46. True . . . . It may not be thrown from behind any obstacle.

47. True . . . . *Part* of the feet must be on or behind the touch-line.

48. False .... The ball must enter the field *at the point it went out of bounds.*

49. True ....

50. True ....

51. CK .... International Board Decision – Dec '69.

52. P.K. .... Play ceases with the 1st violation – no advantage clause because of the 2nd hand-ball.

53. DFK .... Kenastun (FIFA) – 1975

54. IFK .... The player kicked the ball twice in succession. (Rebounded off of the cross-bar.)

55. DB .... The player was not in the field of play when the infraction occurred.

56. GOAL .... A clearing throw is treated the same as a clearing kick.

57. CK .... A penalty-kick would be wrong (ball rebounds off of cross-bar) because it is a form of a Direct Free-Kick.

58. IFK .... This is ungentlemanly conduct.

59. CK .... Ball is in play and the Referee is a neutral object. No goal can be directly scored from a goal-kick.

60. IFK .... The whistle is blown at the instant he played the ball a 2nd time.

61. P.K. .... No advantage clause because it would mean ignoring the play of the ball twice in succession.

62. RETAKE .... The ball has not yet traveled its own circumference and is hence not in play.

63. IFK .... This is considered dangerous play. Had he attempted to kick the goalkeeper then it would be considered Violent Conduct, he would be ejected and a Direct Free-Kick would have been taken.

64. PO or IFK .... It depends upon if the Referee sees the action as being dangerous.

65. PO ....

66. PO .... To be a hand-ball there must be actual contact, attempts aren't considered.

67. DB .... In all other cases when the ball bursts as it is being put into play without a player having touched it . . . RETAKE.

68. RETAKE .... A ball must be thrown into the field of play (in flight). This one was bounced.

69. DB .... No goal can be allowed while the GK is incapacitated.

70. IFK .... From where the ball was when play was stopped. If it had been a *player* instead of a substitute (FIFA) then both would have been cautioned only when the ball went out of bounds.

71. IFK .... Dangerous play. If goes after the man = DIRECT/PENALTY. If goes after ball and plays it 1st = PLAY ON.

George Tiedemann

Holding takes many forms.

225

Sooner or later, you will be tested on the field with an unusual situation, one that you have never even thought of. Just to get your mind working, how about this one? Michael Ryan, 18, of Albuquerque, New Mexico, uses this unique method of throwing the ball in from out of bounds. Mike, co-captain of the Albuquerque Academy "Chargers", thinks it's legal. Never mind the fact that he can throw the ball farther than most professional players.

What's your decision?

After a running start, Mike places the ball on the ground, with both hands, does a complete flip, and, with added momentum from the run and the flip, throws the ball into play. The ball comes from behind and over the head, with both feet on the ground.

It takes work to develop young Referees, but Dick Servaes (top, right) and Nick Mastrella (top, left), of Sunnyvale, California think it's worth the effort. Many of the coaches have asked to have the "Pros" (Player Referee Organization, Sunnyvale) Referee their games.

XII

You
And The Youth

A young Referee asks the question: "Is the ball correctly placed?"

Answer: *Yes, It's for a free-kick.*

Referee lectures must be stimulating for all.

The toss of the coin in a youth game. "Youth soccer," according to John Trapani of San Gabriel, California," is a conspiracy of ignorance." Many would-be Referees are awed by the laws of the game, and by the enthusiasm of parents. Young players usually know when the Referee is being fair.

WHEN YOU REFEREE YOUTH GAMES

Just as most players enjoy their first soccer experience through youth competition, Referees learn by involvement in games of young players. It is here that games are most available and organizers most anxious to "fill the ranks."

At the same time, there is a great need in youth soccer for quality officiating, of a kind that will greatly increase the education and enjoyment of all. Most young players, coaches, and parents have a limited knowledge of the game, and the burden of instruction may fall on the Referee.

Few youth organizations have written charters defining the role of the Referee, and these words seldom mention more than vague ideas such as "interpreter of the laws," "sole authority," or "official league representative." Youngsters and their needs, however, provide many interesting and challenging possibilities for the Referee.

THE REFEREE SHOULD ENCOURAGE PLAYERS WHENEVER POSSIBLE

Examples:

(a) A player makes a mistake, and teammates react negatively. Referee: "That's all right. I once saw Pele miss a shot like that." To the culprit: "Isn't that your teammate? He'll never get better unless you help him."

(b) A goalie makes a good save, giving away a corner kick. There's a lull in play. Referee: (Walking by the goalie): "Good save. I thought that one was going in."

(c) After a goal (the scoring team cannot hear): "That was a good goal, no one's fault.

The game provides many opportunities for this kind of banter. Come alive in the game, always preparing players for the inevitable decision they won't particularly like!

THE REFEREE CAN COACH PLAYERS

Examples:

(a) A youngster is playing dangerously by kicking high or "going over" the ball. Referee: "Keep your feet down and go through the ball, and you won't hurt anyone." You could even make the motion, so everyone knows you're doing your best to prevent a repetition.

(b) A player places the ball in the hole in the corner of the goal area for a goal kick. Referee: "You'll never get it out of that hole. Did you know you could place it anywhere in this side of the area? *Hint*: If you tell the player not to put it in the hole before it is placed, no one will ever guess what you've said, for the ball will not be moved from one place to another.

In most cases, the Referee is to be seen and heard in his instructing, and the instructing must not be such as to directly affect the score.

THE REFEREE SHOULD ADMIT CERTAIN MISTAKES

Examples:

(a) An offside is called, and play is stopped. A second defensive player is seen standing on the goal line. (Don't be smug. It happens to all of us.) Referee: "Oh, no!" I sure missed him over there. Thanks for pointing him out, but the whistle has already blown. We'll have a drop ball." (Note: Some Referees will allow the free kick, even though they know they are in error. This compounds the mistake.)

(b) The foul is called, but the advantage immediately materializes. Referee: (shaking head) "You had the advantage. My mistake. Take the kick."

FURTHER HINTS

1. Almost every injury in youth soccer is genuine and unrehearsed. Unless unusual circumstances prevail, (the ball headed for the net), stop the game immediately when each opponent injury occurs.

2. Many of the nine penal offenses (and obstruction) are committed in innocence, and should therefore not be called.

3. Pushing and dangerous play are the two most common fouls with youth players. You will see a lot of "simultaneous" pushing by two players, where neither gains an advantage. Don't call it, but give some words of advice without stopping play. Dangerous play is more serious, obviously. An experienced youth Referee has said that "the only real job of the youth Referee is to prevent players from hurting themselves."

    Example: Most young players, when late approaching a rolling ball will jump and turn their backs on the kicker (self-preservation). They may land on the opponent's legs, feet, or back (if the opponent also turns!) This habit is not easily stopped by the coach. You may have better luck as a Referee, by calling for dangerous play, or jumping at an opponent."

4. Youngsters become experts on very minor and inconsequential aspects of the laws, such as throw-ins or other out of bounds situations. When you see something that should not be called, such as a player lifting the foot just after the throw-in, say loudly, "That throw-in is OK." Tiny criticism from players is therefore stopped before it starts. You might remember this one for all of your games.

5. Learn the names of at least five players on each team during the first five minutes of play. This will aid your concentration and may help you when you want to address a certain player. "He really knows what he's doing. He even knows my name," the player will think, when spoken to.

232

6. Unless some player has been placed in some physical danger, most "borderline" calls in youth games should not be made. There is nothing more disconcerting than the Referee who calls "goalkeeper steps" perfectly, while disregarding the myriad of fouls that can result when players decide to test the Referee and each other. Most children quickly forget, have little knowledge of what really is allowed, and are innocent in their enthusiasm for the game.

7. Always give the appearance of enjoying yourself. Many youth games are not particularly well-played, and you may suddenly have an urge to be elsewhere. Be seen smiling at least once each game, and try to make a poor game an acceptable experience.

The youth Referee who views himself as a full, firm, authority with a textbook knowledge of the laws may be missing the real joy of the official's soccer experience: that of being a consistent "facilitator" of play and of being a sensible and sensible adult.

Sometimes players will give you a hint on what they 'think' they did.

THE REFEREES OF TOMORROW SHOULD BE REFEREES TODAY

It has already been said that the Referee represents the league, the organization, the game, himself, the spectators, and other Referees. As such, recruiting is important, and vital to growth. Using young players as Referees is a relatively new idea, and has solved Referee shortages in many areas. Also, the adult who sees the youngster on the field may become more anxious to join the ranks of Referees.

The most likely candidates for young Referees are those still playing the game, and should be recruited before the age of 15. Older players develop competing interests and are not as reliable. Moreover, if the youngsters had two or three years' experience at 15, they will most likely go on and take appointments even more seriously.

TRAINING

Youngsters already spend many waking hours in a classroom. Although lectures on the laws are important, field work is even more important, and should be stressed.

Classroom Hints

1. Involve each Referee in each session, and provide more than one instructor.

2. Give a small test, one that they may grade themselves.

3. Informality should govern the classroom. Encourage questions at all times. Adults often ask questions to draw attention to themselves and to trip up the instructor. This is not as true with youth.

4. Deal only with the practicalities of the laws. Illustrations should come only from situations *they* will encounter.

Fieldwork

Give them all a chance to play, but during these informal, small scrimmages stop play often to indicate some fine point of officiating. The action should be confined to a small area at first. Then, graduate to a large-field situation.

Problem Areas to be Covered

1. *Use of the whistle.* This is first. No further activity until they have all shown they can use the whistle with authority. Now, run, stop, use the whistle. Whistle on the run, and while walking.

2. *Using the flag.* Show the various signals for the Referee that will aid in communication. Older Referees often feel that linesmen are second class citizens. If young Referees understand the linesmen's duties, they will excel in this capacity.

3. *Hand and arm signals.* New Referees like to practice in a group. Concentrate on the indirect signal, "play on," goal-kick and corner-kick.

4. *Mechanics.* Decide on one system of control, preferably diagonal or a modified diagonal, and stay with it. More than one system is confusing.

5. *Foul recognition.* Stop the action when the Referee in charge fails to whistle an obvious foul. Find out why it wasn't called. Take a vote on whether the players thought it was a foul. Young Referees will accept friendly criticism.

ASSIGNMENTS

One negative experience will dampen the enthusiasm of young Referees, just as the positive experience will win them over. Always assign young Referees with not only experienced partners, but those partners who are sympathetic with a youth Referee program. A youngster should seldom be asked to officiate players the same age or older. Remember, they return to school in a day or so! A Referee's first game, at least, should be seen by an experienced evaluator.

SYSTEM OF CONTROL

Whatever system is used, be sure the basics are understood, and that the new Referee knows he is being fully supported in decision-making. Each system provides advantages and disadvantages for the beginner. The Modified Diagonal System (see Chapter XV), the authors believe, provides excellent coverage, and will ease the newcomer into the role of Referee with a minimum of stress, while still providing the players with the game control that is always needed.

FURTHER IDEAS

- Minimize the reward system. Young Referees should not be paid. Their reward is an increased understanding of the game.

- Small decisions are easier than larger ones. Have the young Referee make decisions very early in the first game, even though these decisions may only involve balls over the goal line or touch line.

- Abstract concepts of officiating are difficult to absorb. For instance, limit your discussion on "game control," the "advantage," etc.

- Think twice before you issue the red and yellow cards to a new Referee. They are not playthings, and young Referees get "caught up" in discussions on the cards.

- The offside is best taught on the field, with moving players in a dynamic situation. Set up game situations, and work them over and over again.

- When working on mechanics and field positioning, correct the Referee during play, for it will mean more to them. Correcting judgment calls, however, may erode confidence. Be patient. Judgment with most comes only in time.

- Confess your own mistakes to the new Referee. This will break a few barriers.

- This book is not recommended until the young Referee has officiated at least for six months, or a season. Require a small illustrated book on the laws of the game.

- Ask the parent about the Referee's experience. Encourage that it be discussed at home. If the parent wants to watch, perhaps it should be done at a discreet distance, and with no interference. An overzealous parent could add to, rather than relieve pressure.

- Ask the young Referee to recruit others.

Observers will see that participants and spectators are often more inclined to accept the decisions of young Referees than those of older ones. In addition, the player who understands the laws will be sure of adding to his own field performance. There used to be an adage that "a player who was too old to play could ref." Anyone who has watched the enthusiasm, interest, and courage of young Referees would disagree, as well as those many Referees who now play because they learned the game with the laws close at hand.

Two Referees listening to Paul justify one of his calls.

EVERY PLAYER IS DIFFERENT

Each game is different, and dependent on the age group of the participants. Go into each contest with a full understanding of the players. Can you add to this list?

Under 9 *"Age of Innocence"*

- Obedient to all decisions of Referee and coach
- Pressure from parents, most of whom are new to game
- Fear of opponent
- Awkwardness
- No concept whatever of offside.

Under 11 *"The Emerging Skills"*

- Openly, intensively competitive, without intention in fouls
- No dissent
- Parents becoming aware of fair/foul throw-ins, goalkeeper steps, injustices in play
- Game moves more quickly. Less predictable than any other group.

Under 13 *"The Differences in Skills"*

- Intolerance of teammates' incompetence
- Call Referee's attention to minor infractions (throw-ins, etc.)
- Will question "hand balls"
- Team cooperation emerges – Players encourage one another.

Under 15 *"Aggressiveness Toward Opponents and Teammates"*

- Sense injustices, but don't yet know what to do about it
- Widespread difference in abilities
- Game control essential
- Player safety is more important.

Under 17 *"Has More Experience and Dangerous Familiarity with the Laws"*

- Question authority of Referee, coach and parent
- Will retaliate, openly, on intentional foul
- Great frustration with own faults
- Limited parental interest.

Under 19 *"Watch Out"*

- Coach-Referee understanding and cooperation essential
- Everyone thinks he is an expert on all aspects of the game
- Will test Referees very soon in match
- Retaliation common
- Obstruction very common
- Will encroach
- Much "banter" between and among players

Larry Harris, coauthor of FAIR OR FOUL, has written a book called FUTBOL MEANS SOCCER, and Adrian Walsh agrees. Adrian is the Guinness World Recordholder in Ball Control, and has an array of 50 tricks. Referees must be aware of players' tricks, and should possess a few of their own. (From You Can Control the Soccer Ball, by Adrian Walsh.)

A TEST FOR YOUNG REFEREES

It is a rare youngster who, as an experienced player, feels he doesn't know the rules. When they are recruited as apprentice Referees, many appear very reluctant to ask questions in class and to expose their ignorance.

Sooner or later, some kind of a test must be given. The purpose of these tests should be for instruction only, and participants should be allowed to grade their own exams. The items here are offered as samples of the variety of questions that may be posed. An exhaustive test for new, young Referees is not possible within the scope of this book.

1. Draw a picture of the field with all of its markings. Here's a sample of one we received from a ten year old: (Law knowledge)

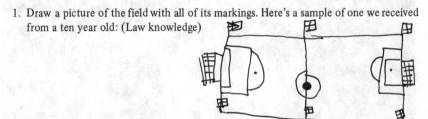

2. Why is it important to dress like a Referee when you have been assigned to a game? (Attitude)

3. Why should the players know you have awarded an indirect free-kick? (Communication with players)

4. Name two instances when a player is guilty of dangerous play. (Imagination)

5. What kinds of things could happen to prevent a game from starting? (Imagination . . . Duties of the Referee)

6. Why is it important for you to know the Referees with whom you will be working? (Cooperation)

7. Name two reasons for stopping your game watch. (Flexibility in application of the laws)

8. Make a diagram to show when a player is not taking advantage of his offside position. (Decision-making)

9. Why is it important to signal when you have given the "advantage"? (Avoid misunderstanding)

10. How can refereeing make you a better player? (Recruiting other Referees)

This unusual photo was taken during a youth game. A game became very much out of control, and the coach attacked the Referee. Fortunately these incidents are few. (From 'Futbol Means Soccer' by Larry Harris)

XIII

For The
Good Of The Game

MAKING SOMETHING OUT OF VIOLENCE

At my first class for the Referee's course I was told, "The functions of the Referee are to insure the safety of the players and to make the game enjoyable to play and watch." It may not be word for word from Law 5, but these words echo inside me every time I put stress on my crippled right knee – that universal and vulnerable joint – and flash back to the incident which ended my professional playing career.

Could the injury have been prevented? Can an accident, looking for a place to happen, ever be avoided? I don't know. But a different Referee may have changed the final result. He might have saved me from surgery, a knee with a half-pound of staples, wires, arthritis and pain.

Another official may have cautioned Mr. X after he pointed his finger at me, and threatened, "I get you." Is that not "ungentlemanly conduct"? A different martinet may have spoken a stern word for all to hear and bear witness, rather than talk with the player in his own foreign tongue. And maybe the gruesome hatchet that was to strike could have been foiled if a word or two had been shared with the captain of Mr. X's team. Who knows? But if a lifetime of pain could have been prevented, isn't it worth a thought? I think it is.

This is not to use the official as a scapegoat, or to blame him for what a greater power may have meant to be, que sera sera. But what about more than a yellow card to penalize someone who has maliciously, and with premeditation, crippled a player for life? The Referee throught a caution was sufficient. Even an ejection would not be a suitable punishment to fit the crime! The Referee's responsibility should not have ended there and certainly not with a caution. The commissioner of the American Soccer League should have held a hearing. Suspend Mr. X for one year or two years or even for life. I am now told that Mr. X has been getting away with the same thing ever since. It reminds me of the folk line, "How many deaths will it take till he knows, that too many people have died?"

"Take up chess," said the orthopedic surgeon.

"What did you want to do when you finished playing soccer?" counseled another doctor. "Start thinking about it now."

My fellow Referees, the health and happiness of those players, young and old, pro and amateur, may someday linger in your whistle, your yellow card and rest with your judgment. With a permanent scar and knee brace, I take my officiating more seriously now. You should, too. Please don't leave the players' safety "blowin' in the wind."

*– The above was written especially for **Fair or Foul** by Stanley Startzell.*

Stanley Startzell (right), had his career cut short by a serious knee injury. He is now directing the soccer program with the Special Olympics in Washington, D.C. Here, he is introducing soccer to one of the Special Olympics participants.

A NOTE ON PROTESTS

"Defeat requires an explanation. Victory covers a multitude of sins."

Soccer is a game of wide-open activity, and a sport where most persons feel they are experts. Although scoring is low, tie games do not often result, and a loser must come to grips with the meaning of defeat. In certain circles where soccer becomes more than recreation, the loser's ire and frustration is taken out on the Referee. This takes the form of physical or verbal abuse or threatened or active protest.

It is well-known that the Referee, with normal human limitations, is remembered for his errors. Fortunately, these errors usually do not occur with the same frequency as player errors, but are a greater subject of discussion among coaches and players. Errors in judgment are at times not even known to the Referee, and errors in interpretation or law application are later discovered through discussions with a rule interpreter or with fellow Referees. Unfortunate as they are, Referee errors must be accepted by everyone connected with soccer.

We are happy to report that since our last edition of this book, more and more soccer organizations have indicated a refusal to consider protests that question the judgment of the Referee. Only those rulings dealing with player eligibility, disciplinary actions, or field conditions are considered, and even then seldom allowed. It is unfair that the Referee's task and performance should be constantly scrutinized, and that games are sometimes won over the bargaining table. Once the Referee is given his authority, he must be backed by the league. If the sport is to progress, league organizers must openly admit that, "The Referee must be supported, even if he is wrong."

From our files, listed below are situations where leagues have chosen not to allow a protest:

1. A twelfth player was on the field and participated in a goal against the opposition. The Referee allowed the goal and the resulting kick-off before discovering the error.

2. The Referee was wearing the patch of another organization. (We're serious, this was actually protested.)

3. The Referee felt a player had sustained an injury which was too serious for continuing the game. He was not allowed to play.

4. The Referee admitted after the game that he made a mistake in awarding a Penalty-Kick. (The goal was scored.)

5. A Referee walked off the field at halftime, leaving his partner for the second half. The partner continued the game.

6. A Referee awarded a Penalty-Kick for Dangerous Play.

7. A game was played without field markings. No protest was made in writing before the game.

8. A Referee allowed eleven players on one side after one of their teammates was ejected.

9. A player was allowed to play with an arm cast, which was against league regulations.

10. The Referee insisted that another series of five kicks from the penalty-spot would be taken, after the original series of five was tied, during a game that was to be settled by such kicks.

The number of obvious and not-so-obvious Referee errors defies the imagination. It will happen to you, and a game will be protested. Whatever your mistake, never make it twice, and if a protest is made, don't become involved in any way after you have made your written report.

Anax Barraza

If you referee and coach, remember that you have certain responsibilities.

NOTES TO COACHES, with Test

This book has been assembled for the purpose of improving soccer refereeing in America. This section, together with words for players and spectators, is for improved Referee-coach relationships and communications, the assumption being that we need each other, and that we are presumably all working for the betterment of the game.

It is an axiom among many college and high school coaches that three teams inhabit a field: the two teams of competitors and the team of officials. These coaches often elaborate by indicating the existence of three teams where game control and discipline are concerned: the two teams of competitors and the team of officials *and* coaches. This is as it should be, for there are many times when a problem on the field needs the support of the coach.

COMMUNICATION WITH THE REFEREE

The Referee's authority begins when he enters the field of play, and carries through until he has left the field at game's end. A Referee is most approachable before a game. Any questions of player eligibility, field conditions, game starting time, etc., should be covered at this time, and irregularities dealt with through written protest prior to kick-off. Few Referees will discuss rule interpretations immediately prior to a game, and for good reason. There are many details necessary to the proper starting of a game, and questions on the laws can only be interpreted as a thorough search for Referee weaknesses.

During the game, only an extreme case requires the coach's addressing the Referee. When there is a substitution or an injury, coaches often despair when they receive no response to their call: "Hey, Ref." Contrast this with a simple, "Substitution, Ref." The latter call is always heeded, when the ball is out of play. The former, seldom.

Half-time belongs to the Referee as well as to the players, and is no time for Referee-contact by a coach. Similarly, game's end is no time for open forum. The coach should not feel insulted when the Referee refuses to discuss the game.

TEAM CAPTAINS

In youth soccer, team captains are not usually mature enough to assume real team responsibility on the field, and they should function only as privileged coin-tossers. They are told by the Referees that their post is a special one, and that the Referee will address the captain in some special circumstances.

Beyond the thirteen year old, however, team captains are often selected on ability alone, the thought being that other players look up to the superior technical players. If the coach has any influence on the selection of his captain, he should consider that player who is most valuable to the team. Personal discipline, a supportive attitude, and individual self-respect are a captain's qualities which aid the team. Since a good Referee will rely on the captain for support in controlling undisciplined players, a captain can be largely responsible for the breakdown or the buildup of a team. The captain, like the goalkeeper in penalty-area play, should be king of all he surveys, and players must respect his every instruction.

246

ON THE SUBJECT OF APPARENT VIOLATIONS

Where coaches and Referees are concerned, apparent violations on the field fall into one of the following four categories:

    a.   Those seen by both the Referee and the coach.

    b.   Those seen by the Referee and not the coach.

    c.   Those seen by the coach and not the Referee.

    d.   Those seen by neither the coach nor the Referee.

In the mind of the coach, in only one of the four above situations can a Referee be really right. (Let's leave those spectators and players out of it!) Dissent resulting from a violation, called or not called, can be active or passive. If it is active, the coach jeopardizes himself and his team through his actions. If the dissent is passive, the "human," positive approach wins out, and the coach acts in the best interests of the game.

HINTS AND OBSERVATIONS

1. It is not wise to ask a Referee to defend himself and his decision.

2. A Referee calls the violation which he first sees, and this takes precedence over everything which happens thereafter, although he may discipline players on all subsequent action.

3. Experienced Referees and experienced players both must come to terms with the advantage clause. Referees apply it, and players expect it. However, even the best of Referees will sometimes choose not to use it.

4. A coach can occasionally call attention to a circumstance on the field without making direct reference to the Referee. Calling to his own player, the coach might explain, "Watch the dangerous play, Joe." The Referee will hear it and say to himself, "Maybe I'd better be more attentive on dangerous plays." In this way, constructive communication has taken place between coach and Referee and player . . . contrast this with, "Watch the dangerous play, Ref."

5. Players' attitudes reflect the attitude of the coach. This is apparent to even the most inexperienced Referee, and needs no further comment.

SIGNALS BY THE REFEREE

Referee signals, as pointed out elsewhere in this book, are meant for spectator, coach, players, and Referees. Coaches are encouraged to learn these signals, as strongly as Referees are encouraged to use them. Particularly important is the signal for the indirect free-kick.

When giving an indirect-kick near the defensive goal the experienced Referee will exclaim, "Indirect," as well as raising an arm until the kick is taken. He has thus anticipated unnecessary questions from players, usually the goalkeeper who is reluctant to take his eyes off the ball in the search for the upraised arm.

No other signals are required (college and high school excepted), and few Referees demonstrate the calls they have made. Until Referees are universally required to signal for each violation, coaches are advised to teach only the indirect free-kick signal to the players, along with the violations which result in indirect and direct free-kicks. (See Law XII.)

NOTES ON COACHING BY AND AROUND THE LAWS

The laws of the game have evolved for more than 100 years of play, and govern half a billion games annually. Part of the beauty of the laws is their simplicity. Some coaches deal with the laws only when players question them or when game situations are presented. Others use the laws in a constant search for methods of gaining unfair advantage over an opponent.

The coach is encouraged to remember that:

1. Many fouls are not called where no competitive edge has been gained through the foul.

2. A player who has fouled has *no* rights. This includes the time it takes to build defensive walls and to engage in other delays of the game.

3. A player who has been fouled has no rights other than his team's taking of the kick, providing the advantage has not been given.

4. All nine penal offenses (Law XII) deal with the intent of the player, and with the Referee's ability to judge this intent.

5. A dangerous maneuver is judged dangerous play if the action places *any* player (even a teammate) in jeopardy.

A certain famous team is still known for its exhaustive and painstaking records on individual performances of its 40 league Referees. Referee weaknesses are probed, with the team convinced that their efforts gain them an extra game won each year in an 80 game schedule. True, there are weaknesses in Referees, as there are weaknesses in players and in coaches. There are, however, no loopholes or weaknesses in the laws, and coaches are going to gain much more through a total knowledge of these laws rather than by probings of Referee failings.

248

COACHES' TEST

A coach who does not familiarize himself with the laws of soccer is doing himself and the team an injustice. Games are won and lost for various reasons, but a team that is confident in the knowledge of what is and what is not allowed will have an advantage. The short test below is to educate the coach and challenge him on some misunderstood laws. The questions represent problem areas. And, even though you may score 100% on the test, your wisdom is of little use unless you pass it on to the players, teaching them to play positively.

1. A player can not be off-side if he receives the ball directly from a: (Circle the letters of your choice.)

   A. Goal-kick

   B. Corner-kick

   C. Indirect Free-kick

   D. Direct Free-kick

   E. Penalty-kick

   F. Throw-in

   G. Drop-ball

2. Offensive players may be located within a defensive wall.   T   F

3. Goal-kicks must be taken from the corner of the goal-area on the side that the ball went out of bounds.   T   F

4. A goalkeeper may leave his penalty-area and play on the forward line.   T   F

5. If a player is out of bounds kicking the ball along the touch-line, the ball is still in play.   T   F

6. Any player may immediately enter the penalty-area following the taking of a penalty-kick.   T   F

7. If for any reason a penalty-kick has to be retaken, a new kicker as well as a new goalkeeper may be named.   T   F

8. A free-kick may be taken without waiting for a signal from the Referee.   T   F

9. A coach who wants to protest measurement or any other field condition must do so before the start of the game.   T   F

10. On any free-kick, one foot may be placed under the ball and the kicker may "lift" the ball to a teammate.   T   F

KEY TO COACHES' TEST

1. A. Goal-kick. . . . .
   B. Corner-kick . . . . Most coaches do not fully exploit all of these
   F. Throw-in . . . . situations.
   G. Drop-ball. . . . .

2. True . . . . An offensive player may occupy any available position on the field he desires on any free-kick. Opponents are not permitted to prevent him from doing so.

3. False. . . . . It may be taken anywhere within that side of the goal-area . . . Why put the ball within a field depression?

4. True . . . . The goalkeeper may play anywhere on the field of play. His handling privileges, of course, pertain only to his being within his own penalty-area. In the last minutes of a match, when down by one goal and desperate measures are called for, the goalkeeper may become like any player to create a goal. This has proven a good tactic.

5. True . . . . The position of the ball is all that counts. Also, to be out of bounds the *whole* of the ball has to be outside of the field, in the air or on the ground.

6. True . . . . As long as he was a minimum of 10 yards away and was outside of the penalty-area prior to the ball traveling its circumference.

7. True . . . . Be sure to notify the Referee of your intentions. Failure to do so will result in a caution for the player(s) involved.

8. True . . . . as long as the team taking the kick hasn't requested 10 yards from the Referee. The Referee, however, may tell any player at any time to wait for a signal. The signal may be a whistle, a hand or arm movement, a nod of the head, or any other indication that it's all right to play.

9. True . . . . and it must be in writing.

10. True . . . . This is an allowable tactic which can result in goals, for the opposition is often caught unawares. The ball may not be "lifted" with both feet.

ADVICE TO PLAYERS

"No Referee can have an excellent game without at least a reasonable degree of cooperation from players."

In 1909, J. W. McWeeney said, in his book, *HOW TO PLAY SOCCER:* "Have no quarrel with the Referee. It is aggravating, I know, to have a goal chalked up against you which ought to have been disallowed, but that is one of the trials which is the test of character. I have played many games in my time, and up till now I have never known a wilfully dishonest Referee."

McWeeney's words, while included in one of America's first soccer books, still apply to the modern game, and should be remembered by the player who wants to progress. Few players realize that a thorough knowledge of the laws of soccer will enhance a player's effectiveness and that most controversial calls on the field deal with the Referee's judgment of a player's intent. While the first point should be obvious, the second is little understood. A famous Referee once said, "I always watch the eyes of the player to judge his intent." While it first sounded ludicrous, it was later accepted as good advice for well-positioned Referees who agaonized over Law XII. Indeed, players are judged by their *intent to play the ball.*

Undisciplined players are advised to consider the Referee's action when the player "goes over the ball" and kicks an opponent. Most players who completely, or who even partially miss a ball with the foot, and who strike an opponent, are not playing the ball. The whistle is sounded, and they should be either warned, cautioned, or ejected. Yet is is very possible that the same player could be struck in the hand by a ball, and his actions judged unintentional.

Players who read and study the laws will have a great advantage over other players. If you are the player who:

1. Places the goal-kick ball in the hole in the extreme corner of the goal-area for a goal-kick,
2. Asks for a Referee's signal before taking free-kicks and corner-kicks,
3. Asks for ten yards to be determined before taking a free-kick near the opponent's goal,
4. Turns and loses the advantage because you were fouled,
5. Asks for "hands" every time a ball touches a hand, or stops because the ball has struck your own hand,
6. Never uses a shoulder charge,
7. Fails to move downfield behind the fullbacks on a throw-in,
8. Fails to read the laws of the game,
9. Fails to accept apparent Referee mistakes as you should your own,

then you are penalizing yourself and your team because you do not understand your rights as described and implied in the Laws of the Game.

After you have read the rules and found how they increase your understanding of soccer and raised your "tolerance level" toward the Referee, you are ready to ask the Referee the question he most likes to hear: "How can I become a Referee?"

251

A COACH LOOKS AT REFEREEING

"O wad some Pow'r the gifte gie us to see oursels as ithers see us."

—Robert Burns

"The Referee is a very important person."

—Graham Ramsay

If the coach is to fully realize his team's potential, he must also understand the role of the Referee. There are many coaches who are understanding of the place of the official in soccer. Few, however, understand more than Graham Ramsay. Known primarily as a coach and clinician, he has conducted courses for Referees. A few quotes from Ramsay, one of America's best-known soccer instructors:

"You must always treat the Referee as a person."

"The game, the Referee, and the coach all belong together, and are not members of separate factions."

"Referees must understand the frustrations of playing. When they do, they can talk to a player who's having a bad game and cool his frustration. This helps the player and prevents him from giving vent to frustrations through fouling."

On Dissent:

- "It wastes all your good coaching work. Good players play."
- "You have to live with bad decisions. They always even themselves out . . . no one's immune."

On Players:

- "Their only responsibility is to play the game to the best of their ability."
- "If a Referee is strict, and the players let his strict posture bother them, they are playing themselves right out of the game. Sometimes a lax Referee will allow players to take justice into their own hands."

On Talking to Referees:

- "Some Referees are approachable after the game. Occasionally I will try to discuss something constructively at this time."
- "A Referee wants to know how *he's* doing. Nobody tells him the good things, at least not at a time when it counts."
- "If you build a mutual respect, the Referee may even talk casually with you at game's end."

On the Referee's Problems:

- "Referees do not understand the pulse, rhythm, and tempo of soccer. They seem surprised when certain things happen."

- "Many Referees pride themselves in being able to detect the foul. Better, they should help the game be a better game."

- "The greatest problem is cooperation. Usually the Linesmen are ignored, even at the highest levels. Probably one game in ten is well officiated."

Graham Ramsay is Director of the SOCCER SCHOOL, an educational and consulting organization for players, coaches, schools, and clubs. He played high-level soccer for 15 years, and was never "booked" by a Referee. Author of *"The Twelfth Player"* (The Little Book of Coaching Youth Soccer), Ramsay represents the coach who totally understands the role and activity of the Referee.

WOMEN REFEREES AND WOMEN'S SOCCER

The involvement of women and girls has brought soccer into true perspective as the "world's game."

FIFA is still encouraging member associations to promote and encourage women's soccer. Within twenty-two European countries now having active competition with women in the sport, and with thousands of girls' teams already active in the United States, it is becoming more apparent that women Referees will be needed as well.

Some countries have already made impressive strides in encouraging women to "take up the whistle." The Netherlands now boasts over 100 qualified women Referees, who are fully sanctioned to referee boys' and youth matches. Moreover, Kenya, Japan, Austria, Uganda, Bermuda, Sweden, Switzerland, New Zealand, France and Rumania have all reported registered female Referees. In the United States, of the 1800 registered USSF Referees, 5 are women, and they may presumably be assigned to men's games.

While women Referees are not required in girls' soccer any more than are men for men's games, it is recommended that they be used. Girls' soccer usually proceeds at a slower pace, and provides the training ground for female Referees, whether they be interested in girls' or boys' soccer.

Since the purpose of this book is only to provide a complete handbook to the universal laws of the game and a guide for Referees and Linesmen, no distinction needs to be drawn between male and female Referees. The laws are the same. In women's soccer, the handball infraction does not apply under Law XII if she uses her hands as an "instinctive" fending-off of the ball for the purpose of avoiding hurt or injury. This applies to instinctively protecting the chest. To use this movement as a tactic would result in a hand ball being whistled.

It should be noted here that the same interpretation applies with respect to boys' and men's soccer. A reflexive movement to protect the groin or face does not result in a whistle.

". . . . Just don't tell the other kids that I'm your big sister."

Players feel comfortable with a decisive Referee.

It helps to keep your socks pulled up.

"Where is the centerfold?"

THE INDOOR GAME

Indoor soccer is a conditioner for players, and a new dimension of the game which is popular and vital to the growth of all of soccer.

The demands made upon the Referee are considerably different when the game is played indoors. The ball is seldom out of play, creating an almost frantic tempo among the 4-6 players on each team. The play changes quickly from one side to another, and the eyes, not the feet of the Referee, must keep up with play.

Fortunately, the premediated, expected foul seldom exists in indoor soccer, for the ball is rapidly played away before the act is perpetrated. The reason for the infrequency of fouls in indoor soccer is simple . . . . there is no time for such foolishness. However, the flurry of activity, the disappearance of most advantage calls, and the closeness of play demand a high level of concentration on the part of the Referee. Games should be officiated alone, as neither the off-side nor difficult out of bounds situations will occur. Help in timing should be given from the sideline.

Positioning and anticipation are important. The majority of the action takes place on the perimeters of the arena, another contrast to the outdoor game. Therefore, the Referee should seldom roam in those areas.

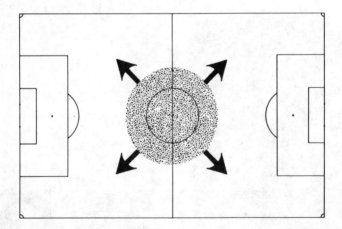

A final note of caution: Some players feel that indoor soccer is "hockey without ice," and that roughness can overcome skill. The pushing that goes on is usually harmless, but the "arms-out" dribble can lead to elbows being thrown and a flare of tempers. Indoor soccer is a game of high skill, and the Referee must make sure that skill is best displayed in this exciting, growing game.

The indoor game is growing in popularity at all levels. At this point, not much is known about officiating indoors. Many of the requirements of good refereeing must prevail: decisiveness, an understanding of play, and good positioning for critical calls.

257

These are not intentional . . . they are deliberate.

XIV

The Laws
Of The Game

LAW I. – THE FIELD OF PLAY

(1) **Dimensions.** The field of play shall be rectangular, its length being not more than 130 yards nor less than 100 yards and its breadth not more than 100 yards nor less than 50 yards. (In International Matches the length shall be not more than 120 yards nor less than 110 yards and the breadth not more than 80 yards nor less than 70 yards.) The length shall in all cases exceed the breadth.

(2) **Marking.** The field of play shall be marked with distinctive lines, not more than 5 inches in width, not by a V-shaped rut, in accordance with the plan, the longer boundary lines being called the touch-lines and the shorter the goal-lines. A flag on a post not less than 5 ft. high and having a non-pointed top, shall be placed at each corner; a similar flag-post may be placed opposite the half-way line on each side of the field of play, not less than 1 yard outside the touch-line. A halfway-line shall be marked out across the field of play. The centre of the field of play shall be indicated by a suitable mark and a circle with a 10 yards radius shall be marked round it.

(3) **The Goal-Area.** At each end of the field of play two lines shall be drawn at right-angles to the goal-line, 6 yards from each goal-post. These shall extend into the field of play for a distance of 6 yards and shall be joined by a line drawn parallel with the goal-line. Each of the spaces enclosed by these lines and the goal-line shall be called a goal-area.

(4) **The Penalty-Area.** At each end of the field of play two lines shall be drawn at right-angles to the goal-line, 18 yards from each goal-post. These shall extend into the field of play for a distance of 18 yards and shall be joined by a line drawn parallel with the goal-line. Each of the spaces enclosed by these lines and the goal-line shall be called a penalty-area. A suitable mark shall be made within each penalty-area, 12 yards from the mid-point of the goal-line, measured along an undrawn line at right-angles thereto. These shall be the penalty-kick marks. From each penalty-kick mark an arc of a circle, having a radius of 10 yards, shall be drawn outside the penalty-area.

(5) **The Corner-Area.** From each corner-flag post a quarter circle, having a radius of 1 yard, shall be drawn inside the field of play.

(1) In International matches the dimensions of the field of play shall be: maximum 110 x 75 metres; minimum 100 x 64 metres.

(2) National Associations must adhere strictly to these dimensions. Each National Association organising an International Match must advise the visiting Association, before the match, of the place and the dimensions of the field of play.

(3) The Board has approved this table of measurements for the Laws of the Game:

130 yards	. . . . . 120 Metres
120 yards	 110
110 yards	 100
100 yards	 90
80 yards	 75
70 yards	 64
50 yards	 45
18 yards	. . . . . 16.50
12 yards	 11
10 yards	. . . . . 9.15
8 yards	. . . . . 7.32
6 yards	. . . . . 5.50
1 yard	 1
8 feet	. . . . . 2.44
5 feet	. . . . . 1.50
28 inches	. . . . . 0.71
27 inches	. . . . . 0.68
9 inches	. . . . . 0.22
5 inches	. . . . . 0.12
3/4 inch	. . . . . 0.019
1/2 inch	. . . . . 0.0127
3/8 inch	. . . . . 0.010
14 ounces	. . . . . 396 grams
16 ounces	. . . . . 453 grams
15 lb./sq.in.	. . . . . . 1 kg/cm^2

(4) The goal-line shall be marked the same width as the depth of the goal-posts and the cross-bar, so that the goal-line and goal-posts will conform to the same interior and exterior edges.

(5) The 6 yards (for the outline of the goal-area) and the 18 yards (for the outline of the penalty-area) which have to be measured along the goal-line, must start from the inner sides of the goal-posts.

(6) The space within the inside areas of the field of play includes the width of the lines marking these areas.

(7) All Associations shall provide standard equipment, particularly in International Matches, when the Laws of the Game must be complied with in every respect and especially with regard to the size of the ball and other equipment which must conform to the regulations. All cases of failure to provide standard equipment must be reported to F.I.F.A.

(8) In a match played under the Rules of a Competition if the cross-bar becomes dis-

LAW 1 (continued)

(6) **The Goals.** The goals shall be placed on the centre of each goal-line and shall consist of two upright posts, equidistant from the corner-flags and 8 yards apart (inside measurement), joined by a horizontal cross-bar the lower edge of which shall be 8 ft. from the ground. The width and depth of the goal-posts and the width and depth of the cross-bars shall not exceed 5 inches (12 cm). The goal-posts and the cross-bars shall have the same width.

Nets may be attached to the posts, cross-bars and ground behind the goals. They should be appropriately supported and be so placed as to allow the goal-keeper ample room.

placed or broken play shall be stopped and the match abandoned unless the cross-bar has been repaired and replaced in position or a new one provided without such being a danger to the players. A rope is not considered to be a satisfactory substitute for a cross-bar.

In a Friendly Match, by mutual consent, play may be resumed without the cross-bar provided it has been removed and no longer constitutes a danger to the players. In these circumstances, a rope may be used as a substitute for a cross-bar. If a rope is not used and the ball crosses the goal-line at a point which in the opinion of the Referee is below where the cross-bar should have been he shall award a goal.

The game shall be restarted by the Referee dropping the ball at the place where it was when play was stopped.

(9) National Associations may specify such maximum and minimum dimensions for the cross-bars and goal-posts, within the limits laid down in Law I, as they consider appropriate.

(10) Goal-posts and cross-bars must be made of wood, metal or other approved material as decided from time to time by the International F.A. Board. They may be square, rectangular, round, half-round or elliptical in shape Goal-posts and cross-bars made of other materials and in other shapes are not permitted.

(11) 'Curtain-raisers' to International matches should only be played following agreement on the day of the match, and taking into account the condition of the field of play, between representatives of the two Associations and the Referee (of the International Match).

(12) National Associations, particularly in International Matches, should
- restrict the number of photographers around the field of play,
- have a line ("photographers' line") marked behind the goal-lines at least two metres from the corner flag going through a point situated at least 3.5 metres behind the intersection of the goal-line with the line marking the goal area to a point situated at least six metres behind the goal-posts,
- prohibit photographers from passing over these lines,
- forbid the use of artificial lighting in the form of "flashlights".

Footnote:

Goal nets. The use of nets made of hemp, jute or nylon is permitted. The nylon strings may, however, not be thinner than those made of hemp or jute.

LAW II. – THE BALL

The ball shall be spherical; the outer casing shall be of leather or other approved materials. No material shall be used in its construction which might prove dangerous to the players.

The circumference of the ball shall not be more than 28 in. and not less than 27 in. The weight of the ball at the start of the game shall not be more than 16 oz. nor less than 14 oz. The pressure shall be equal to 0.6-0.7 atmosphere, which equals 9.0-10.5 lb./sq.in. (= 600-700 gr/cm^2) at sea level. The ball shall not be changed during the game unless authorised by the Referee.

(1) The ball used in any match shall be considered the property of the Association or Club on whose ground the match is played, and at the close of play it must be returned to the Referee.

(2) The International Board, from time to time, shall decide what constitutes approved materials. Any approved material shall be certified as such by the International Board.

(3) The Board has approved these equivalents of the weights specified in the Law: 14 to 16 ounces = 396 to 453 grammes.

(4) If the ball bursts or becomes deflated during the course of a match, the game shall be stopped and restarted by dropping the new ball at the place where the first ball became defective.

(5) If this happens during a stoppage of the game (place-kick, goal-kick, corner-kick, free-kick, penalty-kick or throw-in) the game shall be restarted accordingly.

LAW III. – NUMBER OF PLAYERS

(1) A match shall be played by two teams, each consisting of not more than eleven players, one of whom shall be the goalkeeper.

(2) Substitutes may be used in any match played under the rules of an official competition at FIFA, Confederation or National Association level, subject to the following conditions:

(a) that the authority of the international association(s) or national association(s) concerned, has been obtained,

(b) that, subject to the restriction contained in the following paragraph (c) the rules of a competition shall state how many, if any, substitutes may be used, and

(c) that a team shall not be permitted to use more than two substitutes in any match.

(3) Substitutes may be used in any other match, provided that the two teams concerned reach agreement on a maximum number, not exceeding five, and that the terms of such agreement are intimated to the Referee, before the match. If the Referee is not informed, or if the teams fail to reach agreement, no more than two substitutes shall be permitted.

(4) Any of the other players may change places with the goalkeeper, provided that the Referee is informed before the change is made, and provided also, that the change is made during a stoppage in the game.

(5) When a goalkeeper or any other player is to be replaced by a substitute, the following conditions shall be observed:

(a) the Referee shall be informed of the proposed substitution, before it is made,

(b) the substitute shall not enter the field of play until the player he is replacing has left, and then only after having received a signal from the Referee,

(c) he shall enter the field during a stoppage in the game, and at the half-way line.

Punishment:

(a) Play shall not be stopped for an infringement of paragraph 4. The players concerned shall be cautioned immediately the ball goes out of play.

(b) For any other infringement of this law, the player concerned shall be cautioned, and if the game is stopped by the Referee, to administer the caution, it shall be re-started by an indirect free-kick, to be taken by a player of the opposing team, from the place where the ball was, when play was stopped.

(1) The minimum number of players in a team is left to the discretion of National Associations.

(2) The Board is of the opinion that a match should not be considered valid if there are fewer than seven players in either of the teams.

(3) A competition may require that the referee shall be informed, before the start of the match, of the names of not more than five players, from whom the substitutes (if any) must be chosen.

(4) A player who has been ordered off before play begins may only be replaced by one of the named substitutes. The kick-off must not be delayed to allow the substitute to join his team.

A player who has been ordered off after play has started may not be replaced.

A named substitute who has been ordered off, either before or after play has started, may not be replaced (this decision only relates to players who are ordered off under Law XII. It does not apply to players who have infringed Law IV.)

(5) A player who has been replaced shall not take any further part in the game.

(6) A substitute shall be deemed to be a player and shall be subject to the authority and jurisdiction of the Referee whether called upon to play or not. For any offence committed on the field of play a substitute shall be subject to the same punishment as any other player whether called upon or not.

LAW IV. – PLAYERS' EQUIPMENT

(1) A player shall not wear anything which is dangerous to another player.

(2) Footwear (boots or shoes) must conform to the following standard:

(a) Bars shall be made of leather or rubber and shall be transverse and flat, not less than half an inch in width and shall extend the total width of the sole and be rounded at the corners.

(b) Studs which are independently mounted on the sole and are replaceable shall be made of leather, rubber, aluminium, plastic or similar material and shall be solid. With the exception of that part of the stud forming the base, which shall not protrude from the sole more than one quarter of an inch, studs shall be round in plan and not less than half an inch in diameter. Where studs are tapered, the minimum diameter of any section of the stud must not be less than half an inch. Where metal seating for the screw type is used, this seating must be embedded in the sole of the footwear and any atachment screw shall be part of the stud. Other than the metal seating for the screw type of stud, no metal plates even though covered with leather or rubber shall be worn, neither studs which are threaded to allow them to be screwed on to a base screw that is fixed by nails or otherwise to the soles of footwear, nor studs which, apart from the base, have any form of protruding edge rim or relief marking or ornament, should be allowed.

(c) Studs which are moulded as an integral part of the sole and are not replaceable shall be made of rubber, plastic, polyurethene or similar soft materials. Provided that there are no fewer than ten studs on the sole, they shall have a minimum diameter of three eights of an inch (10 mm.). Additional supporting material to stabilise studs of soft materials, and ridges which shall not protrude more than 5 mm. from the sole and moulded to strengthen it, shall be permitted provided that they are in no way dangerous to other players. In all other respects they shall conform to the general requirements of this Law.

(d) Combined bars and studs may be worn, provided the whole conforms to the general requirements of this Law. Neither bars nor studs on the soles shall project more than three-quarters of an inch. If nails are used they shall be driven in flush with the surface.

(1) The usual equipment of a player is a jersey or shirt, shorts, stockings and footwear. In a match played under the rules of a competition, players need not wear boots or shoes, but shall wear jersey or shirt, shorts, or track suit or similar trousers, and stockings.

(2) The Law does not insist that boots or shoes must be worn. However, in competition matches Referees should not allow one or a few players to play without footwear when all the other players are so equipped.

(3) In International Matches, International Competitions, International Club Competitions and friendly matches between clubs of different National Associations, the Referee, prior to the start of the game, shall inspect the players' footwear, and prevent any player whose footwear does not conform to the requirements of this Law from playing until such time as it does comply.

The rules of any competition may include a similar provision.

(4) If the Referee finds that a player is wearing articles not permitted by the Laws and which may constitute a danger to other players, he shall order him to take them off. If he fails to carry out the Referee's instruction, the player shall not take part in the match.

(5) A player who has been prevented from taking part in the game or a player who has been sent off the field for infringing Law IV must report to the Referee during a stoppage of the game and may not enter or re-enter the field of play unless and until the Referee has satisfied himself that the player is no longer infringing Law IV.

(6) A player who has been prevented from taking part in a game or who has been sent off because of an infringement of Law IV, and who enters or re-enters the field of play to join or re-join his team, in breach of the conditions of Law XII, shall be cautioned. If the Referee stops the game to administer the caution, the game shall be restarted by an indirect free-kick, taken by a player of the opposing side, from the place where the ball was when the Referee stopped the game.

LAW IV *(continued)*

(3) The goalkeeper shall wear colours which distinguish him from the other players and from the referee.

Punishment: For any infringement of this Law, the player at fault shall be sent off the field of play to adjust his equipment and he shall not return without first reporting to the Referee, who shall satisfy himself that the player's equipment is in order; the player shall only re-enter the game at a moment when the ball has ceased to be in play.

LAW V. – REFEREES

A Referee shall be appointed to officiate in each game. His authority and the exercise of the powers granted to him by the Laws of the Game commence as soon as he enters the field of play.

His power of penalising shall extend to offences committed when play has been temporarily suspended, or when the ball is out of play. His decision on points of fact connected with the play shall be final, so far as the result of the game is concerned. He shall:

(a) Enforce the Laws.

(b) Refrain from penalising in cases where he is satisfied that, by doing so, he would be giving an advantage to the offending team.

(c) Keep a record of the game; act as

(1) Referees in International Matches shall wear a blazer or blouse the colour of which is distinct from the colours worn by the contesting teams.

(2) Referees for International Matches will be selected from a neutral country unless the countries concerned agree to appoint their own officials.

(3) The Referee must be chosen from the official list of International Referees. This need not apply to Amateur and Youth International Matches.

(4) The Referee shall report to the appropriate authority misconduct or any misdemeanour on the part of spectators, officials, players, named substitutes or other persons which take place either on the field of play or in its vicinity at any time prior to,

LAW V *(continued)*

timekeeper and allow the full or agreed time, adding thereto all time lost through accident or other cause.

(d) Have discretionary power to stop the game for any infringement of the Laws and to suspend or terminate the game whenever, by reason of the elements, interference by spectators, or other cause, he deems such stoppage necessary. In such a case he shall submit a detailed report to the competent authority, within the stipulated time, and in accordance with the provisions set up by the National Association under whose jurisdiction the match was played. Reports will be deemed to be made when received in the ordinary course of post.

(e) From the time he enters the field of play, caution any player guilty of misconduct or ungentlemanly behaviour and, if he persists, suspend him from further participation in the game. In such cases the Referee shall send the name of the offender to the competent authority, within the stipulated time, and in accordance with the provisions set up by the National Association under whose jurisdiction the match was played. Reports will be deemed to be made when received in the ordinary course of post.

(f) Allow no person other than the players and linesmen to enter the field of play without his permission.

(g) Stop the game if, in his opinion, a player has been seriously injured; have the player removed as soon as possible from the field of play, and immediately resume the game. If a player is slightly injured, the game shall not be stopped until the ball has ceased to be in play. A player who is able to go to the touch or goal-line for attention of any kind, shall not be treated on the field of play.

(h) Send off the field of play, any player who, in his opinion, is guilty of violent conduct, serious foul play, or the use of foul or abusive language.

(i) Signal for recommencement of the game after all stoppages.

(j) Decide that the ball provided for a match meets with the requirements of Law II.

during, or after the match in question so that appropriate action can be taken by the Authority concerned.

(5) Linesmen are assistants of the Referee. In no case shall the Referee consider the intervention of a Linesman if he himself has seen the incident and from his position on the field, is better able to judge. With this reserve, and the Linesman neutral, the Referee can consider the intervention and if the information of the Linesman applies to that phase of the game immediately before the scoring of a goal, the Referee may act thereon and cancel the goal.

(6) The Referee, however, can only reverse his first decision so long as the game has not been restarted.

(7) If the Referee has decided to apply the advantage clause and to let the game proceed, he cannot revoke his decision if the presumed advantage has not been realised, even though he has not, by any gesture, indicated his decision. This does not exempt the offending player from being dealt with by the Referee.

(8) The Laws of the Game are intended to provide that games should be played with as little interference as possible, and in this view it is the duty of Referees to penalise only deliberate breaches of the Law. Constant whistling for trifling and doubtful breaches produces bad feeling and loss of temper on the part of the players and spoils the pleasure of spectators.

(9) By para. (d) of Law V the Referee is empowered to terminate a match in the event of grave disorder, but he has no power or right to decide, in such event, that either team is disqualified and thereby the loser of the match. He must send a detailed report to the proper authority who alone has power to deal further with this matter.

(10) If a player commits two infringements of a different nature at the same time, the Referee shall punish the more serious offence.

(11) It is the duty of the Referee to act upon the information of neutral Linesmen with regard to incidents that do not come under the personal notice of the Referee.

(12) The Referee shall not allow any person to enter the field until play has stopped, and only then, if he has given him a signal to do so, nor shall he allow coaching from the boundary lines.

LAW VI. – LINESMEN

Two Linesmen shall be appointed, whose duty (subject to the decision of the Referee) shall be to indicate when the ball is out of play and which side is entitled to the corner-kick, goal-kick or throw-in. They shall also assist the Referee to control the game in accordance with the Laws. In the event of undue interference or improper conduct by a Linesman, the Referee shall dispense with his services and arrange for a substitute to be appointed. (The matter shall be reported by the Referee to the competent authority.) The Linesmen should be equipped with flags by the Club on whose ground the match is played.

(1) Linesmen, where neutral, shall draw the Referee's attention to any breach of the Laws of the Game of which they become aware if they consider that the Referee may not have seen it, but the Referee shall always be the judge of the decision to be taken.

(2) National Associations are advised to appoint official Referees of neutral nationality to act as Linesmen in International Matches.

(3) In International Matches Linesmen's flags shall be of a vivid colour, bright reds and yellows. Such flags are recommended for use in all other matches.

(4) A Linesman may be subject to disciplinary action only upon a report of the Referee for unjustified interference or insufficient assistance.

LAW VII. – DURATION OF THE GAME

The duration of the game shall be two equal periods of 45 minutes, unless otherwise mutually agreed upon, subject to the following: (a) Allowance shall be made in either period for all time lost through accident or other cause, the amount of which shall be a matter for the discretion of the Referee; (b) Time shall be extended to permit a penalty-kick being taken at or after the expiration of the normal period in either half.

At half-time the interval shall not exceed five minutes except by consent of the Referee.

(1) If a match has been stopped by the Referee, before the completion of the time specified in the rules, for any reason stated in Law V it must be replayed in full unless the rules of the competition concerned provide for the result of the match at the time of such stoppage to stand.

(2) Players have a right to an interval at half-time.

Laws of the Game

LAW VIII. – THE START OF PLAY

(a) **At the beginning of the game,** choice of ends and the kick-off shall be decided by the toss of a coin. The team winning the toss shall have the option of choice of ends or the kick-off. The Referee having given a signal, the game shall be started by a player taking a place-kick (i.e., a kick at the ball while it is stationary on the ground in the centre of the field of play) into his opponents' half of the field of play. Every player shall be in his own half of the field and every player of the team opposing that of the kicker shall remain not less than 10 yards from the ball until it is kicked-off; it shall not be deemed in play until it has travelled the distance of its own circumference. The kicker shall not play the ball a second time until it has been touched or played by another player.

(b) **After a goal has scored,** the game shall be restarted in like manner by a player of the team losing the goal.

(c) **After half-time;** when restarting after half-time, ends shall be changed and the kick-off shall be taken by a player of the opposite team to that of the player who started the game.

Punishment. For any infringement of this Law, the kick-off shall be retaken, except in the case of the kicker playing the ball again before it has been touched or played by another player; for this offence, an indirect free-kick shall be taken by a player of the opposing team from the place where the infringement occurred. A goal shall not be scored direct from a kick-off.

(d) **After any other temporary suspension;** when restarting the game after a temporary suspension of play from any cause not mentioned elsewhere in these Laws, provided that immediately prior to the suspension the ball has not passed over the touch or goal-lines, the Referee shall drop the ball at the place where it was when play was suspended and it shall be deemed in play when it has touched the ground; if, however, it goes over the touch or goal-lines after it has been dropped by the Referee, but before it is touched by a player, the Referee shall again drop it. A player shall not play the ball until it has touched the ground. If this section of the Law is not complied with the Referee shall again drop the ball.

Decisions of the International Board

(1) If, when the Referee drops the ball, a player infringes any of the Laws before the ball has touched the ground, the player concerned shall be cautioned or sent off the field according to the seriousness of the offence, but a free-kick cannot be awarded to the opposing team because the ball was not in play at the time of the offence. The ball shall therefore be again dropped by the Referee.

(2) Kicking-off by persons other than the players competing in a match is prohibited.

LAW IX. – BALL IN AND OUT OF PLAY

The ball is out of play:

(a) When it has wholly crossed the goal-line or touch-line, whether on the ground or in the air.

(b) When the game has been stopped by the Referee.

The ball is in play at all other times from the start of the match to the finish including:

(a) If it rebounds from a goal-post, cross-bar or corner-flag post into the field of play.

(b) If it rebounds off either the Referee or Linesmen when they are in the field of play.

(c) In the event of a supposed infringement of the Laws, until a decision is given.

(1) The lines belong to the areas of which they are the boundaries. In consequence, the touch-lines and the goal-lines belong to the field of play.

LAW X. – METHOD OF SCORING

Except as otherwise provided by these Laws, a goal is scored when the whole of the ball has passed over the goal-line, between the goal-posts and under the cross-bar, provided it has not been thrown, carried or intentionally propelled by hand or arm, by a player of the attacking side, except in the case of a goalkeeper, who is within his own penalty-area.

The team scoring the greater number of goals during a game shall be the winner; if no goals, or an equal number of goals are scored, the game shall be termed a "draw".

(1) Law X defines the only method according to which a match is won or drawn; no variation whatsoever can be authorised.

(2) A goal cannot in any case be allowed if the ball has been prevented by some outside agent from passing over the goal-line. If this happens in the normal course of play, other than at the taking of a penalty-kick: the game must be stopped and restarted by the Referee dropping the ball at the place where the ball came into contact with the interference.

(3) If, when the ball is going into goal, a spectator enters the field before it passes wholly over the goal-line, and tries to prevent a score, a goal shall be allowed if the ball goes into goal unless the spectator has made contact with the ball or has interfered with play, in which case the Referee shall stop the game and restart it by dropping the ball at the place where the contact or interference occurred.

LAW XI. – OFF-SIDE

A player is off-side if he is nearer his opponents' goal-line than the ball **at the moment the ball is played unless:**

(a) He is in his own half of the field of play.

(b) There are two of his opponents nearer to their own goal-line than he is.

(c) The ball last touched an opponent or was last played by him.

(d) He receives the ball direct from a goal-kick, a corner-kick, a throw-in, or when it was dropped by the Referee.

Punishment. For an infringement of this Law, an indirect free-kick shall be taken by a player of the opposing team from the place where the infringement occurred.

A player in an off-side position shall not be penalised unless, in the opinion of the Referee, he is interfering with the play or with an opponent, or is seeking to gain an advantage by being in an offside position.

(1) Off-side shall not be judged at the moment the player in question receives the ball, but at the moment when the ball is passed to him by one of his own side. A player who is not in an off-side position when one of his colleagues passes the ball to him or takes a free-kick, does not therefore become off-side if he goes forward during the flight of the ball.

LAW XII. – FOULS AND MISCONDUCT

A player who intentionally commits any of the following nine offences:

(a) Kicks or attempts to kick an opponent;
(b) Trips an opponent, i.e., throwing or attempting to throw him by the use of the legs or by stooping in front of or behind him;
(c) Jumps at an opponent;
(d) Charges an opponent in a violent or dangerous manner;
(e) Charges an opponent from behind unless the latter be obstructing;
(f) Strikes or attempts to strike an opponent;
(g) Holds an opponent;
(h) Pushes an opponent;
(i) Handles the ball, i.e., carries, strikes or propels the ball with his hand or arm. (This does not apply to the goalkeeper within his own penalty-area);

shall be penalised by the award of a **direct free-kick** to be taken by the opposing side from the place where the offence occurred.

Should a player of the defending side intentionally commit one of the above nine offences within the penalty-area he shall be penalised by a **penalty-kick**.

A penalty-kick can be awarded irrespective of the position of the ball, if in play, at the time an offence within the penalty-area is committed.

A player committing any of the five following offences:

1. Playing in a manner considered by the Referee to be dangerous, e.g., attempting to kick the ball while held by the goalkeeper;
2. Charging fairly, i.e., with the shoulder, when the ball is not within playing distance of the players concerned and they are definitely not trying to play it;
3. When not playing the ball, intentionally obstructing an opponent, i.e., running between the opponent and the ball, or interposing the body so as to form an obstacle to an opponent;
4. Charging the goalkeeper except when he
   (a) is holding the ball;
   (b) is obstructing an opponent;
   (c) has passed outside his goal-area;
5. When playing as goalkeeper,
   (a) takes more than 4 steps whilst holding, bouncing or throwing the ball in

(1) If the goalkeeper either intentionally strikes an opponent by throwing the ball vigorously at him or pushes him with the ball while holding it, the Referee shall award a penalty-kick, if the offence took place within the penalty-area.

(2) If a player deliberately turns his back to an opponent when he is about to be tackled, he may be charged but not in a dangerous manner.

(3) In case of body-contact in the goal-area between an attacking player and the opposing goalkeeper not in possession of the ball, the Referee, as sole judge of intention, shall stop the game if, in his opinion, the action of the attacking player was intentional, and award an indirect free-kick.

(4) If a player leans on the shoulders of another player of his own team in order to head the ball, the Referee shall stop the game, caution the player for ungentlemanly conduct and award an indirect free-kick to the opposing side.

(5) A player's obligation when joining or rejoining his team after the start of the match to 'report to the Referee' must be interpreted as meaning 'to draw the attention of the Referee from the touch-line'. The signal from the Referee shall be made by a definite gesture which makes the player understand that the he may come into the field of play; it is not necessary for the Referee to wait until the game is stopped (this does not apply in respect of an infringement of Law IV), but the Referee is the sole judge of the moment in which he gives his signal of acknowledgement.

(6) The letter and spirit of Law XII do not oblige the Referee to stop a game to administer a caution. He may, if he chooses, apply the advantage. If he does apply the advantage, he shall caution the player when play stops.

(7) If a player covers up the ball without touching it in an endeavour not to have it played by an opponent, he obstructs but does not infringe Law XII para. 3 because he is already in possession of the ball and covers it for tactical reasons whilst the ball remains within playing distance. In fact, he is actually playing the ball and does not commit an infringement; in this case, the player may be charged because he is in fact playing the ball.

(8) If a player intentionally stretches his arms to obstruct an opponent and steps

LAW XII *(continued)*

the air and catching it again without releasing it so that it is played by another player, or

(b) indulges in tactics which, in the opinion of the Referee, are designed merely to hold up the game and thus waste time and so give an unfair advantage to his own team

shall be penalised by the award of an **indirect free-kick** to be taken by the opposing side from the place where the infringement occurred.

A player shall be **cautioned** if:

(j) he enters or re-enters the field of play to join or rejoin his team after the game has commenced, or leaves the field of play during the progress of the game (except through accident) without, in either case, first having received a signal from the Referee showing him that he may do so. If the Referee stops the game to administer the caution the game shall be restarted by an indirect free-kick taken by a player of the opposing team from the place where the ball was when the referee stopped the game. If, however, the offending player has committed a more serious offence he shall be penalised according to that section of the law he infringed;

(k) he persistently infringes the Laws of the Game;

(l) he shows by word or action, dissent from any decision given by the Referee;

(m) he is guilty of ungentlemanly conduct.

For any of these last three offences, in addition to the caution, an **indirect free-kick** shall also be awarded to the opposing side from the place where the offence occurred unless a more serious infringement of the Laws of the Game was committed.

A player shall be **sent off** the field of play, if:

(n) in the opinion of the Referee he is guilty of violent conduct or serious foul play;

(o) he uses foul or abusive language

(p) he persists in misconduct after having received a caution.

If play be stopped by reason of a player being ordered from the field for an offence without a separate breach of the Law having been committed, the game shall be resumed by an **indirect free-kick** awarded to the opposing side from the place where the infringement occurred.

from one side to the other, moving his arms up and down to delay his opponent, forcing him to change course, but does not make "bodily contact" the Referee shall caution the player for ungentlemanly conduct and award an indirect free-kick.

(9) If a player intentionally obstructs the opposing goalkeeper, in an attempt to prevent him from putting the ball into play in accordance with Law XII, 5(a), the referee shall award an indirect free-kick.

(10) If after a Referee has awarded a free-kick a player protests violently by using abusive or foul language and is sent off the field, the free-kick should not be taken until the player has left the field.

(11) Any player, whether he is within or outside the field of play, whose conduct is ungentlemanly or violent, whether or not it is directed towards an opponent, a colleague, the Referee, a linesman or other person, or who uses foul or abusive language, is guilty of an offence, and shall be dealt with according to the nature of the offence committed.

(12) If, in the opinion of the Referee a goalkeeper intentionally lies on the ball longer than is necessary, he shall be penalised for ungentlemanly conduct and

(a) be cautioned and an indirect free-kick awarded to the opposing team;

(b) in case of repetition of the offence, be sent off the field.

(13) The offence of spitting at opponents, officials or other persons, or similar unseemly behaviour shall be considered as violent conduct within the meaning of section (n) of Law XII.

(14) If, when a Referee is about to caution a player, and before he has done so, the player commits another offence which merits a caution, the player shall be sent off the field of play.

LAW XIII. – FREE-KICK

Free-kicks shall be classified under two headings: "Direct" (from which a goal can be scored direct against the offending side), and "Indirect" (from which a goal cannot be scored unless the ball has been played or touched by a player other than the kicker before passing through the goal).

When a player is taking a direct or an indirect free-kick inside his own penalty-area, all of the opposing players shall remain outside the area, and shall be at least ten yards from the ball whilst the kick is being taken. The ball shall be in play immediately it has travelled the distance of its own circumference and is beyond the penalty-area. The goalkeeper shall not receive the ball into his hands, in order that he may thereafter kick it into play. If the ball is not kicked direct into play, beyond the penalty-area, the kick shall be retaken.

When a player is taking a direct or an indirect free-kick outside his own penalty-area, all of the opposing players shall be at least ten yards from the ball, until it is in play, unless they are standing on their own goal-line, between the goal-posts. The ball shall be in play when it has travelled the distance of its own circumference.

If a player of the opposing side encroaches into the penalty-area, or within ten yards of the ball, as the case may be, before a free-kick is taken, the Referee shall delay the taking of the kick, until the Law is complied with.

The ball must be stationary when a free-kick is taken, and the kicker shall not play the ball a second time, until it has been touched or played by another player.

Punishment. If the kicker, after taking the free-kick, plays the ball a second time before it has been touched or played by another player an indirect free-kick shall be taken by a player of the opposing team from the spot where the infringement occurred.

(1) In order to distinguish between a direct and an indirect free-kick, the Referee, when he awards an indirect free-kick, shall indicate accordingly by raising an arm above his head. He shall keep his arm in that position until the kick has been taken.

(2) Players who do not retire to the proper distance when a free-kick is taken must be cautioned and on any repetition be ordered off. It is particularly requested of Referees that attempts to delay the taking of a free-kick by encroaching should be treated as serious misconduct.

(3) If, when a free-kick is being taken, any of the players dance about or gesticulate in a way calculated to distract their opponents, it shall be deemed ungentlemanly conduct for which the offender(s) shall be cautioned.

LAW XIV. – PENALTY-KICK

A penalty-kick shall be taken from the penalty-mark and, when it is being taken, all players with the exception of the player taking the kick, and the opposing goalkeeper, shall be within the field of play but outside the penalty-area, and at least 10 yards from the penalty-mark. The opposing goalkeeper must stand (without moving his feet) on his own goal-line, between the goal-posts, until the ball is kicked. The player taking the kick must kick the ball forward; he shall not play the ball a second time until it has been touched or played by another player. The ball shall be deemed in play directly it is kicked, i.e., when it has travelled the distance of its circumference, and a goal may be scored direct from such a penalty-kick. If the ball touches the goalkeeper before passing between the posts, when a penalty-kick is being taken at or after the expiration of half-time or full-time, it does not nullify a goal. If necessary, time of play shall be extended at half-time or full-time to allow a penalty-kick to be taken.

Punishment:

For any infringement of this Law:

(a) by the defending team, the kick shall be retaken if a goal has not resulted.

(b) by the attacking team other than by the player taking the kick, if a goal is scored it shall be disallowed and the kick retaken.

(c) by the player taking the penalty-kick, committed after the ball is in play, a player of the opposing team shall take an indirect free-kick from the spot where the infringement occurred.

(1) When the Referee has awarded a penalty-kick, he shall not signal for it to be taken, until the players have taken up position in accordance with the Law.

(2) (a) If, after the kick has been taken, the ball is stopped in its course towards goal, by an outside agent, the kick shall be retaken.

(b) If, after the kick has been taken, the ball rebounds into play, from the goalkeeper, the cross-bar or a goal-post, and is then stopped in its course by an outside agent, the Referee shall stop play and restart it by dropping the ball at the place where it came into contact with the outside agent.

(3) (a) If, after having given the signal for a penalty-kick to be taken, the Referee sees that the goalkeeper is not in his right place on the goal-line, he shall, nevertheless, allow the kick to proceed. It shall be retaken, if a goal is not scored.

(b) If, after the Referee has given the signal for a penalty-kick to be taken, and before the ball has been kicked, the goalkeeper moves his feet, the Referee shall, nevertheless, allow the kick to proceed. It shall be retaken, if a goal is not scored.

(c) If, after the Referee has given the signal for a penalty-kick to be taken, and before the ball is in play, a player of the defending team encroaches into the penalty-area, or within ten yards of the penalty-mark, the Referee shall, nevertheless, allow the kick to proceed. It shall be retaken, if a goal is not scored.

The player concerned shall be cautioned.

(4) (a) If, when a penalty-kick is being taken, the player taking the kick is guilty of ungentlemanly conduct, the kick, if already taken, shall be retaken, if a goal is scored.

The player concerned shall be cautioned.

(b) If, after the referee has given the signal for a penalty-kick to be taken, and before the ball is in play, a colleague of the player taking the kick encroaches into the penalty-area or within ten yards of the penalty-mark, the Referee shall, nevertheless, allow the kick to proceed. If a goal is scored, it shall be disallowed, and the kick retaken.

The player concerned shall be cautioned.

(c) If, in the circumstances described in the foregoing paragraph, the ball rebounds into play from the goalkeeper, the cross-bar or a goal-post, the Referee shall stop the game, caution the player and award an indirect free-kick to the opposing team from the place where the infringement occurred.

(5) (a) If, after the referee has given the signal for a penalty-kick to be taken, and before the ball is in play, the goalkeeper moves from his position on the goal-line, or moves his feet, and a colleague of the kicker encroaches into the penalty-area or within 10 yards of the penalty-mark, the kick, if taken, shall be retaken.

The colleague of the kicker shall be cautioned.

(b) If, after the Referee has given the signal for a penalty-kick to be taken, and before the ball is in play, a player of each team encroaches into the penalty-area, or within 10 yards of the penalty-mark, the kick, if taken, shall be retaken.

The players concerned shall be cautioned.

(6) When a match is extended, at half-time or full-time, to allow a penalty-kick to be taken or retaken, the extension shall last until the moment that the penalty-kick has been completed, i.e. until the Referee has decided whether or not a goal is scored.

A goal is scored when the ball passes wholly over the goal-line.

(a) direct from the penalty-kick,

(b) having rebounded from either goal-post or the cross-bar, or

(c) having touched or been played by the goalkeeper.

The game shall terminate immediately the Referee has made his decision.

(7) When a penalty-kick is being taken in extended time:

(a) the provisions of all of the foregoing paragraphs, except paragraphs (2) (b) and (4) (c) shall apply in the usual way, and

(b) in the circumstances described in paragraphs (2) (b) and (4) (c) the game shall terminate immediately the ball rebounds from the goalkeeper, the cross-bar or the goal-post.

LAW XV. – THROW-IN

When the whole of the ball passes over a touch-line, either on the ground or in the air, it shall be thrown in from the point where it crossed the line, in any direction, by a player of the team opposite to that of the player who last touched it. The thrower at the moment of delivering the ball must face the field of play and part of each foot shall be either on the touch-line or on the ground outside the touch-line. The thrower shall use both hands and shall deliver the ball from behind and over his head. The ball shall be in play immediately it enters the field of play, but the thrower shall not again play the ball until it has been touched or played by another player. A goal shall not be scored direct from a throw-in.

Punishment:

(a) If the ball is improperly thrown in the throw-in shall be taken by a player of the opposing team.

(b) If the thrower plays the ball a second time before it has been touched or played by another player, an indirect free-kick shall be taken by a player of the opposing team from the place where the infringement occurred.

(1) If a player taking a throw-in, plays the ball a second time by handling it within the field of play before it has been touched or played by another player, the Referee shall award a direct free-kick.

(2) A player taking a throw-in must face the field of play with some part of his body.

(3) If, when a throw-in is being taken, any of the opposing players dance about or gesticulate in a way calculated to distract or impede the thrower, it shall be deemed ungentlemanly conduct, for which the offender(s) shall be cautioned.

LAW XVI. – GOAL-KICK

When the whole of the ball passes over the goal-line excluding that portion between the goal-posts, either in the air or on the ground, having last been played by one of the attacking team, it shall be kicked direct into play beyond the penalty-area from a point within that half of the goal-area nearest to where it crossed the line, by a player of the defending team. A goalkeeper shall not receive the ball into his hands from a goal-kick in order that he may thereafter kick it into play. If the ball is not kicked beyond the penalty-area, i.e., direct into play, the kick shall be retaken. The kicker shall not play the ball a second time until it has touched – or been played by – another player. A goal shall not be scored direct from such a kick. Players of the team opposing that of the player taking the goal-kick shall remain outside the penalty-area whilst the kick is being taken.

Punishment: If a player taking a goal-kick plays the ball a second time after it has passed beyond the penalty-area, but before it has touched or been played by another player, an indirect free-kick shall be awarded to the opposing team, to be taken from the place where the infringement occurred.

(1) When a goal-kick has been taken and the player who has kicked the ball touches it again before it has left the penalty-area, the kick has not been taken in accordance with the Law and must be retaken.

LAW XVII. – CORNER-KICK

When the whole of the ball passes over the goal-line, excluding that portion between the goal-posts, either in the air or on the ground, having last been played by one of the defending team, a member of the attacking team shall take a corner-kick, i.e., the whole of the ball shall be placed within the quarter circle at the nearest corner-flagpost, which must not be moved, and it shall be kicked from that position. A goal may be scored direct from such a kick. Players of the team opposing that of the player taking the corner-kick shall not approach within 10 yards of the ball until it is in play, i.e., it has travelled the distance of its own circumference, nor shall the kicker play the ball a second time until it has been touched or played by another player.

Punishment:

(a) If the player who takes the kick plays the ball a second time before it has been touched or played by another player, the Referee shall award an indirect free-kick to the opposing team, to be taken from the place where the infringement occurred.

(b) For any other infringement the kick shall be retaken.

278

THE INTERNATIONAL BOARD . . .
HOW SOCCER'S LAWS ARE CHANGED

The laws of the game are quite static, and few people connected with the game expect changes from year to year. The Off-Side law was brought to its present form in 1925. The Penalty-Arc was added in 1935. It is apparent that there is almost a sacrosanctity about the laws governing play.

The International Board consists of representatives from the four British Associations and one from FIFA. The countries — England, Ireland, Scotland, and Wales — each have one vote. FIFA, representing 142 countries, has four. No change takes place without a clear 75% majority. Therefore, no law or wording in the law may be changed without the approval of FIFA, and vice versa.

Any country may propose a change. If the National Association in Brazil, for instance, wanted to suggest a rule change eliminating the center circle, it would first be sent to the FIFA Referees' Committee, a group of seven, which screens all requests. The Committee may either reject the request, or submit it as a FIFA proposal (4 votes). The remaining four votes (countries) are advised of the proposal and the reasons ("because the circle serves only one function, one that is easily administered by the Referee) and the Board will then meet on the change.

The Board, of course, carries a great responsibility. The Referees' Committee naturally performs much of their work by dispensing with proposals that have already failed, and which would have no chance of passing.

An Editorial Board also exists, one which aids in the precise phrasing of law changes. Ken Aston of England, noted Referee authority and former long-time FIFA representative on the International Board, feels that the Board functions well, though the British dominance may seem unfair to some individuals and countries. "The conservatism of the British toward the laws of soccer keep these laws from constantly changing. Wide-sweeping changes in the laws would bring confusion to those who write, those who teach, and to those who must abide by and enforce the laws," he declares.

It should be noted that FIFA does give permission to National Associations from time to time where an experiment in the laws is desired. For example, the North American Soccer League has been given permission to experiment with Law 11 (Off-Side). A line, 35 yards from, and parallel to each goal-line, defines an area in which players may be judged off-side, as opposed to a player's own half of the field.

Experiments with the laws of the game are authorized by FIFA only if first authorized by the International Board. Presently, FIFA has granted permission for experiments in the following areas: (1) the short, or mini-corner (taken at the intersection of the penalty-area line and goal-line); (2) kick-in instead of a throw-in (used in America in college play in the 1950's; and (3) temporary expulsion for certain misdemeanors which are normally punished with a caution.

The Two Referee System has several advantages.

Joe Bonchonsky of Torrance, California. In 1973, Joe originated the Modified Diagonal System.

XV

The

American Scene

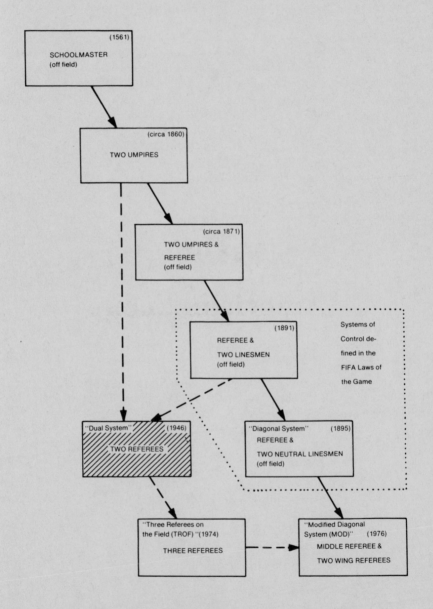

THE TWO REFEREE SYSTEM (DUAL SYSTEM)

The Two Referee System of control was first adopted for refereeing in colleges in 1946 by Earle C. Waters, coach of West Chester State Teachers' College in Pennsylvania. Here are three statements he made in the 1948 NCAA soccer guide. (The 'Fact' and 'Fiction' desigations in the margin are our own.)

Fact   *"They (the two Referees) should be friends and respect the ability of the other, an attitude which will eliminate any tendency toward jealousy. They should work in pairs during the season, as the more they work together the more they will learn the habits of the other and the better team they will become."*

Fiction   *"Since they have only a little over a half a field to cover, they do not get weary toward the end of the game and thus lag behind play at the most exciting time."*

Fact &   *"The trend toward two-on-the-field is due partly to the fact that it is more eco-*
Fiction   *nomical than the three-paid-officials and due partly to the fact that it seems to operate more satisfactorily."*

In this same NCAA guide, Harry Rogers, then secretary of the Pennsylvania Referees Association said the following:

Fact   *"It is quite possible for one of the officials to be screened from an infringement even though he may be closer to the play, therefore his co-official who is moving up with the play, will see the infringement and call it."*

Fiction   *"The off-side is easily handled by the two-man system. Not once during all the games played in this area under this plan has an off-side decision been called incorrectly. This and goal-line plays have done more than anything else to put this system across to all the coaches and their players."*

Fact &   *"Summing up the entire procedure, the two-man system has proven itself to be*
Fiction   *close to 100% perfect and from all reports is here to stay."*

Today the two Referee system is an accepted reality in youth, high school, and college soccer in the United States. Our purpose here is to examine the system, dispel some myths, point out advantages, disadvantages, and take an in-depth look at field positioning.

Two Relevant Acronyms

All of the following indicates that you are in the **game**.

    Give partner trail support.

    Attitude is positive.

    Mechanics.

    Eye contact.

If any of the following apply, you should go **home**.

    Hug the touch-line.

    Off-Side oriented.

    My half, your half philosophy.

    Ego trip.

EXPLOIT ITS STRENGTHS AND GUARD AGAINST ITS WEAKNESSES

Advantages

- A good system for fouls off of the ball.

- Reduced mental strain. Help is given by your partner to take off any of the weight that players or a coach may try to place upon your shoulders.

- Psychological advantage of two officials *on* the field acting together. The Referee team can often overpower a player. If there is any trouble on the field, both officials are there. When a foul is whistled, both officials normally signal in accord.

- Referee teams of two men are easier to assign than three.

Disadvantages

- There is a feeling of being on the outside of the action. It lacks the total feel and and involvement of the diagonal or MOD systems. You must try to get into the game without getting in the way of the players.

- Physical demands. If done properly, the Dual System requires *more* running and sprinting than any other system. It is only an "old man's" or "lazy man's" system when it is operated improperly.

- Off-side coverage. How many times have you heard, "There is no excuse for missing the off-side in the dual system of control." Nothing could be further from the truth. In fact it is the *worst* system for off-sides and out-of-bounds monitoring. If it should become one of the better systems in this respect, then it is being used incorrectly. Game control must take precedent. It's like going to a distant location to stomp on ants while elephants are overrunning your campground.

- A Referee will sometimes hesitate to call an infraction nearer to his partner than to himself.

- It requires disciplined partnerships (like basketball). Otherwise there may be incompatibilities with the two Referees not being in agreement on all law interpretations.

TEAMWORK

Your partner is the most important person at the game.

- You should go everywhere together . . . . . field entry/exit, net checking, equipment checking, etc.

- Nothing is more satisfying than a well-oiled partnership. You can take on the world (and quite often you have to).

- If the best in your partner is not being brought out, then you yourself are usually to blame.

- Develop rapport with your partner, and a difficult game can be easier. Don't do it and an easy one can become drudgery; a tough one, disaster.

Be in constant communication with your partner.

- Continually have eye contact with him. This suffers the most after a layoff between seasons.

- There is nothing wrong with verbalizing to your partner. Often it does a lot of good. "Nice call, Fred" . . . . . "I've got the wall, you take the goal-line." Smiling at each other occasionally also strengthens the officiating bond.

- Flash the time remaining in the period to each other.

- Go towards partner when he is cautioning. Be there when he is ejecting, or if it looks like someone is giving him a hard time.

- Do not allow him to take any abuse from players, coaches, or spectators. The abuse that is heaped upon him falls every bit as heavily upon you, though it's just not that apparent at that moment.

Give partner the trail support that you want him to give you.

AREA OF RESPONSIBILITY

Out of Bounds

- *Touchline* on your side of the field.

- *Goal-line* you move toward as a Lead Referee.

Each Referee works toward his right during one of the periods. He then has the responsibility for monitoring off-side when the attacking team goes toward the goal on his right. The shaded portion indicates his prime area of responsibility. This territorial flow complements the existing FIFA Diagonal System of Control. When the attack is made toward the goal on his right he is known as the Lead (**L**) Referee. When the attack is made toward the goal on his left he is referred to as the Trail (**T**) Referee.

Each Referee works toward his left for the other period. As play moves toward *his* right goal he is in a Trail (**T**) mode and when play goes to his left, he is in a Lead (**L**) capacity.

The partner of each of the above illustrated Referees is on the diagonally opposite side of the field, working in a like manner.

To minimize confusion, all subsequent discussions and illustrations will assume each Referee is working toward his right (top diagram).

285

To begin the 2nd period, the Referees merely move across to the opposite side of the field. They always retain the same end of the field. This is a high school and college requirement. The same philosophy is followed in the NASL whereby the Referee runs the right-wing diagonal during the first period and then changes to the more conventional left-wing diagonal for the 2nd period. There are reasons for this switch:

- Off-side calls are equalized (staying where you are is the only way to do this).

- You are placed by a new subset of players. If you run to your right the left wings and right fullbacks have no one near them. When you change to begin the 2nd period, they are now closely under surveillance. "Presence lends conviction."

- Environmental conditions are equalized. (Sun, field, wind, etc.)

- You get away from a particular team bench/coach/group of spectators. This burden is now shared with your partner. Quite often you will discover that his chemistry doesn't agitate them like yours did, or vice versa. If both benches are on the same side of the field, too many pressures are placed upon the Referee who has to contend with them for a complete game.

- Most of us have experienced the problem of pointing in the wrong direction during the first few minutes of the 2nd period. Changing sides of the field eliminates that problem. (e.g., If the blue team went to your right during the 1st period, it still does in the 2nd.)

The only exception to the above required side changes would be:

- A very poor quadrant of the field that is difficult to run in.

- An extremely weak partner.

BASICS

Jurisdiction

Both officials have equal authority and are responsible for whistling fouls and violations on any part of the field at any time. Fouls are normally not called immediately in front of your partner unless it is clear that he is shielded.

Monitoring Play

Play should be contained between the two Referees, much as it is in basketball. Eye contact should be maintained, particularly in conjunction with advantage clause situations. (L) keeps ahead of play and keeps fairly close to the touch-line. As the ball moves closer to his goal, he moves closer to the touch-line. When play moves into his penalty-area he should be on the goal-line closer to the goal, depending on the position of the last-but-one defender.

(T) is in the field approximately 10 to 20 yards inside the touch-line. He follows beyond midfield as close to the play as possible, taking into consideration field conditions, kicking strength of the players, their speed, his own speed, and that of his partner. He is in a position to reverse his field immediately should a counterattack develop, yet still be ahead of play.

286

The chief shortcoming of the poor Referee is the hugging of the touch-line. He thinks that the job is:

- Out-of-bounds
- Off-side
- Fouls in his half of the field

. . . . . and he does them in that order. The priorities *should* be

1. Game Control — Call fouls anywhere. Get rid of the my ½, your ½ philosophy. That can destroy the game, your partner, and ultimately you yourself.
2. Off-Side
3. Out-of-Bounds — If you are going to miss something, it is better to miss a meaningless out-of-bounds at midfield as opposed to an 'off-the-ball' at the same location.

The toughest areas to monitor are the coffin corners. They are nobody's 'prime' area but rather, the responsibility belongs equally to both officials. It requires very tight trail support for calling fouls in these areas.

Calling the Infraction

- Blow the whistle and point in the direction the kick is to be taken.
- Give auditory (optional) and visual signal for the infraction.
  "PUSHING — NUMBER 14" (Give pushing signal)
- Give auditory (optional) and visual signal for the type of kick or throw-in.
  "BLUE KICK — DIRECT"

Simultaneous Whistle — Rule of thumb: Closer Referee immediately points in the proper direction. Any doubts as to who is closer can be resolved by whose half of the field it is in.

If different infractions are indicated, signal the infraction to each other.

- If dissimilar — the more serious prevails.
- If the same type of foul — DROP-BALL quickly by the closer Referee.

It is very important to signal the nature of all fouls. To fail to do so keeps partner on the outside and unable to attain full involvement in the game.

MECHANICS

The shaded areas   indicate the latitude of (**T**) and (**L**) positioning.

Kick-Off

What to look for on a kick-off.

- Do the players encroach?
- Was the ball played in a forward direction?
- Did the ball travel its circumference?

These questions are best answered by (**T**).

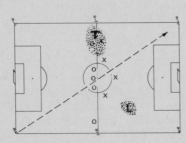

(**T**) whistles for the kick-off after:

- He receives a signal from (**L**) that his GK is ready and his team has the proper number of players.
- (**T**)s team is ready.
- The timekeeper (if used) is ready.

He is watching from the halfway line approximately 5-15 yards in from the touch-line.

(**L**) is approximately 20-25 yards downfield and 10 yards in from the touch-line. He watches for left wing encroachment when he is behind (**T**).

Monitoring Off-Side

The dual system is the *worst* system for off-sides.

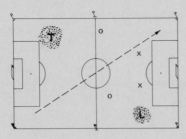 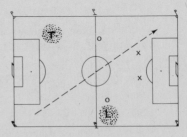

(**L**) may stay parallel with the next-to-last defender.

or

He may stay with the most advanced offensive player. This allows deeper penetration as a trail and puts you closer to play. However, you must be sure that you can get to the next to last defender before any offensive player does.

..... or, because the extensive use of either of the above results in a poor visual perspective, (L) may use a mixture of the two. This consists of staying even with the lead attacker *until he passes* the next-to-last defender; then he stays even with this next-to-last defender until *he re-passes* the lead attacker. Then (L) would switch back and stay with the lead attacker.

(T) comes in from behind and monitors play.

Read the game carefully for a team's off-side philosophy. If they extensively implement the 'trap', then it must be watched closely. The monitoring of play in general as well as off-side may be accomplished by pulling to the center of the field and much backwards running.

Goal-Kick or Corner-Kick?

As previously mentioned, the ends of the diagonal (referred to as the coffin corners) are the most troublesome areas to cover because of the distance away from their respective (L)'s. As the ball crosses the goal-line, the distinction between goal/corner-kick is sometimes a difficult one to make.

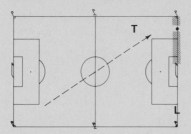 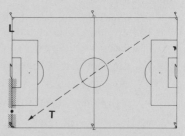

(T) can take some of the pressure off in one of the two ways:

He Makes the Call — If (T) is advanced enough into (L)'s half and clearly sees which man the ball came off of, he may make the call, provided he signals and indicates it quickly and decisively enough. (L) has signaled almost simultaneously the instant the ball went over the goal-line. (L) may now take his cue from (T) because he has him within his line of sight.

or . . .

He Gives a Subtle Indication — If he saw it as a corner-kick he continues his forward momentum and trots toward the corner.

A goal-kick is indicated by falling back toward the halfway line.

To stand perfectly still says, "I have no idea." Once (L) makes the call, (T) immediately becomes supportive in his movements.

Goal-Kick

What to look for in the goal-kick:

- Part of the ball within the goal-area.

- In correct half of the goal-area.

- Ball passing beyond the penalty-area before it is played.

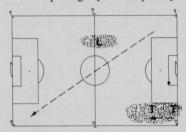

(T) checks for correct ball placement, then rapidly moves to a position at the front of the penalty-area to ensure that the ball leaves the area.

(L) is usually just inside the halfway line for a possible development at midfield and in line with the side of the penalty-area so he can see the ball in relation to the line.

Corner-Kick

(T) assumes the duties of the Referee who is operating under the diagonal or modified diagonal system of control. He is the main official for calling fouls within the goal area. This is because (L) is diluted with:

- Ball in and out of play, particularly the outswinger.

- Off-side potential.

- A goal being scored (100% of ball in?)

- Encroachment, if it is a near side corner-kick.

(T) must come down to the vicinity of the penalty-area. If he doesn't come within 25 of his partners' goal-line, then he should not accept an assignment with the system.

Nearside Kick

(L) checks out ball placement, then . . .

- Is between intersection of goal-area and penalty-area line.

- Is approximately 1 foot behind the touch-line.

- As the ball is played, he pivots 180° on his inside foot following the flight of the ball and stepping into the field.

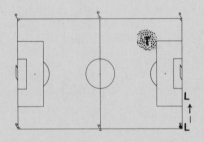

Farside Kick

(T) normally hates the farside corner-kick because it necessitates more running. He checks out ball placement, then moves back to his normal position, but not too close to the goal-area so as to get in the way of the kick.

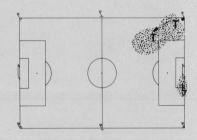

(L) is in similar position as the nearside kick; only after the ball is kicked, he moves a little closer to the goal and perhaps a step or two into the field.

A problem area (L) must be aware of is recovery in sufficient time in order to monitor the off-side.

Both officials should know where 10 yards in from the side-line is so they can cope automatically with attempted encroachment.

Penalty-Kick

The Referee who whistled the penalty immediately moves toward the penalty-spot, pointing at it. He then gives the signal for the type of foul.

Things to do before the penalty-kick can be taken:

- Everyone out of the penalty-area and penalty-arc.
- Correct ball positioning.
- Correct GK positioning.

(L) . . .

- Takes possession of the ball and makes sure that it is properly placed (either by himself or the kicker).
- Identifies the kicker to the GK.
- Makes sure GK is correctly positioned.
- Takes up position on the goal-line somewhere between the intersection of the goal-area and penalty-area lines.
- Gives the signal for the taking of the kick (after GK has indicated that he is ready).
- Watches for the ball entering the goal and GK foot movement (mostly forward/backward).

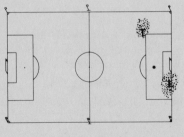

(T) . . .

- Clears out all but the kicker from the penalty-area and penalty-arc.
- Watches for encroachment and
- Lateral movement of the GK's feet.

291

Throw-Ins

On Opposite Touch-Line

If (**T**), try to be opposite the point of the throw-in. Come well into the field.

If (**L**), get downfield and well into the field of play.

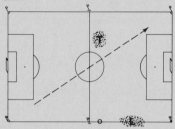 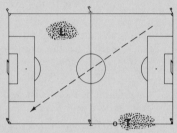

On Your Touch-Line

If (**L**), lead the throw by 10-20 yards. Stand either straddling or just outside of the touch-line.

If (**T**), be within 10 yards of the thrower, either straddling the touch-line or just inside the field of play.

Duties

If the throw is from the farside touch-line — be careful in whistling foul throw-ins. Try to limit your calls to those dealing with:

- Not starting from behind the head when the thrower presents his profile to you.

- Obviously releasing the ball from the side of the head.

. . . Otherwise call only the most *blatant* infractions when your partner is inattentive.

(**T**) has primary responsibility for seeing that the throw-in enters the field at the point it went out of bounds.

Free-Kicks

(**L**) is either even with the last-but-one defender for the possible off-side and in anticipation of the development of the play, or on the goal-line. As distance to the goal is shortened, he should move nearer to the goal for closer view.

(**T**) sees that the kick is properly taken. He places the ball if necessary.

The free-kick which results in the forming of a wall presents the Referee with one of his biggest challenges.

Important ingredients for the Referee are:

- Probability of a goal being scored.

- The wall being at least 10 yards back.

- Correct placement of the ball.

- Off-side monitoring.

292

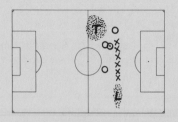

For kicks taken 20-35 yards out from the goal-line:

(T) comes up and monitors ball placement, and assists with pushing the wall back (if necessary).

(L) establishes the wall and monitors off-side.

Kicks taken within 20 yards of the goal-line are the really critical ones. Referees lacking diagonal experience seem to have a lot of trouble with this mechanic. Otherwise, they seem to instrinctively do it properly.

(L) pushes back the wall until (T) comes onto the scene, then he sprints to the end-line to check on the possible scoring of a goal (always top priority).

(T) makes sure that ball placement is OK. Re-pushes the wall back (if necessary) and stays on the wall for off-side monitoring.

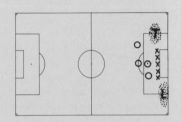

BEFORE, AT HALF, AND AFTER THE GAME

Before the Game

Each Referee identifies the captain and checks out all the players' equipment/apparel of either one or both teams together. The officials inspect field conditions together and verify measurements.

One official might be designated as the Senior Referee. The Senior Referee is responsible for the game report and has final say in matters of dispute. He overrules the other official only relative to interpretation of the laws of the game (not judgment calls). Conventionally he often is the one who delivers any pre-game instructions to the team captains, conducts the coin flips, and is the chief timekeeper.

At Half-Time

The Referee closest to the ball should pick it up. The two Referees run toward each other and then walk off the field together, retiring to an area which is away from players and spectators. The halftime interval should be used to discuss play during the first half and to make any adjustments deemed necessary.

After the Game

The closer Referee picks up the ball. The officials see that it is returned to its rightful owners. Both Referees then leave the field together.

Hint — At all times, avoid the temptation to explain a decision by your fellow Referee.

293

OTHER ASPECTS OF PLAY

Substitutions

New players enter at midfield. Each Referee has a team which reports to him (if required). During play he attempts to maintain a count of players on the team defending his goal as often as possible.

Drop-Ball

Usually conducted by (T). (L) generally only puts into play a drop ball if it is quite near his touch-line and relatively deep into his territory. (See Dynamically Switching Diagonals — on the next page.)

Timekeeping

Time is normally kept by the Senior Referee. His partner keeps backup time. Both Referees should flash the time to one another when it gets down to five or less minutes remaining in the period.

This time is indicated by the hand, using the Referee's black shorts as background. Each finger equals one minute. The closed fist means 30 seconds. To indicate that time has expired, the Referee Badge is covered.

If for some reason the prime timekeeper desires his partner to take over the timing responsibility, he indicates it by pointing from his watch to his partner. The partner acknowledges that he is now official timekeeper by first pointing to his own watch and then to himself.

Goalkeeper Fielding the Ball

Whenever the GK fields the ball, (T) lines up with the penalty-area line where he can observe steps as well as a possble handling of the ball in conjunction with the clearing punt/throw.

(L) is downfield in anticipating of a long clearing punt/throw by the GK (same position as for the goal-kick). He is particularly alert for possible off-side situations. (L) lines up with the *side* of the penalty-area whenever the GK if fielding a ball in that vicinity. This is done as a check in GK handling outside of the penalty-area.

Record Keeping

Scoring of Goals — The number of the player scoring each goal is recorded by the appropriate (L). This information is passed on to the other Referee as quickly as possible before the subsequent kick-off.

Cautions and Ejections — Whenever administered by a Referee, he immediately relays data regarding the number of the player to his partner.

Information relating to any Caution **MUST BE COMMUNICATED** to one's partner before the booking of the player can be considered complete. The partner who is not cautioning must take the majority of this responsibility.

Dynamically Switching Diagonals (For the Very Experienced Team Only)

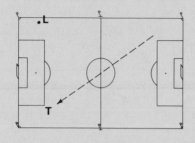

Occasionally a free-kick or a drop-ball occurs relatively deep into (**L**)'s territory near his touch-line. The three aspects which the Referee team must accomplish are correct: (1) ball placement, (2) location of the wall, and (3) position as goal judge.

For (**T**) to come all the way over to the other touch-line for administration or (1) and (2) is impractical, plus the added problem of having both officials on the same side of the field.

The well disciplines Referee team may choose to temporarily change diagonals to overcome this situation. To accomplish this, one of the Referees (usually **T**) signals his partner. (Crossing the index fingers of both hands back and forth accompanied with a vocal "switch" is an acceptable method.) Acceptance can be indicated by a nod of the head.

(**L**) now becomes (**T**). If it is a free-kick he is responsible for the wall and positioning of the ball. He then backpedals 10 to 15 yards to the position of a normal trailer. (**T**), who is now the new (**L**), moves down on the goal-line. The Referees change back whenever it is convenient (usually when the ball is out of play — throw-in, goal/corner-kick, etc.). Implementing this dynamic switching of diagonals requires both Referees being highly disciplined and continually having eye contact.

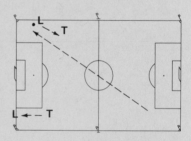

HINTS FOR REFEREES

1. Face the player throwing the ball in from the touch-line, without turning your back on players awaiting the throw-in.

2. Never instruct your partner to "stay out of *my* penalty-area." Rather, remind him that positioning and distance from play are the important factors in whistling under this system.

3. If you are alert, and fifty yards distant, you should be able to call an infraction that occurs in front of your partner, if you believe he was shielded.

4. Use hand signals for the advantage rule. Your partner will know you have seen a foul but have elected to let play continue.

5. Signal for the taking of an IFK especially if the ball went over the end-line. Your partner then knows that it isn't a goal-kick and that the opponents are vulnerable for being off-side.

6. When the Referee is in position for judging off-side, he must know *who* is between him and the touch-line.

7. Practice and be proficient at running backwards quickly.

8. Stay out of the penalty-area as much as possible. When you are there, you are vulnerable to being hit by a surprise shot on goal, and also are in a poor position to call off-side.

9. When a penalty-kick is called by either Referee, the two Referees must act together to administer the penalty. (L) whistles for the kick and acts as goal judge. (T) watches for encroachments and other violations.

Note: The Two Referee System is *recommended* by high school rules. It is mandatory for college.

MASTER SHEET – TWO REFEREES

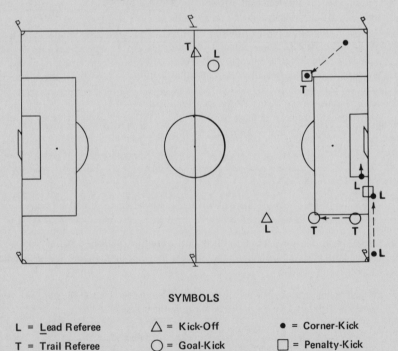

SYMBOLS

L = <u>L</u>ead Referee   △ = Kick-Off   ● = Corner-Kick

T = <u>T</u>rail Referee   ○ = Goal-Kick   ☐ = Penalty-Kick

THE MODIFIED DIAGONAL (MOD)

"The ultimate system for game control, flexibility, and training."

In June 1973, Joe Bonchonsky of Torrance, California conceptualized a new system of soccer officiating. Here are his words indicating the need for such a system:

"The advances on the state-of-the-art in tactics and techniques by the highly skilled, finely tuned player and the professionally-educated coach has placed soccer into the modern-day world of science. The inner game of soccer has advanced tremendously and today 'total soccer' is coming into being. While players and coaches have advanced because of their own unbridled ingenuity, the Referee remains in the archaic times of soccer systems and the big question is 'How long will the sport of soccer be able to live with the old system of refereeing?' The attacking fullback and the quickening pace of the game has outraced the efficiency of one whistle. Modern day technology and its cameras have too often found the Referee allowing the injustices on the field prevailing over the efforts and artistry of better skilled players and coaches. The success of soccer in the future may be fully dependent upon the quality and efficiency of the Referee. With the MOD, the artists on the field will actually experience less whistling, knowing that the guilty will be punished and that his skills can be exhibited.

Bonchonsky, a Referee, originally termed the system "Three Referees on the Field." In 1976 the name was subsequently changed to the Modified Diagonal (MOD) through a suggestion by Bill Mason of Palos Verdes, California, but its principles remain somewhat the same. The system has been used in a variety of settings. It has been used for pre-season games by local NASL teams, in the largest and best known high school tournament in California, and for the past 5 years has been the exclusive means of officiating within the Los Angeles Municipal Soccer League with its major and minor division adult club teams.

More than ever, the system emphasizes the "team" effort in refereeing. The three Referees, all with whistles, must fully cooperate to benefit from the advantages of the system. The Middle Referee, in placing full responsibility with the Wing Referees, will have added control in those areas near the middle of the field where the game takes place and where the majority of incidents occur. Wing Referees are fully aware of their usual duties involving goal-line decisions, off-side, and out-of-bounds. Fouls that may not be seen by the Referee are called, in that same way that flags are used to signal fouls in the traditional Diagonal System.

The whistle in the hand of the Wing Referee means that the game is stopped when it should be; when an infraction occurs. Also, the Middle Referee will be able to concentrate on the important aspects of play without the worry: "What's happening when I'm glancing for my Linesmen?"

The vast majority of Referees who have used MOD have experienced a lessening of fouls, fewer off-side problems, less dissent, and a general acceptance by players, coaches and spectators.

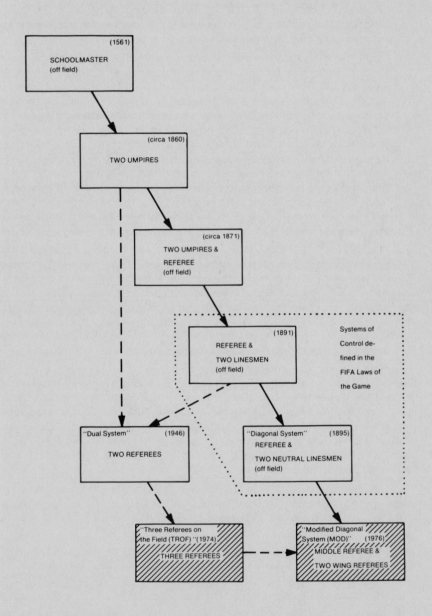

SCHOOLMASTER
(off field)
(1561)

TWO UMPIRES
(circa 1860)

TWO UMPIRES &
REFEREE
(off field)
(circa 1871)

REFEREE &
TWO LINESMEN
(off field)
(1891)

Systems of
Control de-
fined in the
FIFA Laws of
the Game

"Dual System"
TWO REFEREES
(1946)

"Diagonal System"
REFEREE &
TWO NEUTRAL LINESMEN
(off field)
(1895)

"Three Referees on
the Field (TROF)"(1974)
THREE REFEREES

"Modified Diagonal
System (MOD)"   (1976)
MIDDLE REFEREE &
TWO WING REFEREES

298

MOD may be used in a variety of ways.

1. It may be used like a dual system of control plus one. In this mode all officials can and do perform all functions on an equal basis. This suggests not only equivalent ability of all three officials but also a high degree of teamwork.

2. It can be used as an extreme "Referee-Linesman" relationship wherby the wing officials give weak support. . . . calling out-of-bounds, off-sides, and fouls only when they are positive that the middle Referee did not see it. They hug the touch-line and don't dare venture beyond the halfway line. In this mode the wing Referees do not caution or eject, but rather call the misconduct to the attention of the middle Referee.

3. The system might be performed as a mix of the above two approaches. It all depends upon the personnel . . . their abilities and their rapport with one another.

The training of new officials can be accomplished by one of two different means. One way is to put the trainee in the center, flanked by two experienced 'dual oriented' Referees who will carry him. He gets the feel of the game and participates to the degree that he feels comfortable.

The other alternative is to have one or even two trainees on the wing flanking a Referee experienced in the diagonal system of control. He takes over and the wing(s) call out-of-bounds and off-side and increase their participation as they grow into their refereeing role.

The authors feel that the MOD system is the answer to modern day soccer officiating and should be very seriously considered by all Referees and soccer organizers.

BASIC COVERAGE

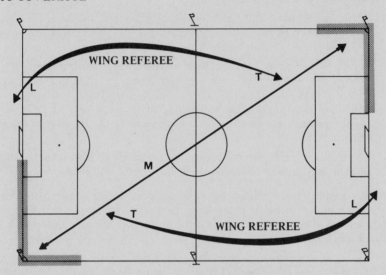

M = Middle Referee. He runs on the diagonal.

The Wing Referees. They are located on the nearside and the farside of the field. One is designated *Lead* Referee (**L**) and the other as *Trail* Referee (**T**). These roles change instantaneously depending upon the direction of play.

OUT OF BOUNDS

One of the weaknesses of other Referee systems is coverage of the coffin corners (ends of the diagonal). This area is partially bounded by the last 18 yards of the touch-line and along the goal-line between the goal-post and the quarter-circle. (▬▬▬▬). Close cooperation between the three officials can somewhat alleviate this condition.

Each Wing Referee (as do linesmen in the diagonal system or two Referees in the dual system) still has prime responsibility for the exact instant the whole of the ball crosses his goal-line or the touch-line on his side of the field.

(**M**) has a strong secondary responsibility for the trouble areas (▬▬▬▬). Because there are three Referees on the field, he is able to penetrate deeper into the corners without worrying about a sudden counter-attack. Whenever he is in a favorable position for judging out-of-bounds in these areas (throw-in and goal/corner-kick) he immediately indicates it. (**L**) and (**T**) are very unlikely to indicate a condition opposite to him because (**M**) is always within their line of sight of the ball.

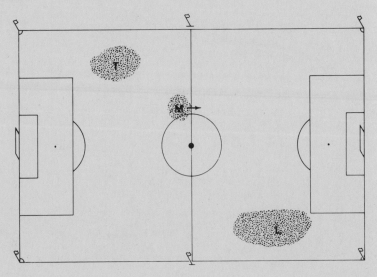

(M) whistles for the kickoff. He stands at the halfway line closest to his corner diagonal. His position allows him to determine:

Ball being kicked forward.

Ball traveling its circumference.

Offense/Defense in own half of the field.

Defensive encroachment into the center circle.

(L) is approximately 5 to 10 yards from the touch-line and equidistant between the halfway line and the Penalty-Area. He is in position to monitor play as well as conveniently pick up the offensive players.

(T) is 5 to 10 yards in from the touch-line and about 35 yards out from the goal-line. He is tracking closely enough to effectively monitor play, yet has a sufficient margin of safety to keep up with offensive players should a counter-attack suddenly develop.

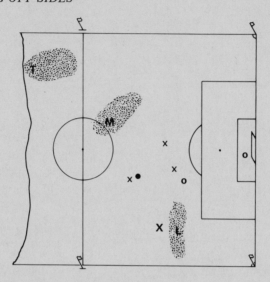

(M) stays up with play along his diagonal. He normally concentrates upon fouls and other types of infractions.

(L) actively monitors off-side usually by staying in-line with either the most-advanced wing or second-to-last defender.

The Wing Referee should not have a player between himself and the touch-line.

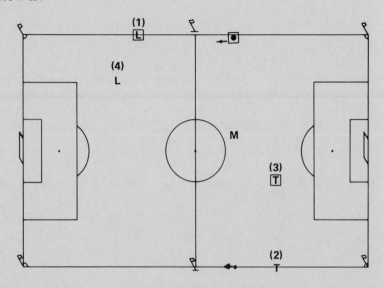

When the Ball Goes Out-of-Bounds in the Middle 40 Yards of the Field

(M) is positioned directly opposite the point where the ball went out of bounds. He makes sure the thrower does not crab along the touch-line. He is in an ideal position to observe the ball coming directly over the head and being delivered equally with both hands.

Nearside Throw-In (On Your Touch-Line)

If (L) – One foot outside the touch-line approximately 15 to 20 yards downfield (if possible. (1)

If (T) – Straddle touch-line within 10 to 40 yards of the thrower. (2) It all depends upon how close the throw is to (M) and his diagonal.

All of the thrower should be watched. Special attention is directed toward feet position, and the onset/culmination of the delivery.

Farside Throw-In

If (T) – Concentrate on play on the field. (3)

If (L) – Downfield from the throw and well into the field of play, waiting for possible off-side after ball has been played. (4)

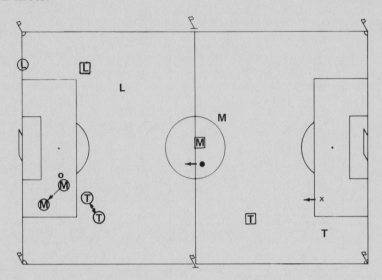

The Referee whistling the infraction immediately points to where the foul was committed and the direction for the kick to be taken. This should be followed by the signal for the type of offense. (The symbol for the ball is either x, o, ●.)

x *Defensive kicks* taken within the vicinity of ones own PA.

    T Administers the kick.*
    M Moves his diagonal downfield.
    L Actively monitors for off-side.

o *Offensive kicks* taken within the vicinity of the opponents PA.

    Ⓜ Administers the kick, then gets in line with the wall for off-side.
    Ⓛ On the goal-line to judge a possible goal.
    Ⓣ Comes up behind the ball and assists Ⓜ in kick administration (if necessary). As the kick is being taken, he retreats in anticipation of the counter-attack.

● *All other situations*

    M̅ Administers the kick.
    L̅ Is downfield actively monitoring off-sides.
    T̅ Watches the field of play in general.

---

*Administering the kick consists of . . .

- Verification that the ball is correctly placed.
- Placement of players 10 yards from the ball, or on their own goal-line between the posts.
- Giving of the signal (if applicable) for the taking of the kick.

GOAL-KICK

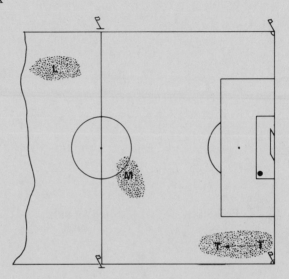

(T) checks for correct placement in goal-area then rapidly moves opposite the front of the PA to ensure that the ball leaves the area.

(M) is in the vicinity of the center circle in preparation for the result of the kick. He shades his position toward the side of the goal-area that the kick is coming from.

(L) is behind the halfway line and in from the touch-line so as to be in line with the side of the PA (10 yards — on the average) to see the ball in relation to the line.

CORNER-KICK

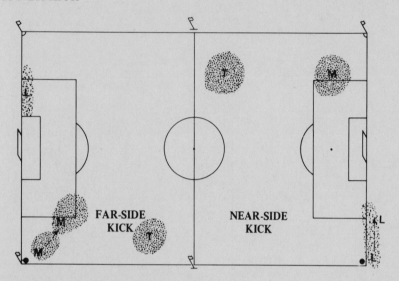

FAR-SIDE KICK   NEAR-SIDE KICK

Nearside Kick (For the Lead Referee)

(**L**) checks the placement of the ball within the quarter-circle, then moves to slightly behind the goal-line and 10 yards in from the corner-area to monitor encroachment. He concentrates upon the flight of the ball.

(**M**) is on the far side of the PA approximately level with the penalty-spot. He is watching for jostling and obstruction within the Goal/Penalty area.

(**T**) comes down and crosses the halfway line about 10 yards from both the touch-line and halfway line.

Farside Kick (For the Lead Referee)

(**M**) checks placement of the ball within the quarter circle, then moves to the position he occupied for the nearside kick. He gives the signal for the kick.

(**L**) is in essentially the same position as the nearside kick except he has now come into the field by 1 to 20 yards.

(**T**) comes down to a point somewhere between the halfway line and the near corner of the PA.

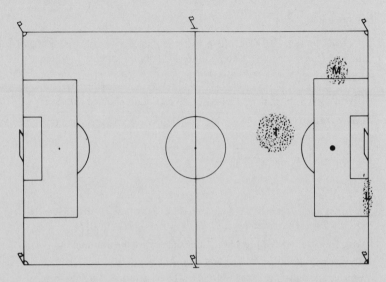

(M) retains possession of the ball until the penalty-area is cleared of all players except the kicker and the goalkeeper. He facilitates the duties of (L) and (T). He identifies who will be the kicker and informs the GK. He retires to his position on the side of the PA in line with the Penalty-Spot. When he receives the signal from (L) that the GK is ready and properly positioned on the line, he then whistles for the kick to be taken, and monitors for encroachment.

(T) clears out players from within the PA (if necessary) and the penalty-kick-arc. He then takes up a position at the rear of the penalty-kick-arc. He has both kicker and GK within his line of sight. He is particularly attentive to lateral movement of the GK.

(L) is responsible for seeing that the GK's feet are positioned correctly on the goal-line. He then goes to his position on the goal-line equidistant between the side of the goal-area and the penalty-area. He judges forward and backwards movement of the GK's feet and whether the ball properly crossed the goal-line. He signals for the goal, but only after first checking with (T) on GK movement and with (M) for encroachment.

MISCELLANEOUS

Before the Game

(L) and (T) each check out the players' equipment/apparel of a different team. All three Referees inspect field conditions and verify measurements together.

(M) delivers any necessary pre-game instructions to the captains.

Designates which teams will report to which Referees for substitution.

Conducts the coin flip.

Is the main timekeeper.

Is responsible for the game report.

Record Keeping

Cautions and Ejections — Administered by any of the three Referees, but, whenever possible, by (M). If given by . . .

(M) — Both (L) and (T) go toward him and receive the information.

(L) or (T) — (M) goes toward him and receives the information. The other side Referee goes near (M)'s original position. (M) then returns and relays the data.

Scoring of Goals — The number of the player scoring each goal is recorded by the appropriate (L). This information is passed immediately on to (M).

Substitutions

Enter at midfield. Each wing Referee has a team which reports to him. During play he attempts to maintain a count of players on his team as often as possible.

Simultaneous Whistles

The closest Referee immediately points in the proper direction.

If the two Referees point in opposite directions, (M) immediately signals *both* infractions then points in the proper direction or gives a drop-ball if they are equal infractions. This should not happen if the Referee who is farther away waits for the decision of the near Referee.

Drop Ball

(M) conducts the majority of drop-balls.

(L) and (T) observe play within their areas. The wing Referees generally only put into play a drop-ball that is in their immediate vicinity near the touch-line. If this is done by a (L), then (M) must get into position for actively monitoring off-sides.

GK Fielding the Ball

(T) is near the corner of his PA where he observes GK steps and a possible handball in conjunction with the clearing punt/throw.

(M) is in the vicinity of the center circle. He is the prime official responsible for monitoring GK steps.

(L) is in line with the side of the PA on his side of the field whenever the GK is attempting to field a ball in that vicinity.

Discipline

If a minor altercation develops between two players the nearest Referee handles it. Play doesn't necessarily have to be stopped because he is secure in the knowledge that both his partners can control the game in the interim.

In an extreme discipline case on the field where large-scale fighting or other disruptive acts take place, (M) attempts to head-up the action, and the wing Referees record events.

MASTER SHEET – THREE REFEREES

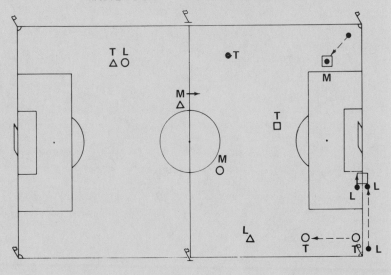

SYMBOLS

M - Middle Referee

L = Lead Referee

T = Trail Referee

△ = Kick-Off

○ = Goal-Kick

● = Corner-Kick

□ = Penalty-Kick

309

Oto Maxmilian

The match should be officiated according to the conditions of play.

YOUTH SOCCER RULES – The American Youth Soccer Organization

The American Youth Soccer Organization (AYSO) began in September 1964, and initiated competition in January 1965, with nine teams. In the 1977-1978 season, more than 9000 teams and 130,000 players in 21 states carried on the tradition of the "Everyone Plays" philosophy.

The philosophy of AYSO includes full participation, and each player plays a minimum of one-half a game, regardless of ability. AYSO has realistically addressed itself to the requirements of youth soccer, and the rules below are highly recommended for youth soccer organizations throughout America.

Players are divided into six age groups for boys' competition, and four for girl's play. Age is determined as of December 31 of the year of competition.

DUTIES AND RESPONSIBILITIES OF COACHES AND OFFICIALS

1. It shall be the duty of each coach and official to:
   a. Conduct himself in a manner becoming a member of AYSO.
   b. At all times encourage clean competition and good sportsmanship.
   c. Train and coach their respective team to the best of their ability.
   d. Enforce the Rules and Regulations of AYSO.
   e. Participate in positive coaching that instructs and encourages players during AYSO games. Negative comments and complaints about refereeing shall not be allowed.
   f. Coaching is restricted to two coaches at the sideline area between the two penalty-areas.

REGISTRATION, DURATION, OVERTIME, SIZE OF BALL

Boys Division	Age Player Must be Under As of 31 Dec.	Girls Division	Law VII. Duration of The Game	Playoff Game Overtime Periods	Law II. The Ball
I	19	I	80 min.	10 min.	No. 5
II	17		70 min.	9 min.	26.5−28 inch circum. 14−16 oz.
	16	II	60 min.		
III	15				
IV	13	III	50 min.	8 min.	No. 4 25−26.5 inch circum. 12−14 oz.
V	11				
	10	IV	40 min.	7 min.	No. 3 13.5−25 inch circum. 9−12 oz.
VI	9				

Half-time is
5-10 min.

SUBSTITUTION

All registered players in attendance at League and AYSO playoff games must participate and play at least half of the game, *excluding overtime*.

Such participation is controlled as follows:

1. Halfway through the first half, and halfway through the second half, during a normal stoppage of play, the Referee halts the game, stops his watch and notes on lineup sheets those players substituting. Stoppage is made when the ball is out of play, such as during a throw-in, corner-kick, goal-kick, following a goal, or before a free-kick is to be taken. Additionally, substitutions may be made at halftime.

2. Respective coaches of each team may substitute any players or none during such interruptions, as long as, at game's end, all players have been substituted.

CORNER-KICKS

Corner-Kicks — Boys' 6th Division and Girls' 4th Division shall be taken from the intersection of the goal-line and the corner of the penalty-area nearest to where the ball crossed the goal-line.

CHARGING THE GOALIE

Charging the goalie shall not be permitted in the penalty-area, nor shall the goalie be harrassed or interfered with while attempting to put the ball into play.

DROP-BALLS

In the event that play has been stopped with the ball in the penalty-area, and the FIFA rules call for play to be resumed with a drop-ball, the game shall be restarted with a drop-ball being taken at the closest point outside the penalty-area.

312

FIELD OF PLAY

Dimensions, the field of play, marking, goal-area, penalty-area, corner-area, and goals will be at the discretion of the particular Region, except where the field is used as the home field during the AYSO championship playoff games.

On open fields, where most youth games are played, the field shall be marked — where possible — with a spectator-control-line parallel to the touch-line (side-line) at a distance of at least three (3) yards from the touch-line. All coaches, Referees, linesmen, and other league officials are asked to ensure that spectators remain behind this line.

IN ALL PLAYOFF GAMES:

1. A minimum of seven (7) players shall constitute a team.

2. In case of conflicting colors, the designated home team shall change uniforms.

3. Failure of both teams to be ready at kick-off shall constitute a double forfeiture and their respective opponents for the next round shall receive a bye.

4. Properly completed lineup forms shall be presented to the Referee prior to the start of the game and shall include the names of all players, present or not, and an explanation of absences.

5. Games shall be played as scheduled and only the Referee in charge or Regional Commissioner shall have authority to cancel such games.

6. In case of a tie at the end of regulation time, *sudden victory overtime* shall be played as follows: 6th Division Boys and 4th Division Girls — two (2), seven (7) minute periods; 4th and 5th Division Boys and 3rd Division Girls — two (2), eight (8) minute periods; 2nd and 3rd Division Boys and 2nd Division Girls — two (2) nine (9) minute periods; 1st Division Boys and 1st Division Girls — two (2) ten (10) minute periods. The first team to score a goal during the *sudden vicotry overtime* shall be declared the winner.

    If a team is playing short because of ejections, they will continue to play short during the *sudden victory overtime.*

7. In case of a tie following *sudden victory overtime*, the winner shall be determined by kicks from the penalty-mark as follows: each team shall alternately take five (5) kicks at the same goal (goal to be chosen by the Referee). Each one of the kicks will be taken by a different player, the team scoring the most goals being declared the winner. If still tied, additional series of five (5) kicks shall be taken (using five (5) different players from the first five (5), until all players are used) until a winner has been determined. The goal-keeper may be changed after any kick.

    All (and only) the players on the field at the termination of the *sudden victory overtime* periods may take the kicks.

8. All Star players must compete only in the division in which they participated during the regular season.

HIGH SCHOOL DIFFERENCES FROM FIFA

1. FIELD OF PLAY

Length — 100 yards to 120 yards.

Width — 55 yards to 75 yards.

Penalty-Kick Line — 2 feet long.

Goal lines are called end lines except for the portion between the goal posts.

An improperly marked Penalty-Area will remain. The home team coach is to be notified so it will not exist in future games.

Corner-flags — May not be removed.

Nets should extend backward approximately 24 inches level with the cross-bar.

Special areas — Marked with a dashed line and 5 yards back of touch-line (minimum).

A coaching area is 20 yards long. It begins 10 yards from the halfway-line. The official area extends 5 yards on each side of the halfway-line (total 10 yards).

When teams are placed on opposite sides of the field, the coaching areas shall extend 10 yards on either side of the halfway-line.

Spectators are not allowed to be behind or within 10 yards of the goal.

2. THE BALL

Leather or similar material which is *weather resistant*.

The home team provides 3 or more of like, legal game balls. If not, the Referee chooses game balls from those offered by both teams.

When dropped from 100 inches onto a cement floor, it should rebound from 60-65 inches.

3. THE PLAYERS

A game may not be started with less than 11 players.

There is no limit to the amount of substitutes. They may be made during stoppage from:

Goal-Kick
Corner-Kick
Ejection
Caution (only for the cautioned player — opposing team may sub a like number)
Between periods
After a goal
Injury (only for the injured player — opposing team may sub a like number)
Throw-In (only in possession)

Repeated substitutions to consume time — Referee may order the clock stopped. If repeat, IFK from where the ball was.

GK changes places with another player. If there is no notification of the Referee — IFK when the ball is handled by the non-reporting GK.

A disqualified player may not play in the next game.

314

4. PLAYERS' EQUIPMENT

It is recommended that the home team wear a light colored shirt and the visitors wear dark colored shirts.

Numbers must be different, worn on the back, and at least 6 inches in height. If not, FORFEIT.

Numbers on front must be 4 inches high.

Numbers are required (except for GK). If not, FORFEIT.

Referee examination of a players' equipment prior to the game being started is mandatory.

Casts (even if padded) are not allowed.

Jewelry may not be worn.

Studs on shoes may not project more than 1/2 inch.

Shoes may not be metal tipped nor have metal cleats.

Female players must wear shin guards.

5. REFEREES

There shall be 2 Referees (one Referee is used only during an emergency).

Referees change sides at halftime, they must dress alike.

He notifies the timekeeper of all Referee called time-outs.

Signals must be given on all fouls. Signals are the same as those in the appendix except:

Direct Free-Kick	— 1 arm forward underarm swing.
Indirect Free-Kick	— Both arms in forward underarm swing.

Suspended game due to unforseen conditions
    If 1/2 or more of the game has been played — It is a complete game.
    If less than 1/2 of the game has been played — Reschedule.

Megaphones, bullhorns, etc. are not permitted as coaching aids..

The coach may approach the Referee if done in a couteous manner.

Coaching from outside the coaching area is not permitted.
    1st offense — WARN
    2nd offense — CAUTION & IFK

If the coach comes onto the field and refuses to leave, a time limit is set by the Referee for him to leave. Non-compliance means forfeit.

If the coach is ejected, and no assistant coach is available, the game is forfeited.

If a team is mre than 30 minutes late without notifying the opponents of the emergency — FORFEIT.

Any physical or verbal attack on an official must be reported to the state high school association.

6. LINEJUDGES

The home team provides at least 2 ball holders.

If there is just one Referee, it is recommended that there be a minimum of two Linejudges who call out of bounds only. The Referee selects the Linejudges.

7. DURATION OF THE GAME/LENGTH OF PERIODS

Two equal periods of 40 minutes each (or four 20 minute quarters if approved by the state high school association). Overtime — Two periods of 5 minutes *may* be played as per league directive.

Interval between quarters
>1st & 2nd, 3rd & 4th, 1st & 2nd overtime periods — Maximum of 2 minutes for changing ends.
>4th period & overtime — 5 minutes
>Haltime — 10 minutes

The above may be shrotened by mutual agreement of the coaches or by order of the Referee, if done before the start of period.

Time-out
>For the taking of a penalty-kick
>Following the scoring of a goal
>When a caution or ejection is given

8. START OF PLAY

The 2nd kick-off violation — IFK.

Temporary suspension — Injury or unusual situation.
>If one team clearly is in possession — IFK.
>If neither team has possession — DROP-BALL.

Drop-Ball
>Dropped at waist level.
>Must be done between two opposing players. (GK can't be one of them.)
>The 2nd violation on the drop-ball — IFK.
>Can't be taken within the penalty-area — Go to nearest point outside the PA.
>A drop-ball resulting from going out of bounds is taken 5 yards from the touch-line.

9. IN AND OUT OF PLAY

The Referee will whistle whenever the ball is out of play.

A second whistle is given after a substituttion, and a PK.

12. FOULS AND MISCONDUCT

The terms warning and caution are interchangeable.

Dangerous play usually results in a caution. (Ejection is possible.)

A sliding tackle is legal when it is made within normal peripheral vision. If not — DIRECT/PENALTY.

The act of moving the hands or arms to protect oneself and making contact with the ball is *intentional* handling. (Except for females who instinctively protect the breast area.)

Goalkeeper

> Any charge of the GK other than when he obstructs (non-intentional) – DIRECT.
> Intentionally charging the GK – DIRECT and EJECT.
> He is considered to be in possession and no one can attempt to play the ball when:
>> Throwing it in the air so he can catch it.
>> Boucing the ball.

13. FREE-KICK

IFK

> Hitch-kick within 6 feet of an opponent.
>
> Persistent coaching from outside the coach's box.
>
> At the point a *coach* makes an unauthorized field entry . . . or at the point the ball was. Penalize whichever is the more severe.

14. PENALTY-KICK

Encroachment and other infringements do not result in an automatic CAUTION. An infringement by the player taking the kick during a penalty-kick results in an IFK from the penalty-spot.

17. CORNER-KICK

The corner-flag post must not be removed.

18. TIMEKEEPERS AND SCORERS

Timekeepers

> One official timer from each school.
>
> The Referee shall designate the official timer.
>
> Time may be kept on a scoreboard by mutual agreement of the coaches.
>
> The last 10 seconds of each period shall be audibly called out. Must say where the ball is and which team last played the ball at the exact end of each period.

Scorers

> One scorer from each team.
>
> Must have teams lineup five minutes prior to game time.
>
> Records all disqualified (ejected) players.

19. FORFEITURE AND TIE GAMES

The Referee shall declare a forfeit:

> If the coach is disqualified (Rule 5-3, Article 2) and no other school faculty representative assumes coaching responsibilities.
>
> A team refuses to play after being instructed to do so.
>
> Gross misconduct by a team or its followers.
>
> Team is more than 30 minutes late without giving prior notification.
>
> Uniforms do not meet the proper standards.
>
> A team has fewer than 7 eligible playeers.

A forfeit is 1-0 unless the winning team is ahead, then the actual score stands.

COLLEGE DIFFERENCES FROM FIFA

1. THE FIELD AND EQUIPMENT

The field of play

Length 110 to 120 yards.

Width 65 to 75 yards.

Penalty-Kick Line = 2 feet long. Kicks may be taken from any position on the line.

Corner-flags may not be removed. Football style corner-flags or pylons may be used for artificial surfaces.

Nets should extend backward two feet level with the cross-bar.

Goal posts and cross-bars are to be between 4-5 inches and must be painted white.

Team benches and timers' tables — Should be on the same side of the field and at least 15 feet from the side lines.

The ball

Must be made of leather and all balls must be of the same make.

When dropped from 100 inches onto a cement floor, it should rebound from 60 to 65 inches.

Players' equipment

Home team wears white or light colored jersey — Visiting team wears colored jersey.

Numbers on back are mandatory — Minimum height is 6 inches.

Numbers at least 4 inches in height must be worn on the front.

Equipment must be inspected prior to the beginning of the game.

2. PLAYERS AND SUBSTITUTES

A match may continue with less than 7 players.

Substitutes

7 substitutes are permitted. (More are allowed only by special league arrangements.)

Unlimited resubstitution is allowed.

Must first report to the scoring table.

If violate the substitution rule — IFK where the ball was.

An ejected player may be replaced unless for physically assaulting a Referee.

Substitutions on . . .
- Goal-kick and Corner-kick
- After a goal
- Between periods
- Injury (Only the injured player(s) can be replaced.)
- Cautions (Only the cautioned player)

Whenever there is substitution for an injury or caution, the opponents can replace a like number.

318

3. OFFICIALS AND THEIR DUTIES

Referees

The two Referee system is mandatory.

They shall dress alike.

Timekeeper is notified for all time-outs and the players to be credited with goals and assists are confirmed.

All fouls must be signaled. Signals are the same as those in the appendix except that the IFK is both arms in a forward underarm swing.

Red and yellow cards must be used for cautions (called warnings) and ejections.

Forfeit if a coach prolongs a discussion with an official or refuses to leave the field.

Ball Persons

Home team provides two who will carry an extra ball and will act as ball retrievers.

They are to be instructed by and are under the direct supervision of the Referees.

Timekeepers

The official timer is designated by the home team.

Referee instructs timer of duties.

He stops the clock when signaled by the Referee, after a goal, and for a penalty-kick.

He signals Referee when a substitution is to be made.

He notifies the nearest official audibly of a countdown of the last 10 seconds of playing time of any period.

He notifies the Referee and teams 2 minutes in advance of the start of the second half.

4. TIME FACTORS, PLAY AND SCORING

Time factors

Half-time interval — Maximum of 10 minutes (no minimum) unless consent by Referee and both coaches.

If the game is tied, two extra points of 10 minutes each are to be played. Ends of the field are changed without a retossing of the coin.

Ball in and out of play

Whistle is blown when the ball crosses the goal-line or side-line.

No drop-balls in the Penalty-Area. (Nearest point outside the PA.)

Scoring

A forfeit game is 1-0.

6. VIOLATIONS AND MISCONDUCT

Goalkeeper privileges and violations

Goalkeeper is considered to be in possession (ball can't be played) when he is bouncing the ball with his hand and also when he drops the ball for a kick.

Intentionally charging the goalkeeper who has possession of the ball — DIRECT and EJECT.

Misconduct

Dangerous play usually results in a CAUTION. If bad enough, EJECT.

Caution of a non-participant results in an IFK where the ball was.

Team caution for 10 yard encroachment on free-kicks and deliberate hand ball.

Coaching must be *verbal*, directed towards one's own team, done without aids, and confined to the immediate bench area. If violate — CAUTION. A repetition results in IFK where the ball was.

Dangerous Play

Hitch-kick within 6 yards of an oncoming opponent.

7. AWARDED KICKS AND THE THROW-IN

Free-kicks

IFK

- A substitution made at an improper time — where the ball was.
- Unauthorized field entry — where the ball was.
- Illegal coaching — the second time — where the ball was.

Penalty-kick

Encroachments and other infringements do not result in automatic cautions.

Corner-kick

The whole of the ball does not have to be within the corner-circle.

TIMEKEEPER INSTRUCTIONS (COLLEGE)

Duration of game

Two 45 minute periods

Halftime interval

Maximum of 10 minutes

Stop the clock

After a goal	For the Taking of a Penalty-Kick	When Signaled by the Referee

Goal	Penalty-Kick	Time-Out

Start the clock

Kickoff — After the ball has traveled its circumference. (Not by the whistle)

After a Referee stoppage — When the ball is put into play.

When the half or the game is about to end

Notify the nearest Referee audibly with a countdown for the last ten seconds. . .

"Ten . . . Nine . . . Eight . . . . Zero"

Substitution

Notify the nearest Referee. Occurrence . . .

Goal-Kick

Corner-Kick

After a goal

Between periods

Injury

Caution

Paper work

Record all goals and assists — Referee will confirm.

Cautions and Ejections — Reported to timekeeper by Referees between periods and at game's end.

321

THE TIMEKEEPER

The Americanization of certain soccer laws has brought about some difficulties for the experienced Referee who is used to being sole timekeeper on the field.

College Rule 3 requires one timekeeper to be designated from the home school. Unfortunately, this timekeeper is seldom experienced in timing and is unfamiliar with Referee mechanics of signaling. It is therefore advisable to meet the timekeeper before the start of the game to discuss the particulars of his task.

He should be notified that his chief task is to watch the Referee and not to enjoy the game. He must remember the three important signals for (1) a goal, (2) Time Out and (3) the awarding of a penalty-kick. Moreover, he should know when substitutes may be made.

The conscientious Referee should time the game himself, even though his watch is not official. He should tell the timekeeper that he is doing so, but he will communicate discrepancies only if they are great.

The college timekeeper instruction sheet (previous page) is recommended as a hand-out to the timekeeper. Its presence helps establish the authority of the Referee.

Similar sheets for high school rules (Rule 18) may be made, with changes for duration of periods and other differences.

One of the requirements of the college and high school timekeeper is to count down the final 10 seconds of a period. Before the game, the Referee should recommend the use of a megaphone to the timekeeper. This is to help facilitate matters particularly if there is a large noisy crowd and/or the play may be near a goal.

☆★☆★☆★☆★☆★☆★☆★☆★☆★☆★☆★☆★☆★

In any stoppage of the game, you should be the first one ready to resume play. Never hold up the game for your personal convenience.

☆★☆★☆★☆★☆★☆★☆★☆★☆★☆★☆★☆★☆★

UNITED STATES SOCCER FEDERATION
National Referee Development Program

In 1975, the United States Soccer Federation began a major Referee development program to upgrade standards of soccer officiating and to recruit Referees to handle the greatly increased number of soccer games occurring in the United States. The core of this program has been the USSF organizational rules adopted at that time which created a basic administrative structure headed by a Referee Committee having extensive authority to train, grade, and administer soccer officials. The Referee Committee has established five different grades of Referees with standard certification criteria for each grade. The USSF Referee rules, Referee grades, and certification criteria for the Referee grades are contained in the following appendix. These materials are being provided by the USSF through its Referee development program which is designed to train and assess soccer officials at all levels in the FIFA Laws of the Game so that uniformity of interpretation can be achieved for the benefit of all soccer games.

–Don Phillipson
Chairman, Referee Committee

USSF REFEREE COMMITTEE — REFEREE GRADES

In order to provide uniform standards for soccer Referees in the United States, the USSF Referee Committee has adopted the five Referee grades listed below. These grades supercede all grades which have previously been adopted by state associations and leagues so that uniform and comparative grading exists throughout the United States.

1. *USSF Referee Trainee*

   a. Minimum Age: None

   b. Badge: USSF Referee (White — 2")

   c. Competence Level: Beginning Referee for novice youth games

2. *USSF Youth Referee (Class 1 and Class 2)*

   a. Minimum Age: None

   b. Badges: USSF Youth Referee (Light Blue — 4") for Referees under 19; USSF Referee (Blue — 4") for Referees 19 and over

   c. Competence Level: All youth games

3. *USSF State Referee (Class 1 and Class 2)*

   a. Minimum Age: 19 years

   b. Badge: USSF State Referee (Gold — 4")

   c. Competence Level: All youth games and all senior amateur games except inter-state games in senior national competitions

4. *USSF National Referee (Class 1 and Class 2)*

   a. Minimum Age: 19 years

   b. Badge: USSF National Referee (Red — 4"); Brass Pin "USSF National Referee"

   c. Competence Level: All games except formal FIFA international matches

5. *USSF FIFA Referee*

   a. Minimum Age: 19 years

   b. Badge: FIFA or USSF National Referee; FIFA Pin

   c. Competence Level: All games

   d. Citizenship: U.S. Citizenship required (USSF Rule 1209)

The USSF grade and class of an official will be determined solely by the standards and examinations issued by the USSF Referee Committee. Annual re-examinations will be required.

CERTIFICATION CRITERIA FOR USSF REFEREE GRADES

In general, the criteria for certification of Referees at each different grade are divided into four categories: experience, physical fitness, written examination, and field assessment. The requirements in each of these categories differ with each grade. In addition, if a Referee fails the written examination, the entire written examination must be retaken after a minimum waiting period. Special instructions describing the physical fitness tests are summarized at the end of the certification criteria described below.

1. CERTIFICATION CRITERIA FOR USSF REFEREE TRAINEE

NOTE: The philosophy behind the Referee Trainee designation is to give official recognition and encouragement to the many volunteer Referees for youth games.

a. EXPERIENCE

No experience required.

b. PHYSICAL FITNESS

No physical fitness tests required.

c. FIELD ASSESSMENT

No field assessment required.

d. WRITTEN EXAMINATION

Overall minimum score required.

e. RETAKE

A person failing the written examination may not take it again for at least *two weeks.*

2. CERTIFICATION CRITERIA FOR USSF YOUTH REFEREE

a. EXPERIENCE

NOTE: The number of games listed is for the person serving as the Referee in the FIFA three person system. TWO games serving as a Referee in the two person system may be counted as ONE game below, except at least 1/5 the number of games listed must actually be as the Referee in the three person system.

	YOUTH CLASS 2	YOUTH CLASS 1
(1) **Minimum Career Games at Designated Level**	20	100
(2) **Level of Games**	All Levels (high school and college games	All Levels (high school and college games included) Serving as linesman on Senior Game counts as one game.
(3) **Special Requirements**		Must pass field assessment

A person passing all criteria except experience may serve as a PROBATIONARY REFEREE at the youth grade.

b. PHYSICAL FITNESS (Minimum Requirements)

		YOUTH CLASS 2	(Age)	YOUTH CLASS 1
(1)	**Endurance Test**	2200 meters	(under 30)	2400 meters
	(meters run in	2000 meters	(30-37)	2200 meters
	12 minutes)	1800 meters	(38-45)	2000 meters
		1600 meters	(over 45)	1800 meters
(2)	**Speed Test**	17.0 sec.	(under 30)	16.0 sec.
	(100 Meter Dash)	18.0 sec.	(30-37)	17.0 sec.
		19.0 sec.	(38-45)	18.0 sec.
		20.0 sec.	(over 45)	19.0 sec.
(3)	**Maneuverability Test**	50.0 sec.	(under 30)	45.0 sec.
	(Staggered Run —	52.5 sec.	(30-37)	47.5 sec.
	5+10+15+20+25 meters	55.0 sec.	(38-45)	50.0 sec.
		57.7 sec.	(over 45)	52.5 sec.

c. WRITTEN EXAMINATION

A minimum score is required for *each section.* Youth Class 1 requires a greater total score than Youth Class 2 although the minimum scores for each section are the same. The first section on critical Laws of the Game requires a score of 100%.

d. FIELD ASSESSMENT

Passing criteria are listed on the field assessment form. The field assessment is *not* required for Youth Class 2.

e. RETAKE

A person failing the written examination may not take it again for at least *one month.* The entire examination must be retaken. The physical fitness examination must be passed within 6 months of passing the written examination (before or after).

3. *CERTIFICATION CRITERIA FOR USSF STATE REFEREE*

a. EXPERIENCE (Minimum Age: 19 years)

NOTE: The number of games listed is for the person serving as the Referee in the FIFA three person system. TWO games serving as a Referee in the two person system may be counted as ONE game below, except at least 1/5 the number of games listed must actually be as the Referee in the three person system.

		STATE CLASS 2		STATE CLASS 1
(1)	**Minimum Career Games** at Designated Level	50		100
(2)	**Level of Games**	Boys' and Men's Games Over 16 years (boys' varsity high school and men's college games included)		Senior Men's Games Only (men's varsity college games in- cluded) Serving as linesman on profes- sional or interstate USSF national senior cup game counts as one game.
(3)	**Special Requirements**	Two games must be assessed by State Class 1 or higher grade Referee		Must pass special field assessment

A person passing all criteria except experience may serve as a PROBATIONARY REFEREE at the state grade.

b. PHYSICAL FITNESS (Minimum Requirements)

		STATE CLASS 2	(Age)	STATE CLASS 1
(1)	**Endurance Test** (meters run in 12 minutes)	2400 meters 2200 meters 2000 meters 1800 meters	(under 30) (30-37) (38-45) (over 45)	2600 meters 2300 meters 2000 meters 2000 meters
(2)	**Speed Test** (100 Meter Dash)	16.0 sec. 17.0 sec. 18.0 19.0 sec.	(under 30) (30-37) (38-45) (over 45)	15.5 sec. 16.5 sec. 17.0 sec. 18.0 sec.
(3)	**Maneuverability Test** (Staggered Run – 5+10+15+20+25 meters)	45.0 sec. 47.5 sec. 50.0 sec. 52.5 sec.	(under 30) (30-37) (38-45) (over 45)	40.0 sec. 42.5 sec. 45.0 sec. 47.5 sec.

c. WRITTEN EXAMINATION

A minimum score is required for *each section*. State Class 1 requires a greater total score than State Class 2 although the minimum scores for each section are the same. The first section on critical Laws of the Game requires a score of 100%.

327

d. FIELD ASSESSMENT

Passing criteria are listed on the field assessment form.

e. RETAKE

A person failing the written examination may not take it again for at least *two months*. The entire examination must be retaken. The physical fitness examination must be passed within 6 months of passing the written examination (before or after).

4. *CERTIFICATION CRITERIA FOR USSF NATIONAL REFEREE*

a. EXPERIENCE (Minimum Age: 19 years)

NOTE: The number of equivalent games listed is for the FIFA three person system only. No experience credit is given for serving as a Referee in the two person system since national Referees must have adequate experience in the international FIFA system to be able to officiate professional games.

	NATIONAL CLASS 2	NATIONAL CLASS 1
(1) **Minimum Career Games at Designated Level**	(100 must be as Referee)	10
(2) **Level of Games**	Senior Men's First Division League Games in State Association	National Professional League Games as Referee ONLY (exhibitions not included)
	Senior Men's National Cup Games	
	Professional League Games (exhibitions included if two professional teams)	
	International Exhibition Games involving at least one professional or national team if the appointment is made by USSF	
	National Playoff Men's Games in NCAA (all 3 divisions) and NAIA, but only if FIFA system used	
	Linesman in Professional League Game (exhibitions included if two professional teams) counts as ½ game, but may not be counted toward the 100 minimum games as Referee	
(3) **Special Requirements**	Must pass special field assessment	Must also meet all Class 2 criteria

328

b. PHYSICAL FITNESS (Minimum Requirements)

NOTE: The physical fitness requirements for National Referees are essentially the same as required by FIFA for FIFA Referees and are the same for Class 1 and Class 2.

		(Age)
(1) **Endurance Test**	2600 meters	under 30
(meters run in	2300 meters	30-39
12 minutes)	2000 meters	over 39
(2) **Distance Speed Test**	75.0 sec.	
(400 meter run on track)		
(3) **Sprint Speed Test**	8.0 sec.	
(50 meter dash)		
(4) **Maneuverability Test**	11.5 sec.	
(shuttle run 4 x 10 meters)		

c. WRITTEN EXAMINATION

Two examinations are given. One examination is comprehensive to test overall knowledge of the Laws of the Game (a section on critical Laws of the Game requires 100%). A second examination tests the Referee's knowledge of officiating mechanics and philosophy as well as game control psychology and judgment.

d. FIELD ASSESSMENT

Passing criteria are listed on the field assessment form.

e. RETAKE

A person failing either written examination may not take the written examinations again for at least *three months*. Both examinations must be retaken even if only one was failed. The physical fitness examination must be passed within 6 months of passing the written examination (before or after).

5. *CERTIFICATION CRITERIA FOR USSF FIFA REFEREE*

The Referees selected to represent the United States on the FIFA panel of international Referees are limited in number to seven by FIFA regulations, so only the very best Referees are selected. To be eligible for consideration, a Referee must be a United States citizen, the age of 25 years or older but under the age of 50 years on December 31 of the year of selection (selections are reported to FIFA in July each year), and a Class 1 USSF National Referee. Final selections are based on field assessments, experience, physical fitness, and present ability of the Referee candidates. All FIFA Referees are reevaluated each year along with the other FIFA Referee candidates so that only the best Referees at the time of selection become FIFA Referees for the following year.

Conversations between reasonable Referees and players can take place even after a game. Alan Merrick plays in the North American Soccer League, and is noted for his fair play and sportsmanship. When he treats Referees fairly, he will find them willing to listen to a reasonable question on the laws.

THE HIGHEST LEAGUE IN AMERICA — North American Soccer League

The most watched Referees in America are the 130 Referees and Linesmen who work in the North American Soccer League. Their season runs from April through mid-August. Many soccer people think that this is the most difficult league in the world in which to referee. Werner Winsemann of Vancouver, Canada, a veteran of World Cup and Olympic play, and one of the most respected officials in the league, sums it up: "The players are all out there, trying to prove something in a very short period of time. I would say that the games are the most difficult to handle anywhere, though the crowd is seldom a problem."

In existence since 1967, the League lists five categories for their officials, with a sliding scale for pay. They are: (1) Premier Referees ($120.00 per game). They are at the top of the list, and are expected to whistle the majority of the important games. (2) Referees ($100.00). They will handle the remainder of the games in the league, with very few exceptions. (3) Supplemental Referees ($60.00). Also called "Senior Linesmen," they are the most likely candidates for elevation to Referee status. Toward the end of the season, they may receive a game that has no bearing on standings, but they could be a Linesman in a playoff. (4) Linesmen ($50.00). They probably have two years or more experience in the league, and would never be called upon to Referee a game. (5) Trialist Linesmen ($40.00). These beginners in the NASL will probably receive two or three games in the season, and will be watched carefully.

In most cases the NASL officials are recommended by their State Associations, and have had extensive experience with the game at both semi-professional and professional levels. They are finally approved through a series of written and physical tests. Referee attitude, personality, physique, age, and cooperativeness also weigh heavily on the selection of Referees.

For the reader who is a self-appointed Referee Assessor, you will notice NASL officials engaging in some unfamiliar practices, all part of the league's new system of Referee-Linesman communication, designed to improve game control and spectator enjoyment:

1. The Senior Linesman (designated by the Referee), carries a red flag.

2. After an off-side has been flagged and whistled, the Linesman points to the offender with his free arm.

3. For other infractions, an indication with the free arm or with body movements will tell the Referee what type of infraction is being called.

4. Linesmen are instructed to keep up with the second to last *player*. (Not necessarily the defender.)

5. Linesmen are to cover the left wing first half, and right wing second half, after having changed sides of the field at halftime. This allows all four corners to be covered in the course of the game. The Referee must, of course, reverse his diagonal at halftime. Premier Referees are excepted from this requirement.

Rules in NASL play are somewhat different from FIFA, and place another burden on officials who are used to FIFA as a standard of play:

1. Off-sides are to be sanctioned only in the attacking area from a line 35 yards from the goal-line to the goal-line itself.

2. Any foul committed from the back receives an automatic caution.

3. Any foul "over the top" of the ball results in an automatic caution.

4. A game is legal after 44 minutes of playing time.

5. Tie games are to be decided after two 2½ minute sudden death overtime periods by a "shootout." The ball is placed on a line 35 yards from the goal-line, directly in front of the goal. The designated kicker must shoot at goal within five seconds. The goal-keeper may move off the line immediately after the "five second" clock begins, and the kicker may dribble the ball prior to shooting. After the ball touches the goal-post, cross-bar, or goalie, it may not be played a second time by the kicker. As with kicks from the penalty-mark, each team alternately has five shooters. If the score is tied after the first series of five shootouts, sudden death will prevail.

The standardization, but not stereotyping of officials needed for NASL is stressed. Each Referee will develop his own personality and method of control, as in all other levels of the game.

APPENDICES

GLOSSARY, DEFINITIONS, AND TERMS

AYSO — The AmericanYouth Soccer Organization.

Bicycle-kick — See scissor-kick.

Bridging — Stooping in front or behind an opponent in an effort to gain an advantage, usually on a high ball.

Caution — An official disciplinary action by the Referee to a player who (a) persistently infringes on the Laws of the Game, (b) shows dissent by word or action from any decision given by the Referee, (c) is guilty of ungentlemanly conduct and (d) enters or leaves the field without the permission of the Referee.

Charging — Bodily contact, usually consisting of one shoulder against another shoulder. A charge may be fair or foul. See Section X, The Rules Almanac, Charging.

Club Linesman — A Linesman with a flag who has been appointed by the Referee to indicate out of bounds balls. He is usually a club official or supporter.

Continental Federations — There are six Continental Federations under the direction of FIFA. They are: (1) CONCACAF (Confereracion Norte-Centroamericana y del Caribe de Futbol); (2) Confederacion Sudamericana de Futbol (CONMEBOL) (SOUTH AMERICA); (3) Asian Football Confederation (ASIA); (4) Union of European Football Associations (UEFA) (Europe); (5) Oceania Football Confederation (OFC) (Oceania); (6) The African Football Confederation (AFRICA).

Dead Ball — The ball is dead whenever it is not in play. This occurs when the ball is outside of the field of play or due to any temporary suspension of the game due to an infringement of the rules or when the game is otherwise stopped by the Referee.

Deliberate foul (see intentional foul) — These two terms are often confused, and should not be carelessly bandied about by the Referee. A deliberate foul is more extreme, and more purposely planned, than an intentional foul. Deliberate handling of the ball (catching it as a defensive measure) for instance, is planned, against the spirit of the game, and should be dealt with by a caution for the first offense. Intentional handling (where the hand moves with intent toward, and has contact with the ball) should be called, but the player penalized without the caution.

Diagonal System — The internationally recognized system of game control, involving a Referee and two neutral Linesmen.

Direct Free-Kick — A free-kick awarded for an opponent's infraction. A goal may be scored directly into an opponent's goal.

Double-Kick — See Scissor-Kick.

Drop-Ball — A ball which is dropped on the field by the Referee after he has stopped the game due to an injury, foreign object on the field, or due to a similar circumstance when no breach of the laws has occurred.

Dual System of Control — The Two Referee System of Control, where two Referees with equal authority are on the field.

End-line — The entire goal-line from touch-line to touch-line.

FIFA — The Federation Internationale de Football Association, which is the international governing body of soccer. Address: FIFA, 11 Hitzigweg, 8032 Zurich, Switzerland.

Formations — The lining up of players into certain prescribed locations on the field, according to style of play and team objectives. The GK is not mentioned in formation discussions, for his is the only fixed position on the field. Players located immediately in front of the GK are listed first. The most common formations are 2-3-5, 4-2-4, and 4-3-3. Sometimes it helps if the Referee knows a team's basic formation, particularly with regard to judging the off-side.

Forwards — The front line of a team, usually consisting of an outside left and right (wings), inside left and right, and center forward.

Free-Kick — An unchallenged kick in any direction. It is awarded for an infringement by the opposing side.

   Indirect . . . A goal may not be scored directly.

   Direct . . . A goal may be scored directly into an opponent's goal.

Fullback — One of two players (normally) who are positioned in front of the goalkeeper.

GK — The goalkeeper.

Goal — (a) That area between the upright posts and under the cross-bar, (b) the two posts and the cross-bar themselves, (c) the unit of scoring. A ball passing completely over the goal-line and in the area termed "goal" is a "goal."

Goal-Kick — The kick that puts the ball in motion after it has gone behind the goal-line of the defense and was last touched by a member of the offensive team. A goal-kick is not in play until it has passed out of the penalty-area.

Goalkeeper (goalie) — Sometimes called "goaldie" by seven year olds just beginning soccer. The player who guards the goal. He may use his hands within his own penalty-area. He has all the privileges of every other player on the field, plus a few of his own.

Goal-Line — The end-lines (width of the field) which extend from touch-line to touch-line, passing directly under the cross-bars of the two goals.

Goal-Mouth — That area immediately in front of the goal.

Going Over the Ball — The practice of raising one's foot above and over the ball in such a manner that when the opponent attempts to kick the ball, he is likely to be cleated in the shin. This is dangerous play, and players should be cautioned.

Halfbacks — The middle line of a team. The first line of defense, or the second line of offense.

Halfway-Line — The line in the center of the field extending from touch-line to touch-line and dividing the field into two equal parts.

Hand-Ball — A ball touching the hand or arm of any player on any part of the field, with the exception of the goalkeeper within his own penalty-area. The player must have intentionally moved the hand toward the ball, or must have been carrying the hand or arm in an unnatural position in order for the "hands" to be called. (See section on women's soccer for exception.)

Hidden fouls — Those fouls that usually go undetected by the Referee, and are therefore unpunished. They are usually committed by experienced players and can cause unpleasant incidents in a game.

Hitch-kick — (See scissor-kick)

Holding — Grasping an opponent with any part of the hand or arm.

Hungarian Off-side — Fullbacks deliberately moving forward to put an opposing forward in an off-side position. This is legal.

IFK — Indirect Free-Kick.

Indirect Free-Kick — A free-kick awarded for an opponent's infraction. A goal may not be scored directly.

Inswinger — A term used in conjunction with a corner-kick which hooks in toward the goal. (See outswinger)

Intentional foul (see deliberate foul) — Intentional fouls are not always deliberate. In officiating a game, the Referee must judge the premeditation of the player. If a player willfully and repeatedly tries to gain an advantage by unfair means, then his acts are deliberate. However, if his violations are sporadic and generally non-disruptive to the continuance of the game without incident, his acts are to be judged intentional, and penalized, but not subject to disciplinary action.

'Keeper — The goalkeeper.

Kick-off — A kick at the center of the field at the start of each period and after each score.

Laws of Soccer — The rules of the game, as set down by FIFA, broken down into 17 laws.

Law 18 — An unwritten law sometimes used rather blatantly by Referees to justify any type of decision which deviates from the laws of soccer, international board rulings, or common interpretations. It should be viewed as a common sense law pertaining only to those aspects and situations of the game not previously documented.

Modified Diagonal System — A new system of game control which has won favor with many Referees, coaches, and players. It places three Referees on the field, each with a whistle. It is generally acknowledged that fewer fouls result from this system.

Neutral Linesman — A fully qualified Referee who is assigned to act as Linesman on the diagonal system of control.

336

Obstruction — The deliberate action of one player as he prevents another's movement on the field. It is sanctioned by an indirect free-kick. When the ball is within playing distance of the player who obstructs, the obstruction is legal.

Off-side — Being illegally in advance of the ball. The off-side law has remained unaltered since 1925 (except in the North American Soccer League).

Off-side Position — Being illegally in advance of the ball, but not sanctioned by the Referee. Usually, this is due to a player's not taking advantage of this off-side position.

Outswinger — A term used in conjunction with a corner-kick which hooks out and away from the goal toward the center of the field. (See also inswinger.)

Pass — To kick, head, or otherwise advance the ball deliberately to a teammate.

Penalty-Area — That 18 x 44 yard rectangular area in front of each goal, in which the goalkeeper may touch the ball. Any defensive action committed in this area which would have resulted in a direct free-kick if committed elsewhere results in a penalty-kick.

Penalty-Kick — An unchallenged kick taken by the offense from a spot or line 12 yards from the goal-line. The goalkeeper is the only defensive player allowed in the penalty-area until the ball has been put in play (traveled its circumference) by the kicker.

Pitch — The field of play.

Periods — The quarters or halves of a game.

Place-Kick — A kick at the ball while it is stationary and on the ground. All free-kicks, corner-kicks, goal-kicks, and kick-offs must be place-kicks.

Playing Distance — That distance between the player and the ball that would allow the player to reach out with a part of his body (usually his foot) and play the ball.

Pushing — Use of the hands to move an opponent. Resting a hand on an opponent is pushing.

Quarter Circle — The corner-area, from which corner-kicks are taken.

Referee — The appointed official in charge of a game. Notice that throughout this book the Referee begins with a capital "R." The capital "R" stands for Respect by players and Respect for players.

Reference System — An experimental system of officiating used in Russia with two Linesmen on one side of the field and the Referee on the other. (We're told it hasn't worked out!)

Sanctioned — Penalized.

Sandwiching — Two teammates converging on an opponent simultaneously. This type of "boxing in" is penalized with a direct free-kick, as it is regarded as holding.

Save — A move by the goalkeeper that prevents a score.

Scissor-Kick — A move whereby the kicker's feet leave the ground, causing his body to be parallel with the ground with his feet at a higher elevation than his head. The intent is to kick the ball over his head in a single motion. If the ball is within playing distance of an opponent, this attempt is dangerous play, and results in an indirect free-kick. This is true even if no contact was made with this opponent, even though the intent was to kick the ball. Also known as a bicycle-kick, hitch-kick, reverse-kick, and double-kick.

Senior Linesman — Designated by the Referee, the Linesman who will take over for the Referee if needed.

Senior Referee — The Referee in charge when the Dual (Two Referee System) is being employed. The identity of the Senior Referee should be known only to the two Referees, and this should be determined before game time.

Short Corner — Making a quick pass instead of a long cross toward the goal when taking a corner-kick.

Strikers — The two inside forwards in a 3-3/4 offense/defense.

Touch — That space outside of the field of play, separated from it by the touch-lines.

Touch-line — The side-lines traveling the length of the field on both sides of the field which extend from goal-line to goal-line.

Tripping — Intentionally throwing, or attempting to throw an opponent by use of the legs.

USSF — The United States Soccer Federation. The USSF, the governing body of soccer in the United States, is located at 350 Fifth Avenue, Room 4010, New York, N.Y. 10001.

Violent Conduct — Intentional rough play which should carry both technical and disciplinary sanctions at the same time.

Volley — To kick a ball before it bounces, as one does in tennis after having double-faulted.

Warning — A "soft caution" given by the Referee to a player who is guilty of some infringement of the laws. If the infringement is repeated, a caution usually results (yellow card).

Wings — The two outside players of the forward line.

Worrying the Goalkeeper — Interfering with the goalkeeper's progress by word or action, usually while he has possession of the ball. This is sanctioned by an indirect free-kick and a caution.

INDEX OF FILMS

The following films are available through FIFA. These are the only known audio-visual materials on officiating in soccer.

1. *Referee and Linesman – A Team*

   FIFA Film concerning diagonal system of control and positioning of Referees. Color film, English commentary, 16 mm.

2. *Allowed or Forbidden*

   West German F.A. film on Law XII with FIFA commentary in English. Black & White, 16 mm.

3. *Swiss Test Film for Referees*

   No commentary. Black & White, 16 mm. 70 scenes.

4. *Law XII Incidents*

   FIFA film on Law XII. Black & White, 16 mm. English commentary.

5. *Four Step Rule for Goalkeepers*

   FIFA film with English commentary. Color, 16 mm.

6. *Towards Uniformity of Interpretation*

   50 incidents from the 1970 World Cup. Excellent for instruction. 16 mm, color, 25 minutes. Available through Overseas Production Services, 70 Wardour St., London W1v3AB.

7. *The Referee*

   Available through the United States Soccer Federation or your local Coca Cola Bottling Company. 16 mm, color, 25 minute movie, plus 140 slides, Instructor's Guide, script for slides, and Handbook for Youth Soccer.

   Designed to be inspirational and to recruit new Referees.

8. *Laws and Refs*

   Available through your local Dr. Pepper Bottling Company. A 25 minute color 16 mm film which takes you through the basics of the laws, also with presentations on the Referee's duties. No charge, but small rental deposit required. #10 in a series of 13 films on the game.

BIBLIOGRAPHY

1. Federation Internationale de Football Association, *Laws of the Game and Universal Guide for Referees.* Published annually, with up-to-date decisions of the International Board. Also available in French, Spanish, and German. The United States Soccer Federation now publishes its own version for the United States.

2. FIFA, *Signals by the Referee and Linesman,* 26 pp. Write for their latest price list.

3. Football Association, 22 Lancaster Gate, London W2. *F.A. Guide for Referees and Linesmen,* 75 pp. Covers many areas of Referee conduct and signaling, with many questions on the laws of the game, with diagrams. Published annually.

4. *Handbook for Referee Instructors,* available through FIFA. Approved and Recommended by the FIFA Referee's Committee. An excellent guide for Referee instructors. 1976.

5. Harris, Paul, *THE LITTLE BOOK OF SOCCER, Everyone's Illustrated Guide to the Laws of the Game,* 48 pp, 78 illustrations. The complete summary of what is important about the laws of the game. Very popular with newcomers and coaches. Available through Soccer for Americans, Box 836, Manhattan Beach, California 90266. $2.50.

6. Harris, Larry, *FÚTBOL MEANS SOCCER, Easy Steps to Understanding the Game,* 160 pp, heavily illustrated. Teaches the laws painlessly and effectively, with some humor. An excellent device to bring you up to snuff. Soccer for Americans, Box 836, Manhattan Beach, California 90266. $4.95.

7. Hill, Gordon and Thomas, Jason, *GIVE A LITTLE WHISTLE, The Recollections of a Remarkable Referee.* 1975, 157 pp. The whole book centers around the English FA Leagues, where Hill had a remarkable career. A refreshing approach by a very human Referee, one who prided himself in knowing players. Excellent reading. Available through the Tampa Bay Rowdies, 1311 North Westshore Blvd., Tampa, Florida 33607. $7.95.

8. Lover, Stanley, *Association Football Laws Illustrated.* Pelham Books, London, 1970, 128 pp. The excellent illustrations provide the graphic emphasis that is absent in so many books. Deals particularly well with Laws XI and XII, the most discussed laws in the game.

9 Maisner, Larry and Mason, Bill, *The Rules of Soccer: Simplified.* 1978, 12 pp. The essentials of the rules are summarized and made simple. An excellent handy companion for what is important. Available from the authors, 2163 Ronsard Road, San Pedro, California 90732. $1.00.

10. Mullen, Ken, *A Case in Mind,* 61 pp. Published privately, and available through the author, 2500 Lucy Lane, Walnut Creek, California 94595. A collection of fifty knotty problems in soccer, this book is a challenge for those who think they know the rules.

11. National Collegiate Athletic Association *SOCCER GUIDE* (The official rulebook and guide). Published annually by College Athletics Publishing Service, 349 East Thomas Road, Phoenix, Arizona.

12. National Federation of State High School Associations, 400 Leslie Street, Elgin, Illinois 60120. *Soccer Rules Book*, National Federation Edition. Complete rules, comments, interpretations, and suggestions for tournament progression. Published annually.

13. Paine, Reg, *The Referee's Quiz Book*, 93 pp. 1976 Pan Books, London. Many questions and answers on the laws of the game, presented in an interesting fashion. Available from Mr. Soccer, 14027 Floyd Road, Dallas, Texas.

14. *Referee Magazine*, Box 161, Franksville, Wisconsin 53126. Published monthly. If you study officiating in other sports, you'll do better at soccer.

15. Rous, Sir Stanley and Ford, Donald, *A History of the Laws of Association Football*. Published by FIFA, 1974. Contains all you ever wanted to know about the history of the laws of the game but were afraid to ask.

16. Sellin, Eric, *The Inner Game of Soccer*. 1976, 343 pp. A conversational, incisive treatment of all aspects of refereeing including numerous comments on the laws. The serious Referee should have a copy, as Sellin leaves no stone unturned. Available through the author, at 312 Kent Road, Bala-Cynwyd, Pa. 19004. $6.95.

17. Taylor, Jack (with David Jones), *Jack Taylor, World Soccer Referee*. 1976, 183 pp. Pelham Books, London. The Referee who so masterfully handled the 1974 World Cup Final tells about his experiences in the game. The cover shows Taylor with a vise-like grip on a World Class player. If you want to go far in refereeing, read this book. Available from Mr. Soccer, 14027 Floyd Road, Dallas, Texas.

18. United States Soccer Federation, *Official Rule Book*. Available through USSF at 350 Fifth Avenue, Suite 4010, New York, N.Y. 10001. Published annually for USSF affiliated competitions.

MEET FARAH FOUL!

INDEX

Advantage 70-71, 87, 153,
                        161, 232, 247
  definition 153
  the other — Law V, IBD 8 . 72, 73, 87
  the signal 71
  through trifling offenses 233
Almanac of Rules 135-197
American Youth Soccer Organization
  (AYSO) 311-313
  corner kicks 312
  changing goalie 312
  drop ball 312
  duration of game 311
  duties of coaches and officials .. 311
  field of play 312
  play off games............. 313
  substitution 312
Assignments
  youth................... 235
Attitude
  of players reflected by coach ... 247
Ball....................... 143
  becoming inflated 156
  college 318
  FIFA Laws 264
  high school 314
  in and out of play (college) 319
  in and out of play (FIFA) 270
  in and out of play (high school) . 316
  in and out of play........... 160
  inspection................ 142
  law requirements 143
  legally in play 154
  lost 154
  youth (AYSO)............. 311
Ball Persons (college) 319
Beausay, William 84
Bonchonsky, Joe 280, 297
Captains.......... 13, 144, 171, 246
  rights of 152
Card system
  origin of................. 53
Carvalho, Jose 122, 130, 131
Cast
  permitted and not permitted ... 150
Cautions............... 53, 54, 94
  and advantages 71
  Law XII, Section K and....... 90
  reasons for 173
  second................87, 174
  third in season 173

Charging
  conditions for 185
  definition 185
  the goalkeeper........148, 196, 312
  judging fair charge 88
Club Game 152
Coaching
  and referee relationships. 238, 246, 252
  AYSO 311
  from sidelines 173
  from sidelines (FIFA) 152
  influencing Referee.......... 247
  players (by Referee) 231
  test 249
Coin Toss.................14, 155
  in overtime 155
Communication
  with Referee by coach 246
CONCACAF
  recommendations on exceptions
    for advantage 71
College Differences from FIFA . .318-322
  ball 318
  ball in and out of play 319
  ball persons 319
  corner kick 320
  dangerous play 320
  field of play 318
  free kicks 320
  goalkeeper privileges
    and violations 320
  misconduct................ 320
  penalty kick 320
  player's equipment 318
  Referees.................. 319
  scoring................... 319
  substitutes 318
Concentration 79, 82-84
Conditioning 4, 5
Confused Referee............. 197
Corner Flag Post 196, 197
Corner Kick 196
  AYSO (youth)............. 312
  college 320
  conditions for taking of 196
  diagonal system 20
  FIFA Laws 278
  high school 317
  modified diagonal 306
  two Referee system 289, 290
Criticism of Referees 98

Dangerous Fouls 92, 93
Dangerous Play 248
   college rule 320
   examples of. 181
   judging. 88, 89
Data Card 48, 49
Davies, Ron 95
Defensive Wall 248
Deliberate Foul 172
Deliberate Hand Ball. 178
Diagonal System of
   Control (FIFA) 18-23, 32, 282
   advantages and disadvantages 32
   corner kick 20
   counter attack 21
   development of attack. 20
   free kick near goal 22
   free kick near midfield 21
   goal kick. 21
   penalty kick 22
   throw-in 22, 23
Direct Free Kick (basic) 183
   signals 182
   examples of 183
   comments on 183
Dissent 252
Drop Ball 91, 156, 157, 160,
              161, 171, 173, 287
   after injury 65, 146
   high school 316
   modified diagonal 308
   outside agent 159
   placement of 157
   two Referee system 294
   youth 312
Duration of Game
   FIFA Laws 268
   high school 316
   youth (AYSO) 311
Ejections 53
   and ejected players 159
   conditions for 174
   miscellaneous 174
   of player 174
Encouragement
   of players by Referees 231
Entering and Leaving the Field 175
   for equipment adjustment 175
   for injury 175
   if ordered off 175
   result if goal scored 175

Entering and Leaving the Field (Cont)
   ungentlemanly conduct 178
   without permission 161, 175
Equipment 9
   college 318
   FIFA Laws 265, 266
   players' 150
Evaluation
   field. 99
   by coaches 100, 101, 102
Field of Play 138, 139
   college 318
   FIFA Laws 260-262
   high school 314
   measurements 139
   playability 12
   youth (AYSO) 312
FIFA
   championships (kick from
      penalty mark) 192
   differences from colleges . . 318, 319
   differences from high schools 314-317
   editorial board 279
   international board 279
   laws of the game 259-279
   Referee's committee 279
   third caution – season 173
   USSF Referees 120, 324
   World Cup 110
   World Cup Referees 112-118
Fitness. 4, 5, 81
Flag
   use of 30, 31, 234
Foreign object 54, 159, 161
Forfeiture and Tie Games
   high school 317
Fouls. 171
   against teammate 171
   and misconduct (FIFA laws). 271-273
   and misconduct (high school). . . 316
   by substitute 171
   by player outside field 171
   common, in youth games 232
   dangerous 92, 93
   from behind (NASL) 332
   in penalty area 172
   in retaliation 171
   intentional vs. deliberate 172
   over the top (NASL) 332
   point of offense. 171
   recognition (youth) 234

Fouls (Cont)
seen by linesman 171
simultaneous 171
unintentional 171
Free Kick
cautioning on taking of 61
college 320
conditions for 176
diagonal system 21, 22
exact positioning of ball 75
FIFA Laws 274
high school 317
modified diagonal. 304
near goal 54
opponent encroachment on 176
procedure (9.15 meters) 60
two Referee system 292, 293
wall 61, 94
Game Control 50, 51, 237
Game Preparation 81
Game Reports 105-109
Giebner, Dick 84
Goalkeeper
and injury 161
charging 57, 148, 149, 185
definition of possession 57, 148
delaying tactics 148
injury 146, 149
fielding ball (two
Referee system) 294
obstruction 58
possession 59
privileges and violations
(college) 320
rights 57
rolling the ball 58
steps 73, 94, 148
substitution 149
Goal Kick 195
Conditions for taking 195
FIFA Laws 277, 278
diagonal system 21
modified diagonal 305
retaking of 195
two Referee system 289, 290
Halftime 67
duration 154
two Referee system 293
Handling the Ball 183
deliberate 178, 183

High School Differences from FIFA
ball 314
corner kick 317
field of play 314
forfeiture and tie games 317
free kick 317
penalty kick 317
players 314
Referees 315
timekeepers and scorers 317
Hill, Gordon 83, 122, 128, 129
Indirect Free Kick 177, 247
definition 177
infractions resulting in 177
on opponent's goal line 173
signal 177
Indoor Soccer 256, 257
Infringement of the Laws
persistent 90
Injuries 65, 66, 146
and drop ball 156
treatment of 154
Inspection
of field 12
Instructions
to players 12, 13, 14
Intent 251
Intentional Foul 172
Kick Off 155
diagonal system 20
modified diagonal system 301
two Referee system 288
Krollfeifer, Howard 107, 109
Laws of the Game
(FIFA) 259-278, 323
as applied to girls and women . . . 254
coaching the 248
how they are changed 279
textbook knowledge of 233
Lifted Ball 249, 250
Line Judges
high school 316
Linesmen
FIFA Laws 268
mechanics 25-29
NASL 331
signals 30, 31, 35
substitute 152
Mason, Bill 102, 297, 340
Mechanics 81

Mechanics (Cont)
   modified diagonal 300-307
   two Referee system 288-293
   youth. 234
Metric System
   conversions. 141
Misconduct. 171
   (see cautions and ejections)
Modified Diagonal
   System. 18, 282, 297-309
   corner kick 306
   discipline 309
   drop ball 308
   free kicks 304
   goalkeeper fielding ball 309
   goal kick 304
   kickoff 301
   master sheet of mechanics 309
   offside 302
   out of bounds 300
   penalty kick 307
   record keeping 308
   simultaneous whistle. 308
   substitutes 308
   use of 299
Mullen, Ken 109
NASL (North American Soccer League)
   legal game 332
   offside experiment 279
   Referee and linesman pay scale . . 331
   shootout 332
Neutral Linesman 152, 153
Obstruction. 89, 177
   definition of 177
Offside 162-169
   and goalkeeper 88
   and participation 88, 163
   conditions for 162
   condensed 168, 169
   diagrams to illustrate 164-166
   escaping offside position . . . 168, 169
   FIFA Laws 270, 271
   from drop ball 156
   infrequent occurrences in . . 166, 167
   modified diagonal system 302
   NASL experiment. 279
   on corner kick. 196
   on free kick. 176
   on goal kick. 195
   on throw-in. 193
   position 168, 160

Offside (Cont)
   position and the advantage. 73
   stepping off field to avoid 163
   trap. 163
   two Referee system . . .283, 284, 288
   when taken 156
   youth. 235
One Referee System 34, 35, 37
Overtime 154
Pele 94
Penal Offenses
   in youth games 232
   resulting in direct free kick 183
Penalty Kick
   college 320
   conditions for 187, 189
   definition 187. 189
   dissent from 51
   double standard and 88
   encroachment 190
   FIFA Laws 275, 276
   high school 317
   modified diagonal 307
   outside agent 159
   Referee mechanics 187, 189
   time extension for 191
   two Referee system 291, 296
   whistling for 42
Phillipson, Don (USSF) 323
Players 144
   advice to 251
   differences among 237, 238
   equipment 150
   equipment (high school) 314
   FIFA Laws 264, 265
   fouled, and rights 248
   instructions to 12, 13
   knowledge of 232
   knowledge of laws 251
   safety 237
Playoff Games
   youth (AYSO) 312
Protests 244, 245
Ramsay, Graham 252, 253
Referee
   and indoor soccer. 256
   attitude and proper field
     execution 78, 79, 80
   college 319
   decision to 2
   equipment 9

Referee (Cont)
errors 244
FIFA Laws 267
FIFA, USSF 329
high school 315
meetings............... 98, 99
mistakes........ 73, 221, 232, 248
NASL................ 331, 332
National, USSF 328, 329
perfect game 90
playing the game 91
positioning 256
problems 253
problems (youth).......... 234
substitute 152
State, USSF 326, 327
test for (basic).......... 200-209
test for (advanced) 214-221
trainee, USSF 325
women 254
youth, USSF 325, 326
Referee Characters
agitator 55
cheapskater............... 63
commentator 33
dictator 44
facilitator 103
hesitator................ 140
immitator............... 186
potentator 158
rottentator 151
spectator 85
Reference System of Control 152
Rogers, Harry 283
Scoring
college.................. 319
definition 161
method of (FIFA Laws) 270
premature awarding of score ... 161
Sellin, Eric 15, 341
Senior Linesman (NASL)........ 331
Shoes
illegal and legal 150
Signalling 94, 247, 248
direct free kick 182
hand and arm 45-47
youth 234
Simultaneous Whistle
modified diagonal system 308
two Referee system 287
Smith, Pat 104, 105

Smog 153
Soccer and Television 94
Soft Cautions 172
Somos, Istvan 112
Spitting 174
Start of Play
FIFA Laws 269
Startzell, Stanley 242, 243
Substitutions and Substitutes .. 145, 171
college 318
high school 314
number of 145
outside agent 159
two Referee system 294
System of Control
diagonal 19-23
modified diagonal 235
two Referee system 283-296
youth 235
Termination of Game
conditions for 153
Tests 98, 200-209, 214-221, 249
critique (advanced) 222-225
critique (basic) 210-213
key (coaches') 250
Throw-In 193
conditions for proper taking of.. 193
diagonal system 22, 23
FIFA Laws............... 277
judging "crabbing" by thrower .. 75
miscellaneous occurrences 194
modified diagonal 303
retaking of 194
turnover on 194
two Referee system 292
unorthodox 226, 227
Tie Breaker Kick Record 49
Time
allowance 154
keeping (college) 319, 321, 322
keeping and scoring
(high school) 317
two Referee system 294
wasting 154
Two Referee System.. 18, 152, 153, 280,
282, 283, 296, 298
after game 293
areas of responsibility 285
basics 286
before game 293
communication with 285